ISRAEL: A CONCISE POLITICAL HISTORY

ISRAEL

A CONCISE POLITICAL HISTORY

Yossi Beilin

St. Martin's Press
New York

To Helena, Gil and Ori

All rights reserved. For information, write:
Scholarly and Reference Division,
St. Martin's Press Inc., 175 Fifth Avenue,
New York, NY 10010

First Publication in the United States of America 1993

Printed in Great Britain

ISBN 0-312-09124-9 (Cloth)
ISBN 0-312-12066-4 (Paper)

Library of Congress Cataloging-in-Publication Data

Beilin, Yossi
      Israel: a concise political history / Yossi Beilin.
            p.   cm.
      Includes bibliographical references and index.
      ISBN 0-312-09124-9 (Cl)   0-312-12066-4 (Paper)
      1. Israel—Politics and government.   I. Title.
DS126.5.B3586   1993
956.94—dc20   92-30626
                                                 CIP

Contents

Preface

Israel, July 1992. For fifteen years the Likud had led the government, or had been an equal partner in power. On 23 June 1992 an upheaval occurred in which the Labour Party returned to power. The ongoing uprising (Intifada) in the Occupied Territories (the West Bank and Gaza), the waves of immigration from the former USSR, the Gulf War and the Scud missiles on Tel Aviv and Haifa, the Madrid Conference on peace in the Middle East, and the democratization process which occurred in the Labour Party – all of them had had their impact on the Israeli voter.

In spite of a cautious tradition of non-involvement in internal politics many statesmen in the world were relieved when the almost impossible happened and a hawkish, conservative government was replaced by a pragmatic government which made it a goal to depart from most of the occupied territories.

This new chapter, which began in the summer of 1992, may become a turning point in the annals of the Middle East. Whether or not this happens, we will only know in some years time. In the meantime, we can try to understand the past and the human and the ideological context in which political decisions are made.

When I began to write this book, I could not have foreseen in my wildest dreams that parts of it would be written between one alarm siren and the next, while Scud missiles travelling some 400 miles in six or seven minutes fell on homes in Tel Aviv and the surrounding area. Now, having finished its writing, it is hard to believe, in the midst of boisterous Tel Aviv, that we in fact lived through this nightmare, night after night, for a month and a half – a period which shattered many accepted truths. This sharp passage from war to its absence, to life in the shadow of constant threat, and the great hope of realizing the tremendous potential inherent in Israeli society – the yearning for peace – all this symbolizes the uniqueness of Israel, which is the subject of this book.

I confess that the book is the direct outgrowth of professional deformation. This is a personal view, which presents the changes which have occured in Israeli society from the point of view of what is known in the social sciences as participant observation. Many political scientists who engage in politics find themselves, while caught up in political activity, looking on from the side and saying to themselves: 'Interesting, very interesting. I should write something about it ...'

The following pages are not meant as a reader on Israeli government, nor do they constitute a book of memoirs. They are meant to present the major trends in the development of Israeli society and the issues that occupied a central place on its agenda over the years, some of which rocked its very foundations yet today appear utterly irrelevant. The issue of German reparations after the Holocaust of European Jewry, for example, which caused a deep rift within Israeli society, bringing it to the brink of the delegitimation of its regime by the Herut movement under Menachem Begin, has become meaningless. Following the Scud attacks against Israel, German former Foreign Minister Genscher was among the first to visit the sites hit by the missiles, and his promise of massive financial aid to Israel was accepted without debate.

I have tried in the following pages to describe the decision-making mechanism, to identify the power centres in Israeli society, to sketch the character of the decision-makers which has changed considerably in the course of the past decades, and to define the political norms of Israel, a democracy under siege. The Israeli–Arab conflict, towards which none of us can be objective, naturally occupies an important place in these pages. This conflict, unforeseen by the fathers of the Zionist idea at the close of the last century, became, at the beginning of the twentieth century, the major problem of the Jewish community in Palestine and of the State of Israel since its founding – even more so since its great but fatal victory in 1967. I shall also discuss the heavy price which Israel continues to pay in the absence of peace, and the challenges it will face once the longed-for peace is achieved.

Each of us, of course, has his own personal Israel. For our parents, it was a dream. For them, who fought for its independence, Israel was a fragile object to be handled with care: it was not to be criticized, a bad impression was inadmissible, every flaw was viewed as a youthful error, as a growing pain. For my generation, Israel was a given quantity, an established, unquestionable fact. The generation of statehood even enjoy a certain advantage – the special identification felt by those whose birthday coincides with the birth of the state.

I was born less than a month after the establishment of the state. During the second lull in the war of independence an arms ship called the *Altalena*, arrived at the country's shores unauthorized by Israel Defence Forces. Belonging to the IZL – the organization headed by Menachem Begin which seceded from the Haganah – the ship was viewed as the first test of the integration of the former underground armies into a national fighting force. It seemed as though even before it was a month old, Israel would be plunged into civil war, but this was averted.

With no special effort, I was born into one of the most fascinating periods in history, the mid-twentieth century, three years after the conclusion of World War II. The world had many hopes for peace, the young state of Israel, which had just fulfilled the dream of many generations, faced the greatest challenge – the absorption of immigrants from seventy different countries, twice its total population in number, within a brief space of time.

Not surprisingly, I found myself proud to be a Jew, proud to be an Israeli, an ardent Zionist, a stauch supporter of Prime Minister David Ben-Gurion, and an uncompromising adversary of all those who opposed him, be it Menachem Begin, the moustached and articulate oppositionist on the right, or Moshe Sneh, the moustached and articulate oppositionist on the left. In school, we immersed ourselves in the pre-state period. I supported the Haganah while other children favoured the secessionist underground movements – the IZL and Lehi.

In 1977, several months after the historic defeat of the Labour Party, I joined up. I exchanged my academic and journalistic pursuits for a full-time job as spokesman of the party. I enlisted for a year, and remained for seven. This was for me a unique opportunity to become acquainted with party life, for better and for worse, with its power plays and its ideological debates.

When the national unity government headed by Shimon Peres was formed, I was appointed Government Secretary. These two years provided me with an intensive inside view of the workings of the state from its very heart. I followed such important decisions as the withdrawal of the IDF from Lebanon, the drafting of the 1985 economic recovery plan, and the negotiations with Egypt over the Taba area and northern Sinai.

During the next two years, I served as Director General for Foreign Affairs in the Foreign Ministry. This was an opportunity of a different nature, an opportunity to engage in the conduct of Israeli foreign policy and to meet with the world policy-makers. In addition, from 1984 to 1988, I was a regular observer at the meetings of the inner cabinet, a forum comprising ten ministers – five from the Likud and five from the Labour Alignment – which discussed security issues not brought before the full cabinet.

In 1988 I was elected to the Knesset and served as Deputy Finance Minister in the new national unity government until its fall in March 1990. This was for me a new angle, less familiar than my previous positions, which allowed me a macro look at Israeli society through the allocation of resources.

Intimate knowledge is sometimes disaffecting. Yet despite sharp disappointments – primarily in the area of missed opportunities in the advance of the peace process – my 'journey' of the last few years has reinforced my pride in my country and in its people. They have not yet succumbed to cynicism and materialism, and many are prepared to make supreme sacrifices for the sake of what they view as vital to the realization of their own dream for the State of Israel.

Judging by international standards, Israel is a success story. The gathering of millions of Jews from all corners of the world; the revival of a language which had been dead for thousands of years; the creation of a society which achieved rapid economic growth and set high standards of democracy and social integration: all these are achievements which cannot be ignored. Although economic development and prosperity slowed down significantly after the 1973 Yom Kippur War, the roots of this can clearly be traced back to the outcome of the 1967 Six Day War and the heavy defence burden that this created for Israel. This book has been written out of faith in the ability of Israel to return to the path of economic growth and to become an integral part of international society. The post-Gulf War era will be a decisive time for Israel: will it become part of the new world order and accept the hazards of the peace process, or will it risk the continuation of the status quo, in which it faces both a constant strategic threat from the Arab states and the impairment of the personal security of its citizens by the intifada – the Palestinian revolt in the West Bank and Gaza?

The agreement of the leaders of the Jewish community in Palestine in 1937 to accept the Peel Commission's partition plan, according to which two states – Arab and Jewish – were to be established in the territory to the west of the Jordan River was an historic decision. The 1978 decision by the Israeli government to accept the Camp David Accords and to relinquish the entire Sinai peninsula, viewed by many as providing Israel with vital strategic depth, was also an historic decision. So was the 1985 decision which led to Israel's unilateral withdrawal from Lebanon. Will Israel be able to undertake yet another such decision? Will it prove capable of reconsidering the situation, in order to extricate itself from the morass of the territories and resume the course interrupted in 1967? Will it be possible to achieve peace and security arrangements with the Palestinians and the Arab states? The answers to these questions will determine whither the State of Israel, this long-suffering, fascinating and much loved historical wonder, is headed.

Introduction

The interest aroused by Israel is totally disproportionate to its size. The most up-to-date figures, released on the eve of Independence Day, April 1991, show a state whose population numbers 5 million, including 900,000 non-Jew citizens. The overall territory of Israel within the pre-1967 borders and including all of Jerusalem and the Golan Heights does not exceed 21,501 km². The West Bank, measuring 5,500 km², contains an Arab population of 800,000, while the 1,000 km² Gaza Strip has 700,000 Arab inhabitants.

Media experts know that Israel is the third largest newsmaker in the world, after the United States and the former Soviet Union. A reporter accredited to Jerusalem knows that he will have few holidays. And for any state that maintains diplomatic relations with Israel, the role of ambassador to Israel is one of the most important postings in the foreign service.

Israel is the only Western state in the Middle East. It is marked by constant tension, periodic wars, and such unique social structures as the kibbutz. Moreover, for a nation whose very survival is an enigma, the attempt to renew its national life represents an unprecedented effort: the revival of a dead language and its transformation into a modern means of communication; the immigration of entire diaspora communities to Israel, and an interesting 'melting pot' that combined experiment and deed, many disappointments, and not a few surprising successes.

In the Israeli parliament, the Knesset, situated on a hill in Jerusalem and resembling a Greek temple, hangs a picture of a man who symbolizes the consensus in this diverse and multi-polar society: the portrait is of Dr Theodor Herzl, or by his Hebrew name, Binyamin Ze'ev Herzl. This eccentric man, who passed away in 1904 with a heavy heart at the age of only 44, has been accorded the title of 'father of the Jewish state'. Herzl pre-dated the establishment of parties in the Zionist movement, and hence he remains above party affiliation. He symbolizes Zionism for Zionists and non-Zionists alike. His photograph, which shows a handsome face, a black rectangular beard, and crossed hands, graces many of the state's official institutions.

Would the State of Israel have been established without the vision of this man – a doctor of law, Paris correspondent of the *Neue Freie Presse*, frustrated playwright and heretic, whose children converted to Christianity? At first glance the answer is yes: the first wave of Jewish immigration (*aliya*) to Palestine, which began in 1882, anticipated Herzl's national period by many years. It is doubtful, however, whether such immigration would have led to statehood were it not for the formulation of Herzl's Zionist philosophy.

Herzl epitomized the enlightened, detached Jew that lived at the end of the nineteenth century when, on the one hand, there was the abandonment of Jewish communal life, apostasy, and assimilation into the Christian world, and on the other, the superficial and fragile integration of the Jew in this Christian world. The Dreyfus case, which he covered as correspondent for his newspaper, demonstrated to him the tenuous nature of the integration of the enlightened, secular, liberated Jew, and imbued him with the desire to find a solution to the Jewish problem.

He was a pampered boy from Budapest, son of an attractive, proud and dominant mother and a millionaire merchant who had lost a part of his assets. The boy who left the Jewish primary school to acquire a broader education at the municipal Realschule and the evangelical secondary school grew into a youth who went to Vienna to study law, who frequented the opera houses as well as houses of lesser repute, where he is known to have contracted a venereal disease. This is the young man who admired Wagner and remained unmoved by the manifestations of anti-Semitism in the University of Vienna. It was in his thirties that, old beyond his years, and burdened with an unsuccessful marriage, Herzl abandoned the practice of law and became the Paris correspondent of a prestigious German newspaper. During this period he formulated a detailed plan for the mass conversion of the Jews to Christianity, to be carried out openly and proudly, although he himself and other Jewish leaders remained Jews to their dying day. In the spirit of this plan, he did not have his son circumcised.

At this time Herzl combined an understanding of anti-Semitism, even justifying some of its elements, with a powerful need to free himself from being one of its targets. The idea of mass conversion was one outgrowth of this dilemma. Another idea for a solution to the problem of anti-Semitism – the gathering of world Jewry in Palestine – was not unknown to him, but he rejected it in the belief that the profound differences between the various Jewish communities would not permit the reestablishment of the Jews as a nation.

It was the Dreyfus affair which erupted in the fall of 1894 that altered Herzl's approach to the Jewish question. A Jewish officer of the French army, Alfred Dreyfus, was arrested on charges of treason. In 1895 Herzl became convinced that the Jews had to leave Europe because of the frightening intensity of anti-Semitism prevailing there. His last nine years there were devoted to seeking a solution to the Jewish problem, specifically aimed at settling the Jewish people on some tract of land. Complex, frustrated and talented, and deriving little pleasure from his private life, this man became the father of the Jewish state despite his very marginal ties with the Jewish community.

At first he did not speak of Palestine; he felt that it was too close to Europe. On the contrary, he preferred a more distant location in Africa or South America – a place which could be purchased with money, to be chosen by its geographical, climatic and other qualities. He foresaw a secular, democratic, German-speaking state, and presented this idea to wealthy Jews and non-Jewish statesmen, only to be turned away.

The turning point in Herzl's life came when he returned to Vienna in a year when anti-Semitism in that city reached a new peak. Here he encountered little support for his idea and indeed much rejection, which was echoed by his wife. While his letters to her were addressed 'My big girl' or 'My dear girl', his frequent journeys – to England, to Turkey, and to wherever he hoped to win support for the idea outlined in his book *Der Judenstaat* (The Jewish State) – made relations between them became increasingly distant.

Herzl's astounding success was his convening of the First Zionist Congress in Basle, Switzerland in 1897. Had he not translated his views into an organized movement, he would have remained one of the many thinkers who dreamt of bringing the Jews together in one country – whether in Palestine or elsewhere, whether a religious revival or a new society. Only he, inspired by the force of his belief in the cause and in himself, with his unique charisma, succeeded in founding an organization with branches throughout the Jewish world. He overcame opposition, especially from rabbis of the various denominations and other Jews who feared an increase in anti-Semitism in Europe on charges on dual loyalty.

In an intensive individual effort, which endangered his position with the *Neue Freie Presse*, exacerbated his heart ailment and further aggravated his shaky relationship with his quarrelsome wife, Herzl succeeded in bringing together in Basle 208 Jews from 16 different countries – from that time on known as 'Zionists'. It was the end of a hot August but all the delegates came in frock coats and white ties to the municipal casino; over the doorway was hung the blue and white flag which was later to be adopted by the State of Israel. Every delegate wore a blue badge on his lapel saying, in German: 'The only solution to the Jewish question is the establishment of a Jewish state.'

The success of the First Zionist Congress surprised Herzl himself. The organization was exemplary, enthusiasm ran high, his leadership was convincing and he was naturally elected chairman of the Congress and president of the World Zionist Organization. The event was accorded wide media coverage. Herzl's message to the Congress was very clear: the Jewish people must establish an organizational framework within which to negotiate with the leaders of the great nations in order to obtain a charter for Jewish settlement in Palestine. In saying this, he formulated the idea of 'political Zionism', which called for a political arrangement prior to mass immigration. Thus, he even sharply criticized those of the first *aliya* who had begun arriving in Palestine in 1882 simply because they had entered the country by means of stealth. He opposed individual immigration and spoke of an open, official political arrangement that would license the ingathering of the exiles and the ingathering of the Jewish people in the land of Israel. As a jurist and a formalist, the great revolution which he was proclaiming could not be based on stealth.

The Zionist Congress prompted a broad response both in the Jewish world and beyond. While among Jews it awakened Zionist feeling, among non-Jews it aroused the fear of an international Jewish conspiracy. In his diary, Herzl wrote what he dared not say in his address before the Congress: 'In Basle I founded the Jewish state.'

From this time on, Herzl met with world statesmen as the leader of an important organization, and not as an eccentric trying to convince them of the truth of his idea. The organization could finance a part of his activities, which included intercession with and the bribing of courtiers of the Turkish sultan. Throughout the seven years that he headed the World Zionist Organization, and as he grew physically weaker with progressive heart disease, intercession and organization were his major activities. The Zionist Congress was held annually until his death; he continued to attach importance to the outward forms of the Congress and busied himself with props and other symbols. With the help of David Wolffsohn, he worked to establish a Zionist bank, which was founded in 1902. Most of his time, however, he devoted to meetings with bureau chiefs and with ministers throughout Europe.

The importance of settlement in Palestine continued to be debated at the annual congresses, and Herzl found himself manoeuvring between its enthusiastic supporters and its vehement opponents, of which he was one. The question of the Palestinian Arabs was first raised at the Second Congress. The delegates heard a report on their numbers and where they were living, but the issue was at this stage not yet viewed as problematic. Amos Elon writes:

> None of those who convened in Basle foresaw that the State of Israel would be established through war. The delegates to the Congress saw themselves as working for a goal of unparalleled humanity, justice and honour: the redemption of an alien people, the revival of the most ancient national covenant in the world. More sensitive than their contemporaries to the force of national ideals, they ignored the possible effect of similar ideas on the part of the Arabs. There is nothing more egocentric than a movement of national revival. The delegates were confident that the Arabs of Palestine would welcome them with open arms. Anyone who would have argued otherwise – and no one did – would have been declared insane.

Herzl now embarked on an obstinate search for a protectorate, preferring his idea of German patronage. He succeeded in being received by Kaiser Wilhelm II and impressed him with his idea. The Kaiser did not have very many good words to say for the Jews of his country; he accused them of having joined the camp of his opponents and for engaging in moneylending, Consequently, he viewed their removal to Palestine in a favourable light. Here, as was frequently the case, Herzl's Zionist idea coincided clearly with anti-Semitic interests. The Kaiser agreed to appeal to the Turkish Sultan for his consent to the establishment of a colonial society as a public charter for the settlement of Palestine under German patronage. But when the Turks made it clear to the Kaiser that they had no interest in such a proposal or in the entry of more Jews into Palestine, Wilhelm II abandoned the idea.

After months of high hopes, the German rejection was a bitter disappointment to Herzl who had come to Jerusalem to meet the

Kaiser during his visit there. At the Third Congress held in 1899, the delegates sharply citicized their chairman, and Herzl was forced to seek an alternative to Palestine, entertaining the possibility of Cyprus among others. The Fourth Congress was held in London in 1900, and it now became apparent that Herzl had decided to place his trust in Great Britain in his search for a charter. In the spring of 1901 he received an audience with Sultan Abdul Hamid after years of efforts. Herzl proposed to the Sultan that the Jews purchase Turkish bonds on the European markets, and the Sultan requested aid in repaying his country's debts. The Zionist leader raised the matter of the Palestine charter with members of the Sultan's court, but it soon became clear not only that he would be unable to raise the funds demanded by the Sick Man on the Bosphorus, but also that the Sultan was prepared to offer alternatives to Palestine (such as Syria), but not Palestine itself.

The failure of Herzl's diplomatic efforts was reflected at the Fifth Zionist Congress held in Basle towards the end of 1901. Here the voice of the opposition, which preferred practical Zionism and settlement in Palestine to Herzl's futile travels, gained the upper hand. Herzl remained true to his position. He devoted his remaining years to the search, under British patronage, for alternatives to Palestine. He expressed a preference for Cyprus or the Sinai peninsula, but the chances of obtaining either of these territories were slim; Cyprus had ethnic problems of its own, while the Sinai peninsula was not a British colony. Although it was at one time proposed that the Zionist movement lease the Sinai peninsula for a period of ninety-nine years from the Egyptian government, this idea was ultimately shelved because of the British assessment that it would be impossible to supply the area with water.

In the wake of the pogrom against the Jews of Kishinev (45 dead and over 600 wounded in April 1903) and the abandonment of the idea of a Sinai charter, Herzl was prepared to consider the British proposal to grant a charter in Uganda (British East Africa, today Kenya). This proposal, put forward by the British Colonial Secretary Joseph Chamberlain, became an official British offer, designating a large tract of land to be called New Palestine. At this stage Herzl foresaw about ten centres of Jewish settlement throughout the world, where the Jews would be granted full autonomy and would prepare themselves for eventual settlement in Palestine.

Following his visit to Tsarist Russia in the summer of 1903, Herzl received a promise that the Russian government would encourage

Jewish emigration to the Jewish state in Palestine, but would oppose the organization of a Zionist movement in Russia. But leaving Russia, he found a message awaiting him saying that Britain was prepared to advance the establishment of a Jewish colony in East Africa. A Jewish governor would control the colony's affairs on an autonomous basis, with formal authority resting with the British sovereign.

Herzl, ill, hurt, prematurely old, proposed to the Sixth Congress that the British offer to establish a Jewish colony in Uganda be accepted. Herzl did not prepare the Congress, did not foresee the strong opposition aroused by a proposal to settle anywhere other than Palestine, and relied too much on his personal charisma. The opponents of the proposal were headed by a Russian Zionist delegation under Chaim Weizmann; they reacted sharply, tore up the map of Africa, and held a hunger strike. The religious delegates, along with the Western Europeans, supported Herzl's proposal.

When he realized that he might well be outvoted at the Congress – which he had built with his own hands – Herzl replaced the original proposal by calling for a delegation of experts to be despatched to the region in order to study the terrain. This proposal saved his shaky leadership position, but the outcome was far from a sweeping victory: 295 delegates supported his proposal, 178 opposed it and 99 abstained. After the Russian delegates walked out of the Congress, Herzl promised to resign should the delegation not return from Uganda with a positive recommendation. He also declared to the delegates, in Hebrew: 'If I forget thee, O Jerusalem, let my right hand forget her cunning.' This was the last Zionist Congress which he attended. Less than a year later, on 3 July 1904, Herzl died in Vienna, shortly after his forty-fourth birthday.

Any intensive effort to obtain a charter for Jewish settlement in Palestine – or elsewhere – in effect ended with his death. The delegation sent to Africa came to nought. No leader appeared on the horizon to assume responsibility for the Zionist movement. The rift created at the Sixth Congress remained acute. The Seventh Congress, which was to have been held in 1904, was postponed. However, while many considered the Zionist movement an episode that would pass with the demise of its founder, it proved too strong and rooted to disappear with Herzl's death.

The History of the Zionist movement after Herzl's death is primarily that of practical Zionism. While Herzl achieved astounding success in establishing a national organization out of nothing, he failed in his attempt to obtain the political approval that was to precede actual settlement. Practical Zionism prevailed over political Zionism, and 1904 marked a new chapter in the history of Zionism, that of the second *aliya* and the waves of immigration which followed. Herzl became the symbol of the Zionist consensus immediately after his death. His most vehement opponents of yesterday once again became his admirers, agreeing that there was no one to replace him.

At the Seventh Congress, held in Basle in July 1905, a small Executive Committee headed by David Wolffsohn, Herzl's confidant, was elected. For the first time, a decision in favour of strengthening Jewish agriculture and industry in Palestine was adopted. The composition of the committee symbolized the new approach – three representatives of practical Zionism sat alongside three representatives of political Zionism.

Wolffsohn was an excellent organizer, and a lacklustre realist. He maintained the political contacts with the Turkish leaders before and after the Young Turks revolution, with the courtiers of Tsarist Russia, with Germany and Britain – without success. The Russian opposition which had criticized Herzl severely criticized Wolffsohn also, and in 1911 he ended his tenure. Professor Otto Warburg, an enthusiastic proponent of practical Zionism who represented the antithesis of the approach adopted by his two predecessors, was elected in his stead.

The policy change of the Zionist movement had already begun in 1908, with the establishment in Jaffa of the Palestine Office headed by Dr Arthur Ruppin. This marked the first meeting between the political viewpoint which belittled the practical approach, and the practical approach which had no faith in the political viewpoint. The parallel lines crossed, and the movement began to engage in an organized and intensive manner in the purchase and preparation of land.

The years before World War I and the war years themselves saw no strengthening of the Zionist movement, which was centred in Berlin. A real change occurred on 2 November 1917 with the Balfour Declaration, in which Britain declared itself prepared to view favourably the establishment of a national home for the Jews in Palestine. The Balfour Declaration was issued out of fear that Germany would anticipate Britain and issue a similar declaration to the Jews, thus winning the sympathies of the Zionist movement at a time when the struggle between the European powers over Palestine was at its height.

The Balfour Declaration was to a great extent the realization of Herzl's dream. It aroused great excitement in the Zionist and Jewish world, and shifted the Zionist movement's centre of gravity from defeated Berlin to London. The leader of the movement for the coming decades was Chaim Weizmann, doctor of chemistry, who played a central role in obtaining the declaration through hundreds of talks with British decision-makers. Indeed, Anita Shapira claims that the Balfour Declaration was the combination of a personality (Weizmann) and a situation (the desire to win Jewish support in the struggle for Palestine).

Yet the Balfour Declaration did not take the form envisaged by Herzl. It made no mention of a state, an autonomous area or even a protectorate. Neither did it define the way in which the national home was to be achieved. It was not a festive declaration, nor was it a direct statement to the Zionist Organization, but rather a letter addressed to Lord Rothschild, to whom Balfour wrote:

> I have much pleasure in conveying to you, on behalf of His Majesty's Government, the following declaration of sympathy with Jewish Zionist aspirations which has been submitted to, and approved by, the Cabinet. 'His Majesty's Government view with favour the establishment in Palestine of a national home for the Jewish people, and will use their best endeavours to facilitate the achievement of this object, it being clearly understood that nothing shall be done which may prejudice the civil and religious rights of existing non-Jewish communities in Palestine, or the rights and political status enjoyed by Jews in any other country.'

But despite the nature, content and style of the declaration, it was welcomed as an important achievement by the Zionist movement and as a breakthrough in the realization of a Jewish state. Weizmann henceforth became the central figure in the Zionist movement.

In March 1918 he came to Palestine as a member of the Zionist Commission sent by the British Government to serve as a liaison between the Zionist movement and the British military authorities. He spent five months in Palestine before returning to London. In 1919 Weizmann appeared before the Supreme Allied Commission, where he spoke explicitly of the establishment of a Jewish government in Palestine once a Jewish majority was created there. In 1920, following protracted negotiations between France and Britain, Britain received the mandate over Palestine, thus commencing twenty-eight years of British administration in that country, a period which began with great Zionist hopes and close ties between the Zionist leadership and the mandatory authorities, and ended in conflict, an open rift and an anti-British underground.

In 1920 Weizmann was elected president of the Zionist Organization. In the debate with the American Zionists, led by Justice Louis Brandeis, who called upon the Zionist movement to invest its resources in Palestine and to establish its central office there, Weizmann emerged victorious. Weizmann represented the 'synthetic' approach, combining political and practical Zionism; he supported the political effort to open the gates of Palestine to the Jews, while at the same time supporting Jewish immigration and settlement. He favoured the establishment of the Jewish Agency for Palestine, composed of Zionists and non-Zionists, which was to represent the Jewish people before the mandatory authorities. The establishment of the Jewish Agency, provided for by the terms of the mandate, gave rise to a bitter debate within the Zionist movement, leading groups vehemently rejecting cooperation between Zionists and non-Zionists. Ultimately the non-Zionists played only a marginal role, and the Jewish Agency became the arm of the Zionist Organization in Palestine.

As an advocate of the synthetic approach, Weizmann manoeuvred between right and left, and was criticized by both. In 1931 the Zionist Congress voted no-confidence in his leadership, electing in his stead the elderly leader who had worked alongside Weizmann for many years – Nahum Sokolow. Only four years later Weizmann assumed the presidency again, when the party structure of the Congress had already taken shape and the Zionist Organization was led by a coalition headed by the Labour movement centred in Palestine.

In the 1930s and 1940s, in an atmosphere of growing tension, the Zionist movement was led by Jerusalem and London, by Ben-Gurion and Weizmann, with Jerusalem gaining in strength *vis-a-vis* London and Ben-Gurion *vis-a-vis* Weizmann. Zionist Congresses were held biennially on the odd years until the outbreak of World War II, but the Jewish Agency for Palestine was now the most active and vibrant factor in the Zionist movement. Its centrality became even more pronounced during the course of the war, when the activities of the world movement were in effect paralysed.

The Holocaust of European Jewry destroyed the vast majority of Polish Jewry, thus eliminating the central arena of Zionist activity. With the end of the war, it became clear that the focus of Zionism in the diaspora had now shifted to the United States, and that the centre in Palestine would assume the leadership of the movement. Paradoxically, political Zionism was vanquished in the gas chambers of the Nazi concentration camps. The Jews of Europe who succeeded in reaching Palestine before the outbreak of the war were saved, demonstrating that the decision to defer immigration pending formal international permission to settle in Palestine had for many proved fatal.

1. The Pre-State Jewish Community in Palestine

Even before the national awakening which began in the nineteenth century, Jews had immigrated to Palestine and were living there. At times the community grew stronger and at times weaker, but the land was never devoid of Jews. These were, on the whole, religious Jews engaged in religious worship and study, concentrated in Jerusalem and other holy cities. Even at a relatively late stage, they did not create a communal framework; rather they remained wrapped up in themselves, subsisting primarily on contributions from Jews living in the diaspora. The culture which developed, parasitic in character, became known as the *halukkah* (distribution), denoting the distribution of the donations among the various religious Jewish groups in the country.

In the 1830s and 1840s, with the establishment of foreign consulates in Jerusalem, Jews began to immigrate to Palestine as groups. Under the system of capitulations prevailing in the Ottoman Empire, the immigrants enjoyed the protection of their home countries. These were no longer religious Jews who came to study and pray in the Holy Land, but rather artisans who came seeking a livelihood. They formed ties with the younger members of the existing Jewish community and began to criticise the *halukkah* system, calling for productive labour, modern education, the establishment of agricultural settlements, and they began to move beyond the Jerusalem city walls. The Ottoman subjects among them were represented by the religious head of the community, the Hakham Bashi.

Until the First Aliya, the Jewish community in Palestine was composed of a Sephardi majority (Jews who had come to Palestine from other Middle Eastern countries and their offspring) and an Ashkenazi minority (Jews from Europe). The Ashkenazi Aliya of the eighteenth century, known as the Hassidic Aliya, created what became known in the historiography of Jewish Palestine as the 'Old Yishuv'. The *Halukkah* funds which supported the Ashkenazim were obtained by special emissaries sent to collect the donations in several centres in Eastern and Central Europe; twice yearly these were transferred from there to the four holy cities – Jerusalem, Hebron, Tiberias and Safed – where they were distributed to all the Ashkenazi residents, regardless of whether they actually engaged in religious study. The Sephardi Jews were supported by a different fund, called 'Tiferet Israel', which was distributed only to those engaged in religious study. The difference in the manner of distribution gave rise to friction between the Ashkenazi and Sephardi communities. Even within the Ashkenazi community disputes and dissension arose about this financial support; in addition to the equal distribution of the *halukkah* funds, certain diaspora communities made extra contributions to members of their own paticular communities, who were organized in special frameworks (*kolelim*). Each *kolel* constituted an autonomous unit and provided for the religious needs of its members (synagogues, *kashrut*, burial, etc.). The Va'ad Klali (General Committee), founded in 1866 and on which all the *kolelim* were represented, was the first joint framework to incorporate a large number of the Jews living in the country. The committee dealt with both religious and secular affairs, such as the payment of ransom for exemption from Ottoman military service, a census of the Ashkenazi community, and more.

The Old Yishuv establishment was opposed to Jewish agricultural and rural settlement. Afraid that this might put the settlers under threat of attack, and afraid that it would lead to the loss of *halukkah* funds originally intended to support religious study, the opposition also had religious foundation: the difficulty of observing the religious commandments in a rural environment was foreseen and the objection to achieving national redemption before the coming of the Messiah was also raised. Only in the latter third of the nineteenth century did members of the Old Yishuv begin to settle in agricultural colonies, which then served as a meeting-place between the Old Yishuv and the new immigrants. The gap between the Old and the New Yishuv was wide, however; most of the religious Jews opposed the idea of the national revival of the Jewish people, viewing it as a violation of Jewish religious tradition. The First Aliya, with its explicitly nationalist basis, was perceived by the Old Yishuv as a grave error. The New Yishuv, formed in 1882 by the immigrants of the First Aliya, established its own separate frameworks and lived a life totally different from that of the Old Yishuv, although there were some who joined the Old Yishuv and lived off the *halukkah* funds. There were even some parents, founders of the first agricultural settlements, who chose to send their children to study at the Old Yishuv schools, but this was not a widespread phenomenon.

The envy with which the Old Yishuv beheld the New highlights the hostility between the Old and New Yishuv. In 1911 the ultra-religious daily *HaModi'a* published an article claiming:

'We who observe all the fast days in memory of the destruction of the Temple; we who pray for the rebuilding of Jerusalem, we who founded the Yishuv with our very bodies and souls; we who do not touch (Gentile) wine or bread because of their daughters and are a people sacred to God; we, without whom there would be no Jewish community in the land of Israel; we who, in coming to the land accepted all its sufferings and will never abandon it – we are not nationalists. And those who came and desecrated the Holy Land, they who will up and leave the land – they are nationalists!'

But it is important to go back to the time before the First Aliya. In the mid-nineteenth century the population of Palestine numbered about 400,000; in 1881 there were some 450,000. Of these 25,000 were Jews; 15,000 lived in Jerusalem and the rest in Safed, Tiberias, Hebron and Jaffa. Two philanthropists left their mark on late nineteenth-century Palestine. The first was the British Jew Sir Moses Montefiore (1784–1885): born in Italy, extremely wealthy, a leader of British Jewry and a supreme justice in English who frequently visited Palestine, he built hospitals, purchased the first orchard near Jaffa, and established the first Jewish quarter outside the walls of the Old City of Jerusalem, called Mishkenot Sha'ananim. The second philanthropist, known as the 'father of the Yishuv', was Baron Edmond (Avraham Benjamin) de Rothschild (1845–1934): grandson of the founder of the dynasty. Born in France, he purchased thousands of dunams of land in Palestine and saved the First Aliya from failure. In 1854 the Rothschild family established a hospital, and in 1860 the Alliance Israelite Universelle which they founded began to operate in Palestine, leading to the opening of the 'Mikveh Israel' agricultural school near Jaffa in 1870. All these were pre-Zionist initiatives and, while rooted in a desire to expose the Old Yishuv to new ways of life, were in no way related to the conception which called for the return of the Jewish people to its homeland. Just as philanthropists operated in other Jewish communities throughout the world, so they did in Palestine. The three founders of the first Jewish agricultural settlement in Palestine – Yoel Moshe Salomon, Yehoshua Stampfer and David Gutmann, who founded Petah Tikvah in 1878 – did not do so out of Zionist convictions. In the same way that political Zionism was born out of anti-Semitism in Central Europe, so practical Zionism was born out of anti-Semitism in Eastern Europe.

The so-called First Aliya began in 1882 after an outburst of violence against the Jews of Russia and other East European countries, the most severe attacks following the murder of Tsar Alexander II by the Narodnaya Volya ('Popular Will') movement in March 1881. One month later the pogroms against the Jews in the Ukraine began, climaxing in April 1882 in Balta. The pogroms strengthened Jewish solidarity and prompted a mass wave of emigration. The majority found their way to the United States, following those who had begun to emigrate in the 1860s, and the many more who had departed in the 1870s as compulsory military service was introduced in Russia. Hundreds of thousands of Jews migrated to the United States in the 1880s; there are no exact figures on the scope of immigration to Palestine, but there was a real wave of some 20,000–30,000 persons, which aroused the fears of the Turkish authorities.

The Sick Man on the Bosphorus, who suffered several blows at this time, was not particularly pleased to receive Jewish refugees from Russia and Romania. Coinciding with the British conquest of Egypt, there seemed to be an international plot to tear away parts of the Ottoman Empire. In the Autumn of 1881, Turkey decided to ban Jewish immigration from Russia and Romania, but the immigrants overcame this ban through bribery. The country was not prepared to absorb tens of thousands of newcomers, and many of the immigrants tried to return to Russia. This *aliya* was important, however, not only for the relatively large number of immigrants it involved, but for laying the groundwork for agricultural settlement: colonies whose very names bear witness to primordiality and hopes for the future – Rishon le-Zion ('first to Zion'), Yessud HaMaala ('the beginning of immigration'), Rosh Pina ('cornerstone') and Petah Tikvah ('gate of hope').

The most prominent group in the First Aliya, though not necessarily the most characteristic or the largest, was the Bilu group (Hebrew initials of *Beit Ya'akov Lekhu ve-Nelkhah*, 'House of Jacob, come let us walk,' Isa. 2 v.5) founded in Kharkov in Russia in February 1882. This movement, which numbered about 500 prior to their immigration to Palestine, was unique because of its national programme, which included settlement in Palestine as a national solution and the establishment of agricultural settlements as a way of life, born out of a desire to bring about a real change in Jewish life. Whereas previous immigration had been prompted by religious motives or flight from persecution, here a sense of national mission was perceptible, of pioneers preceding a large camp of followers. The group displayed the characteristics of a vanguard: vision, enthusiasm, and a readiness for self-sacrifice. They were university and high school students and small tradesmen who had not previously visited Palestine and who arrived in the country with no economic means. The first fourteen Bilu immigrants arrived in Palestine in July 1882 following a bitter debate within the organization; some viewed the decision by these young single people to settle in Palestine as irresponsible and hasty, and had urged them to wait. The members of the group resolved not to marry and to share their income, although they were not socialists. Only when they owned land, their statutes stated, would they be permitted to marry.

The Bilu'im arrived at Mikveh Israel agricultural school, where they worked for a time. At the end of 1882, Baron de Rothschild agreed to support the Bilu'im and they joined the settlement in Rishon le-Zion. The religious members of this settlement viewed the arrival of this secular group negatively, and voiced their criticism. Another group of Bilu'im went to Jerusalem to learn a trade, others settled in Jaffa, and several returned to Russia. Only nine of them remained to found the first Bilu settlement of Gedera in November 1884.

In May of that year the ban on Jewish immigration to Palestine was tightened. The Turkish state council decided to permit only pilgrims to enter the country, and then on condition that they did not remain for more than one month. Once again, however, bribery proved an effective means of gaining entry at the ports, and limited illegal immigration ensued. Bribes were financed with the help of philanthropists, reinforced by the founding of the Hovevei Zion ('Lovers of Zion') society, which first convened in Kattowitz in November 1884 and specialized in providing financial support for immigration to Palestine. The conference was held in honour of Sir Moses Montefiore's hundredth birthday, indicating symbolically that the society intended to follow in his footsteps – his love of Zion, help for the needy living in Palestine, and his encouragement of productivity – while it was not an activist national movement. Gradually, over the years, the term Hovevei Zion came to be synonymous in Hebrew parlance with non-commitment; the 'lovers of Zion' were not immigrants and not *aliya* activists. This does a certain injustice to this group of Jews who, like others, worked on behalf of the land of Israel before the establishment of the Zionist movement.

The settling of the nine Bilu'im in Gedera put an end to the wanderings and temporary lifestyle that had characterized their first two years in Palestine. In many respects the Bilu'im failed. Only nine remained to found a settlement of their own, and hundreds of the organization's members never immigrated to Palestine. They did not fulfil their dream of establishing a new social order. At the time of the establishment of Gedera, seven Jewish agricultural settlements had already been founded in Palestine, with the help of philanthropists, and these Jewish farmers had in many cases purchased the land whilst still abroad. Nevertheless, the attempt of the Bilu'im to set up a real movement, and the fact that they left their mark of the Mikveh Israel school, Rishon le-Zion and Gedera accorded them historical importance.

Most of the agricultural settlements in Palestine enjoyed the protection of Baron de Rothschild. Rothschild invested the enormous sum of £1.6 million (as opposed to £82,000 invested by the Hovevei Zion society) in settling the land, and there is no doubt that without his vigorous involvement, the entire settlement endeavour at the end of the nineteenth century would have failed. Even those immigrants who arrived with some capital could not meet the huge outlay required to build an infrastructure, and only a philanthropist such as he could have saved these settlements. He appointed and funded agents in the settlements but the regulations issued by these agents (prohibiting guests for more than forty-eight hours without permission, for example, prohibiting membership in organizations without permission, etc.) aroused considerable anger among the settlers, who became increasingly hostile towards the Baron's bureaucracy. An elite emerged within the settlements of those who, like Rothschild's representatives, spoke French, sent their sons to study in France, and provided their daughters with piano lessons. This elite, which ran counter to the dream woven in the diaspora of self-fulfilment in the land of Israel, aroused the anger of the members of the First Aliya. Rothschild, alarmed by the memory of the Paris Commune, opposed any form of cooperative living. The settlements which he founded were in the spirit of his monarchic and conservative approach.

Gedera was not a Rothschild settlement. It enjoyed the support of Hovevei Zion, but for many years suffered severe poverty and could not support its settlers. Several returned to Russia, and others moved to other settlements. While the Bilu'im were prepared to accept Rothschild's patronage, he refused to enter into an association with them, apparently because of their non-observance of Jewish religious commandments. Be that as it may, Gedera was the only agricultural settlement in the 1880s which did not enjoy his patronage and yet maintained its independence, surviving all the many hardships in its path.

In October 1888 the Turkish government lifted the restrictions on Jewish immigration, and in 1889 this new policy began to be felt. It gave rise in 1890 to a large wave of immigration from Russia. Many newcomers chose to settle in Jaffa and Jerusalem, others in the already established settlements, and the rest in three new settlements: Rehovot, Hadera and Mishmar HaYarden. During that year there were months in which immigration to Palestine exceeded emigration from Russia to the United States, but this 'golden age' came to an end in June 1891 when the Turkish government decided once again to ban Jewish immigration after sharp protest by Muslims and Christians in Jerusalem. A ban was also placed at this time on the sale of land and houses to Jews throughout Palestine, regardless of their nationality, a ban which was enforced more strictly than ever before.

In 1900 Baron de Rothschild ceased his direct involvement in the settlements' affairs. His philanthropy was channelled instead through a newly created association over which he still presided, and to which he accorded a grant of 15 million francs. (The Jewish Colonization Association (ICA), as it was called, was later (1923) reorganized, and settlement activity in Palestine was entrusted to the Palestine Jewish Colonization Association (PICA).) The ICA brought to an end the presence of Rothschild's agents in the settlements, whilst working to ensure their efficiency and profitability. The transfer of the settlements to the ICA and the reduced support for the farmers gave rise to a wave of emigration in the early twentieth century.

The importance of the ICA lay in its allowing a transition – though a painful one – from the 'hothouse' of the Baron's patronage to full independence. With the encouragement of the association, new settlements were established in the Galilee which grew arable crops, in contrast to the settlements in the central part of the country which primarily cultivated grapes.

In the course of the First Aliya (which continued until 1903), close to 6,000 chose to live in agricultural settlements. During this period, 23 such settlements were founded, with the development of the

agricultural sector directly dependent upon the opportunity to purchase land in Palestine.

The First Aliya made a significant contribution to shaping the map
of Jewish settlement in Palestine; educational and cultural institutions
were established, and, most importantly, the character of a new
type of settlement – the *moshava* (agricultural settlement of private
farmers) – was shaped. It was not endowed with prominent leaders,
as most of the leading figures who supported it – I.L. Pinsker, leader
of Hovevei Zion and author of *Autoemancipation,* and of course
Baron de Rothschild himself – did not settle in Palestine. And the
writer Asher Ginsberg (Ahad Ha-Am) only lived there for the few
years before his death. Menahem Ussishkin's attempt to found a
leadership encompassing all the Jews of Palestine – the Great
Assembly (HaKnesset HaGedolah) – failed utterly, despite the banners
and horsemen which graced the gathering at Zikhron Ya'akov. The
Jewish community was governed from abroad. The First Aliya did
not leave a rich historiography, and its literary achievements were
meagre.

The enthusiastic youth of the Second Aliya, who began to arrive
in Palestine in 1904, most of them under the age of twenty, found
religiously observant, conservative farmers who paid Arabs low
wages to work in their orchards and who on the whole supported
the idea of Jewish settlement in Uganda. Only the tale of the small
Bilu group kindled the imagination of the pioneers of the Second
Aliya because they resembled them; they were determined, secular,
independent, favouring a communal way of life rather than Rothschild's patronage. It is for this reason that the Bilu'im were later
presented as the central element of the First Aliya, while the historical
truth was very different. Shulamit Laskov is right in saying that the
myth of the Second Aliya contributed more than anything else to
reshaping the image of the Bilu'im.

The Bilu movement was not characteristic of the First Aliya. Bilu
did not found the first agricultural settlement, they were largely
rejected by the other immigrants of the First Aliya, and the only
settlement they established – Gedera – did not prove a great success.

The awakening of the Bilu'im was related to the abortive initiative
of 1874 when thousands of Russian students appealed to the farmers
and were rejected. The failure of the Narodnaya Volya movement
reinforced the readiness of Bilu's adherents and sympathizers for self-
sacrifice. The principle of self-sacrifice and dedication accorded Bilu
its uniqueness and gave it a place of honour in Israeli historiography.

Bilu was, in effect, a youth movement whose regulations set an upper age limit for membership at twenty-five. It taught its members self-sacrifice and called upon them 'to dedicate all to Bilu's goals and society – with sincerity, devotion and loyalty'. The members of the movement forswore private property, not because they professed Marxism, but because they felt that attachment to property would divert them from their overriding purpose.

The Bilu'im did not leave behind any written social treatise, but their statements as recorded in writing indicate an intention to establish a society composed of agricultural settlements which would operate without hired labour, through cooperative services. This was an outlook very close to the contemporary Narodnaya Volya socialism, and contrasted with the Marxist socialism which characterized the Second Aliya.

The Bilu'im did not found the settlement movement in Palestine, but they marked the beginning of the Zionist movement as a movement of national liberation. They were the first to plan an international organization for the settlement of Palestine. They created an identity between the immigrant settler and the national worldview which believed in changing the fate of the nation. They were less sophisticated than those who came after them, and their political efforts did not bear fruit. While Herzl was a democrat and a liberal, they envisaged a well-disciplined society; while Herzl was modern in his outlook, they sought a return to agricultural romanticism. But both were opposed to Jewish plutocracy.

The First Aliya brought to Palestine only two percent of the 1.5 million Jews who left Eastern Europe. Within twenty-two years, the Jewish community in Palestine doubled in size from 25,000 to 50,000, of whom 6,500 were living in agricultural settlements. This growth was considered sufficient by many members of the First Aliya who envisaged a slow and gradual growth of the Yishuv. Herzl's approach, which gained a foothold in the Jewish world on the eve of the twentieth century, failed to strike a chord in all but a few of them.

The Second Aliya (1904–1914) began after the pogroms in Kishinev (19 April 1903) during which some 50 Jews were killed and 2,000 homes destroyed. The pogroms constituted a climax of anti-Semitism in Russia, during which many Jews were driven from their homes and the admission of Jewish youth to schools became increasingly difficult. During the ten years of the Second Aliya some 40,000 Jews arrived in Palestine, but at least half of them left the country. David Ben-Gurion remained convinced to the last that only a tenth of the

Second Aliya immigrants remained in the country. While there are no exact figures, this was probably an exaggeration. It is clear, however, that immigration to Palestine continued as a thin stream amid the great tide of Jewish migration – 1.2 million during this period. On the eve of World War I, the Jewish community in Palestine numbered 85,000, about twelve per cent of the country's population. Half of them were considered part of the Old Yishuv who lived on *halukkah* funds, and half were of the New Yishuv living in the cities and agricultural settlements.

Looking back, it is hard to dispute the fact that the Second Aliya was the most important immigration wave and the one that left the deepest mark on Israeli society. It brought to the country traits which were not found in either the Old Yishuv or the First Aliya – leadership, a clear worldview, and organizational thinking.

The most prominent group within the Second Aliya was the group of youths who founded the institutions of Jewish society in Palestine. They founded the various workers' parties, the welfare institutions, the labour organizations, the new forms of agricultural settlement – the *kvutza*, the *moshav* and the *kibbutz* – the parliamentary institutions (Asefat HaNivharim, the Elected Assembly), and even the religious institutions (the chief rabbinate). The leaders of the Second Aliya were to govern the Jews of Palestine, and later of Israel, from the 1920s until the 1960s, joined from time to time by later immigrants and those born in the country. The institutions which they founded and the norms which they set in their youth served to perpetuate both their leadership and the institutions themselves.

During the ten years of the Second Aliya, it was decided that Hebrew would be the language spoken in the country. While the so-called 'language war' continued through the 1920s and 1930s, the die had already been cast. During this same period, the first Hebrew high school was established, as was the Technion.

Most of the members of the Second Aliya were middle class, and they settled in cities, especially in Jaffa, preferring urban life. In 1909 the residents of Jaffa founded the first all-Jewish city, Tel-Aviv. Established first as a quiet residential suburb adjoining tumultous Jaffa, it soon became a large, modern city alongside the crowded and antiquated Jaffa. The small village of Haifa began to develop with the arrival of the Hejaz railroad in 1904, and thousands of immigrants settled there. Jerusalem and the holy cities (Safed, Tiberias and Hebron) were reinforced primarily by religious immigrants who joined the Old Yishuv. Young immigrants were attracted to the agricultural settlements, imbued with the idea of replacing the Arab workers hired by the Jewish farmers. The principle of 'Jewish labour' became a cardinal issue in the first decade of the century, and remained important during the decade which followed.

The first decade of the twentieth century was a propitious time in Palestine. Even taking into account the lack of documentation and the effects of nostalgia, it would nevertheless not be far wrong to say that this was one of the brightest periods in the country's history. Immigration continued and hopes flourished with the visit of Kaiser Wilhelm II and his meeting with Herzl; the Young Turks revolution and the subsequent disappointment only came later. The agricultural settlements recovered from the crisis resulting from the severing of their ties with Rothschild. The citrus orchards made Petah Tikvah a success story – citrus fruits beginning even to rival the grape industry – and scenes of poverty became rare.

The beginning of the century witnessed the growth of an industrial momentum which developed out of agriculture. Factories manufactured products from agricultural raw materials (wine from grapes, olive oil, soap from other oils) or farming tools (water pumps and filters for the orchards). The early years were marked by many industrial failures, but there were also significant successes which later Israeli historiography, with its romantic, agricultural slant, tended to gloss over. The first winery founded in Rishon le-Zion in 1890 was a huge success, becoming a diversified enterprise. It was the first plant to use electricity, although this had to be done clandestinely after Abdul Hamid had imposed an explicit ban on its use, a ban which was lifted by the Young Turks in 1908. Another large enterprise was Leon Stein's metal factory in Jaffa, which produced filters for water pumps, metal parts for farming tools and carriage wheels, etc. The factory, with its 150 employees, grew beyond the country's needs and later entered into financial obligations that it was unable to meet. But the very fact that at this early period in the history of the New Yishuv such a factory existed, producing modern tools by modern means and in such large quantities, presents Palestine during these early years of the twentieth century in a different, uncommon light; there was an industrial sector, complete with labour disputes, and there were capitalists – albeit few – who invested both capital and knowledge.

A lost list of reasons, notably the lack of appropriate infrastructure, the inexperience of the workers and a constant scarcity of credit, caused the failure of most of these pioneering efforts prior to World

War I. But their failure does not nullify the importance of these beginnings. The factories that came and went produced experienced workers. Some of these founded factories of their own which proved much more successful than their predecessors.

The decision adopted by the Jewish Agency to favour agriculture over industry transformed the new Jewish community in Palestine into an agricultural success story, at a time when the developed Western countries had already experienced the Industrial Revolution. Had the collective effort been divided between agriculture and industry, the achievements of the 'golden age' of Jewish industry in Palestine during World War II might have been attained earlier. Instead, the decision to promote agriculture left industry, until a relatively late stage, in the hands of private individuals who found it hard to cope with the lack of credit, the poor infrastructure, and marketing problems.

As the Jewish community began to flourish in Palestine, the sceptical Zionist movement came to recognize it. After the founding of the Zionist Anglo-Palestine Bank in Jaffa in 1903, and after land had been purchased by the Zionist movement near the Sea of Galilee, a branch of the movement called the Palestine Office was opened, as mentioned above, in Jaffa in 1908, headed by Dr Arthur Ruppin. This was not an autonomous, elected body, but rather an arm of the Zionist Organization.

Largely through the efforts of Dr Ruppin, the Palestine Office became an important factor within the Yishuv; it purchased land and played a role in defining the new forms of settlement which characterized the Second Aliya – the *kvutza* – and the Third Aliya – the *moshav*. The *kvutza* was developed as an egalitarian collective farm whose members shared in the labour and received their share in services, not in wages; while the later *moshav* emerged as an agricultural settlement whose members were partners both in purchasing the means of production and in marketing, and who were committed to mutual assistance, while each continued to own property of his own.

The new forms of settlement established by the Second Aliya – and indeed, virtually no new forms were added after 1920 – were not the product of a socialist ideology, although most of the settlers who believed in a communal way of life were socialists. The socialists of the Second Aliya did not want to be like the farmers of the First Aliya, who were property owners and employers. They preferred to live at first as hired labourers, without property, and to await the

Marxist revolution which was historically inevitable.

Arthur Ruppin was not a part of the pioneering Zionist wave which arrived in Palestine at the turn of the century – not in age, as he was born in 1876, making him about ten years older than the others, nor origin, for he was born in Prussia while most of the pioneers came from Eastern Europe, nor in his way of life – he had studied economics and law at the Halle and Berlin universities and served as a lawyer and a deputy judge in Berlin. He was nevertheless very close to the young Jewish workers and was considered the leader of Zionist agricultural settlement. Ruppin was the motivating spirit behind the purchase of land by the Jewish National Fund (JNF). He founded several national farms in order to prepare the young immigrants for agricultural work, he participated in the birth of the new settlement efforts, and helped to found the Ahuzat Bayit quarter which later became the city of Tel-Aviv.

Ruppin viewed the pioneers of the Second Aliya – those thousand young men who went to work in the agricultural settlements as soon as they arrived in the country – as the major element within that wave of immigration. These young people, who did not leave the country after two or three years and who, in effect, founded the labour movement in Palestine, did more than any other group to define the character of the Jewish community which developed there. All born in the mid-1880s into the lower middle class, they had all received a religious and secular education, although the various social ideologies prevalent in Eastern Europe had obviously influenced them. Bonded, therefore, by a variety of common factors, they were self-confident, viewing themselves as a vanguard.

In 1905 the first two labour parties were founded in Palestine: HaPoel HaTzair (the 'Young Workers' party) which was a non-socialist party laying special emphasis on the value of labour but opposed to the idea of a class struggle, and Poalei Zion ('Workers of Zion') which was a clearly Marxist-oriented labour party – even adopting slogans later used by the socialist parties. The unification of these two rival parties a quarter of a century later created the ruling party of the Yishuv, and later of the state.

Undoubtedly the most avant-garde aspect of the Second Aliya was the establishment of a miniature military organization. This was a kind of secret society and was called Bar-Giora after one of the leaders of the great revolt of the Jews against the Romans, who was put to death after Titus's victory parade in Rome in 71 CE. The aim of the organization was to take over from the Arabs the task of guarding the Jewish settlements and to place it in the hands of the pioneers. It was founded in 1907 within the Poalei Zion framework and did succeed in transferring several settlements to Jewish guards. Less than two years later, the HaShomer ('The Watchman') organization came into existence, founded by members of the Bar-Giora society and others – forty in all. Placing the maintenance of security in Jewish hands remained the goal and indeed it was achieved in the Galilee, and was extended to the settlements of Samaria and Judaea. The organization expanded to some 100 members and founded two settlements in the northern part of the country over the years up to 1920 when it ceased to operate.

HaShomer had a romantic aura, emulated the lifestyle of the Arabs and the Bedouins, and to a great extent shaped the character of Israel's security doctrine. The mystery which surrounded the organization's activity, the new Jewish heroism, the self-confidence: all these were a source of attraction and admiration. Jewish youth movements abroad saw HaShomer as the realization of the modern Jewish dream, and even adopted its name – the important youth movement named HaShomer HaTzair, for example. There was for a time tension between HaShomer, as an armed organization, and Poalei Zion to the point that members of HaShomer were expelled from the party. They were, however, only to be reinstated three months later.

Many of the institutions which characterize the Israeli labour movement have their origins in the second decade of the century against a background characterized by young, single, homeless, idealistic and enthusiastic immigrants. This reality led to the establishment of laundries, workers' kitchens, and a health service.

While the communal idea was present among the early waves of immigration, its implementation was less ideological than practical. The absence of a supportive family required some communal alternative. The contracting groups, the kitchens and the health funds were all related to this lack of family, to poverty, and to the need to make efficient use of the few available resources. Ideology was to follow reality.

It was the allocation of work on Jewish publicly-owned land by the Palestine Office that encouraged the collective structures. The work was contracted out, and the most practical means of carrying it out was through cooperation in consumption and production. *Kvutzot* (cooperative groups) were formed, generally for a period of several months to a year, and on the completion of the work were disbanded. This was a commonly accepted method, and those involved did not view it as a permanent social solution but rather as a convenient work arrangement. The first agricultural *kvutza*, Degania, was founded at the end of 1910, its permanent format representing a new social outlook.

The cooperative groups were in effect founded as a result of the failure of the young people of the Second Aliya to take over the agricultural job market. The Jewish farmers preferred cheap Arab labour to the more expensive Jewish labour. Work in the orchards required a large labour force but, despite considerable effort and partial success, these jobs were on the whole not filled by Jews. The Jewish workers could realize their goal of Jewish labour only through contracted work. This ultimately led to the establishment of the *kvutza*, which ran counter to the original intention of a class struggle against the Jewish farmers, by according its members private property, albeit in a cooperative framework.

In one way, the story of the Second Aliya can be portrayed as the ongoing struggle between imported doctrines and a complex reality: the principle of the unity of the working class versus the need to ensure the use of Jewish workers and guards; the principle of the rejection of private property versus the establishment of the cooperative *kvutzot*: the principle of the class struggle versus the creation of a new type of settlement which, in effect, obviated the need for such a struggle.

The cooperative workers' group was a copy of a group which operated in Russia under the name of 'artels'. In the early years of the century they were convenient for employers and workers alike. The employers were happy because the workers were intelligent, and wages were paid not by the hour or the day but for completion of the task; and the workers liked the system because they were not subject to overseers or foremen, and they could work independently at their own pace and as they saw fit.

Even Degania, the 'mother of the *kvutzot*', was not originally established as a permanent organization. It was Arthur Ruppin who suggested that the group cultivate the land known as Umm Juni near the Sea of Galilee, east of the Jordan River. The group was composed of ten youths and two young women who had arrived from the Ukraine and who had already been operating as a commune on the Kinneret farm and in Hadera for two years before they undertook to farm the Umm Juni land together. One of the proofs that there was no original intention to function on a long-term basis is the composition of the group: the two women did the cooking and washing, six of the youths worked – with the help of mules – two engaged in guard duty, one served as secretary and treasurer, and one was reserved for *ad hoc* tasks. They intended to move to a new site after two years, as was common at the time, but Yosef Busel, the leader of the group, proposed remaining where they were. His proposal was accepted, thus in effect establishing the first *kvutza*, the structure of which has not changed significantly to this day. Busel himself defined the *kvutza* as 'a form of settlement which obliges us to perform the work ourselves, not by others, and without outside management.' Even today the uniqueness of the *kvutza* (or the kibbutz, as it is more commonly known) lies in its being a social and geographical enclave whose members enjoy social equality. The members work according to the immediate local needs and to a work schedule set by a work steward. This position rotates frequently. There are no wages for the labour but only services – housing, schools, food, culture, medical care, etc. Everyone enjoys an equal standard of living, and members are given money – equally – only to purchase goods and services outside the kibbutz. The individual electing to live in a *kvutza* relinquished a considerable portion of his privacy for a communal way of life. Children were raised in 'children's houses' from birth, for example, and not in their parents' homes; their daily needs were attended to by members assigned to child care and teachers, and they spent only a few hours in the afternoon and on the Sabbath with their parents. Meals were eaten in a common dining room and not at home, and the living quarters therefore had only an alcove to serve as a small kitchen for light refreshments.

While this experimental framework has stood the test of time, it never became a way of life for the majority. The percentage of Israelis living in such communities has always been between three and four per cent. It is a way of life that is suitable for those who choose it and who are prepared to accept its conditions. But, in fact, many of those born into this way of life accept it and choose to remain even after having becoming acquainted with city life, studying at university, and living a part of their lives outside the kibbutz.

The *kvutzot* of the mid-twentieth century were ascetic in nature. Many were far removed from the urban centres. They suffered from poverty and temporary conditions, lacked basic services and proper health care, and had to defend themselves against robbers and Arab gangs. In the 1960s their situation began to undergo a change for the better; the small administrative cadre, self-employment and diligence bore fruit, and, together with the partial shift from agricultural to industry and the improvement of the standard of living, many of the kibbutzim joined the Israeli middle class.

On many kibbutzim today children live with their parents, homes are larger, and many have televisions, telephones and other modern conveniences. Kibbutzim permit their members to study at university as well as to travel abroad – both on a queue basis. There is still a common dining room, and everybody is still required to do whatever work is needed. A new *modus operandi* has evolved between the cooperative spirit and the national desire for private ownership, family ties, etc. The kibbutzim are still considered the elite of Israeli society within the framework of the labour movement. They are prominently represented in the upper echelons of government and particularly in the Israeli army, where their members hold positions of command and volunteer for special duties.

The success of the kibbutz and its identification with the miracle of Israel's rebirth is attributed first of all to its adaptability while it retained its uniqueness. The kibbutz has evolved into a multi-generational society concentrated in a single geographic location, at a time when the modern world is dividing the extended family into its component cells. It is an ideological society which inculcates its children from the very first with clearly defined goals and values. It is a society which is capable of undertaking national tasks because of its homogeneity, and is almost completely free of delinquency. Yet it does have serious problems. The distance from the centre which in the past characterized the kibbutz has been shortened by the improvement of roads and an increase in the use of motor vehicles. Industrial development led to a need for hired labour, primarily from the immigrant towns established in the 1950s and 1960s, thus creating growing tension between the kibbutzim as employers and the residents of the development towns. The capital which accumulated in the kibbutzim was invested during the 1980s on the stock exchange in order to ensure its value during the difficult inflation years (100–400 per cent annually), and a large portion of this money was lost, exposing the weakness of the kibbutz.

The kibbutzim of the 1980s are still a fascinating, unique phenomenon, still a cooperative island in a materialistic society, a socio-economic success story, and an example of a social experiment which grew out of objective necessity and became part of an ideology, but they are facing a very serious economic crisis which can be solved only by massive government aid.

At the beginning of the second decade of the century, agricultural workers founded Kupat Holim – a health fund. These young people, many of whom were barely twenty years old and single, needed medical attention for frequently recurring bouts of malaria. Kupat Holim was based on the principles of mutual aid, with payment according to the number of workers in the family. The intimate nature of the founding group was reflected in one of its principles: each member undertook to care for an ailing co-member for one night, or to send someone in his stead. Over the years, the nature of the health fund underwent considerable change. In 1920 it became part of the Histadrut (the General Federation of Labour in Israel). Central clinics were opened where doctors received patients; pharmacies where the patients received medication prescribed by a doctor free of charge; and hospitals owned directly by Kupat Holim. Despite the changes, however, Kupat Holim retains its special character to this day. Most Israelis are members of the Histadrut and receive medical services from its health fund, while others choose other forms of health insurance. Israel has no national health insurance law.

The Third Aliya lasted from 1919 to 1923, and numbered some 35,000 immigrants. In many respects, this was a continuation of the previous wave of immigration, with the time gap between them due primarily to the outbreak of World War I, which precluded population movement. During the war Palestine was transferred from Ottoman to British rule; at first this was military rule, but this was replaced by the temporary mandate accorded to Britain by the League of Nations over the territory east and west of the River Jordan. The change of government in Palestine, the Bolshevik Revolution in Russia and the Balfour Declaration were all among the factors which prompted the Third Aliya.

The immigrants of the Third Aliya were optimistic, believing that World War I would also be the last. It was composed largely of young pioneers who joined the workers of the Second Aliya, ten to fifteen years their seniors. Several important institutions were founded during the Third Aliya, some which remain to the present day and others which were later dissolved, mostly in cooperation with veteran immigrants of the Second Aliya: the Gedud HaAvodah (the 'Labour Legion'), the Histadrut HaKlalit ('General Federation of Labour'), the Hevrat HaOvdim (umbrella organization of Histadrut-owned enterprises), the Haganah (official underground organization of the Jewish community in Palestine) and *moshav ovdim* (cooperative smallholders' settlements).

The first moshavim were founded in 1921. Based on the principles of self-employment, mutual aid, collective purchase of equipment and raw materials, and joint marketing of agricultural produce, they entitled each member to a separate farm on state land. Unlike the kibbutz, in which the means of production were collectively owned and the individual was assigned his task according to the work schedule, receiving services (housing, food, education, culture, etc.) rather than cash, the moshav formed an intermediate model, a number of collective elements standing alongside a significant emphasis on privacy.

The moshavim attracted farmers who objected to the social intimacy of the kibbutz, and there are today over two hundred such communities throughout Israel. Their disadvantage emerged only after the establishment of the state and the mass waves of immigration from the Middle Eastern and North African countries: each farm on the moshav can pass into the hands of a single son only, and if a family has more than one son, the others must leave the moshav. This did not pose a serious problem during the 1920s and 1930s when families were small. But the new immigrants, with families of 8–10 children and with a close-knit family structure, found it hard to adapt to these conditions. In the 1970s and 1980s the moshav movement continued to face a crisis which may lead eventually to a structural change and perhaps even the abandonment of its collective principles: the stronger farms will sustain themselves while the weaker will go under.

In June 1920 the Irgun HaHaganah HaIvri BeEretz Israel (the 'Jewish Defence Organization in Palestine'), or the Haganah as it was known, was established by the new labour party, Ahdut HaAvoda, as a popular volunteer army which trained primarily on weekends. Although the Haganah was ostensibly an underground army, it was accorded semi-official recognition even by the British authorities. In its early years it operated on a local basis, and only during the Arab riots of 1936–39 did it become a permanent organization. The organizational structure and the strategic perceptions which characterized the Haganah formed the basis for the Israel Defence Forces (IDF) established in 1948, most of whose officers emerged from the Haganah.

Six months after the founding of the Haganah, the Histadrut accepted responsibility for it. The Histadrut, founded in Haifa in December 1920, was an alternative to the unification of all the labour parties in Palestine. Attempts at such unification were made in the wake of World War I and the beginning of the Third Aliya, but they proved unsuccessful because of the ideological differences between the socialists and Marxists, and those who opposed a class struggle, seeking only to highlight the value of labour and to improve working conditions. Thus, instead of establishing one labour party which would also serve as a trade union, it was decided to establish an umbrella organization which would include all the Jewish workers of Palestine, which would supply all the workers' needs. Kupat Holim and the Haganah immediately became part of the Histadrut. The Histadrut decided also to involve itself in culture and education; a labour exchange was opened for new immigrants and unemployed workers, a worker's bank was established, together with a workers' newspaper, a workers' sports association, pension funds, old-age homes, and a network of schools. In 1923 the Histadrut founded Hevrat HaOvdim as an overall framework for the cooperative enterprises under its ownership. Over the years Hevrat HaOvdim became a central factor in the Israeli economy, representing about one quarter of the country's labour force and GNP, and symbolizing more than anything else the Histadrut, as a synthesis between a trade union and the ownership of the means of production.

The Histadrut, with its many varied functions, was a kind of 'state in the making' and retained much of its role even after the establishment of the state. Thus, for example, a state labour exchange was established only in 1959, and the 'labour stream' – the network of schools affiliated to the Histadrut – was abolished only in 1953, becoming subsumed into the state school system. Kupat Holim remains part of the Histadrut to this day. Thus, structures whose existence had been justified by the absence of a sovereign state continued to find justification even after statehood had been achieved.

Several issues that were raised in the third decade of the century were translated into organizations designed to serve society at large and to solve general problems. The first and most far-reaching was the Gedud HaAvodah (the 'Yosef Trumpeldor Labour and Defence Legion') founded in 1920. The aim of the Gedud HaAvodah was to establish a single commune of all workers in Palestine, which would engage in defence and settlement tasks. The entire Gedud had a common treasury, and its members shared income equally. At the peak of its strength, the Gedud numbered 3,000 workers who engaged in drying swamps, paving roads and various public works. In the course of the decade it underwent several splits, its leaders returned to the Soviet Union, and some of its members settled on various kibbutzim. It ceased to function completely in 1930.

Hevrat HaOvdim, founded in 1923, was also designed as a framework to incorporate all the workers in Palestine. It was based on a renunciation of the class war and the establishment of an egalitarian classless society in which the means of production would remain in the hands of the public, and even private smallholders would belong to cooperatives and be part of an egalitarian society. The Hevrat HaOvdim proposal, as put forward by David Ben-Gurion, stated that all organizations created by the workers – kibbutzim, moshavim, productive cooperatives, etc. – would be incorporated within one framework, the Histadrut. The Histadrut would coordinate all labour demands in Israel and divide them among the various labour groups, while supplying the workers' needs at its own expense. This far-reaching vision was realized only in part. Hevrat HaOvdim, which became an important factor in the country's economy, founding many new enterprises and acquiring existing ones, was never a workers' society in which the individual worked in accordance with his ability and received compensation in accordance with his needs, with money being unnecessary. The Histadrut, reconciling itself to reality, adopted the pluralistic view which recognizes the role of private, government and Histadrut enterprise, forgoing the attempt by the Histadrut to control the entire economy. Pluralism was thus transformed from necessity into ideology.

In 1927 the HaShomer HaTzair kibbutzim (dating from 1920 onwards) established their umbrella organization, known as HaKibbutz HaArtzi. The story of HaShomer HaTzair is one of the most interesting and unique in the history of the Zionist movement. This was a youth movement founded in Poland during World War I, as mentioned above, named after the HaShomer society in Palestine which caught the imagination of the young Zionists in the diaspora. As the leaders attained maturity, they immigrated to Palestine at the beginning of the Third Aliya, and adopted Marxist ideology. They foresaw the realization of their dream in the founding of radically egalitarian agricultural communes, and dreamt that the entire country would some day be a network of such communes, beginning in the beautiful landscape of the Galilee. The name they chose, HaKibbutz HaArtzi ('*artzi*' meaning countrywide), is indicative of the worldview of this movement.

HaShomer HaTzair participated in the Histadrut elections, and its entire membership lived on the various kibbutzim. When an urban group sought to join the movement in order to increase its political influence, the movement's leaders objected and the group was forced to stand apart as the Socialist League. Only in 1946 did HaShomer HaTzair stand for election as a bona fide party, with branches in the cities. The dream of transforming Jewish society in Palestine into a large community composed of kibbutzim proved to be utopian.

Of course, there was never any official admission of the failure of the original goal. Although the Gedud HaAvodah itself was dismantled, it left behind permanent kibbutzim. The Histadrut performed many of its original functions, thus fulfilling – more than any other organization – the role of the state in the making. Hevrat HaOvdim was never a workers' society in the full meaning of the term. Immediately upon its establishment, it became an economic force which owned various enterprises and invested its profits in these enterprises rather than accumulating private capital. After the establishment of the State of Israel and in the decades since then, Hevrat HaOvdim became a central factor in the economy, holding part-ownership of many leading firms. If the criterion for the success of Hevrat HaOvdim is the very ability of a large economic enterprise to develop without the motivation of individual profits, then Hevrat HaOvdim is a success story (or at least was, until the late 1980s.) If, however, it represented an attempt to create a new labour framework which would do away with alienation and employer–employee relations, this is a dream that was never realized.

HaKibbutz HaArtzi became part of the Israeli landscape and constitutes one third of the kibbutz movement. Mapam, its political party, not only reconciled itself to the urban reality – even its leader lives in the city – but the issues which most concern it today are political. In many respects HaKibbutz HaArtzi is a success story – economically, culturally and educationally – although the dream of creating a society composed solely of kibbutzim of course proved unachievable, and the movement has reconciled itself to a much more pluralistic vision of urban–rural cooperation in a common struggle.

Unlike the Second and Third Aliya, the Fourth Aliya (1924–1928) was not ideological in nature. It was called the 'Grabski Aliya', by many, after the Polish minister who adopted a policy of heavy taxation, and it was characterized by middle-class people who preferred large cities to rural settlement. Some 80,000 Jews arrived in Palestine during this period, about 20,000 of whom left shortly after their arrival. They experienced a period of economic prosperity in 1925 but this was immediately followed by economic depression. Although they introduced no ideological or structural innovations in Jewish society in Palestine, their greatest contribution was a sense of normalization: during the years when the gates to the United States were virtually closed, Palestine became the focal point for Jewish immigration. Those who came were not only idealists and pioneers, but ordinary people who wanted to live an ordinary life; this went to show how successful the pioneers had been in establishing social institutions that were capable of absorbing such a large number of new immigrants.

There were five major waves of immigration between the beginning of modern Jewish settlement in Palestine and the establishment of the State of Israel. The Fifth Aliya was the largest of all, lasting from 1930 until 1939; during this period 145,000 Jews arrived in the country. Some were young and idealistic, but most were professionals and well-to-do people fleeing Europe on the eve of World War II. Many of them would not have dreamt of leaving Central and Eastern Europe had not the skies of Europe been covered by darkening clouds. Prominent among them were the German Jews who left their imprint in the cultural field both in music and architecture, and most notably in the academic field. Once again the new immigrants mostly settled in cities, and they arrived without new social structures or ideologies to introduce. Their absorption into society was slower than that of their predecessors, and they remained virtually outside the political system, which was already filled with earlier immigrants.

The Holocaust of European Jewry changed the face of world Jewry. Until then, there had been a gradual but continuous stream of Jewish emigration from Eastern Europe; most chose to settle in the United States, and some in Palestine. This process might, within several decades, have produced a change in the demographic balance in Palestine between Jews and Arabs. The establishment of the Jewish state – the ultimate goal of the Zionist movement – was to be achieved either by waiting until there was a Jewish majority in Palestine, or by dividing western Palestine, so as to create a Jewish majority in that part under Jewish control. Such a partition proposal was put forward in 1937 by the British, but they themselves retracted it before the Jews in Palestine had a chance to respond. The Holocaust created a new situation: most of the potential reservoir for Jewish immigration was destroyed, and because of the strict immigration laws imposed by the British mandatory government, the survivors were not permitted to settle in Palestine. It was no longer practical to await a Jewish majority in all of western Palestine and, at the same time, there was an urgent need to establish Jewish sovereignty, thus providing the survivors with a place to live. A readiness to accept a Jewish state in part of Palestine began to take shape within the Zionist establishment, and in 1947 the United Nations, accepting this approach, voted to establish two states – Jewish and Arab – west of the Jordan River. The Arab states rejected the UN resolution, and in May 1948 attacked the newly declared State of Israel. The outcome of this war was a Jewish state with wider borders than those originally drawn by the United Nations. The remaining territory was later annexed to Jordan.

2. The State – Major Events

The young state, of which many generations had dreamt, was born in an atmosphere of mixed emotions; profound grief over the Holocaust was combined with gladness at the great change in the life of the Jewish people.

The organizations and institutions operating in the Yishuv prior to the establishment of the state had functioned as national bodies. The Jewish Agency, headed by David Ben-Gurion, which had represented the Jewish people before the British mandate authorities, ceased to exist as such, but its central figures moved to the Prime Minister's office and to the foreign ministry. The Va'ad Leumi ('National Council'), which had served as a kind of government for the domestic affairs of the Yishuv, was abolished, and those who held portfolios in it moved into the various government ministries. Central figures in the Histadrut filled the new social government ministries. And the Haganah became the Israel Defence Forces.

The transition from Yishuv to state was thus relatively simple. For decades the Yishuv had lived an autonomous life which prepared it for the establishment of a state with stable institutions and high-level personnel. While there were cases during the War of Independence (1948–1949) in which the legitimacy of the new regime was brought into question, primarily on the part of the two right-wing underground organizations, these were swiftly quashed.

The new state had a population numbering 630,000 Jews and about 150,000 Arabs. The Jewish community was educated and highly developed. Its main challenge was to absorb a very large wave of immigration. The first immigrants to arrive after the establishment of the state were the refugees from the DP camps in Europe, as well as a large group of illegal immigrants who had been held by the British in temporary camps in Cyprus. Some of these even managed to participate upon their arrival in the War of Independence.

In 1949 and 1950 the Jews of Yemen were brought to Israel in an operation known as 'Operation Magic Carpet'. While the operation was legal at the outset, by the end it was carried out against the wishes of the Yemenite authorities, at considerable risk, and only with the help of world Jewry. During those years, a total of 99,000 Jews arrived in Israel from Yemen, on the initiative and under the direction of the Israeli government.

Although for years a death sentence had been imposed on Jews seeking to leave Iraq for Palestine, the Iraqi authorities in 1950 permitted their departure, on condition that they left their property behind. Once again, Israel organized a large-scale operation, known as 'Operation Nehemiah', which reached its peak in 1951, during which some 100,000 Iraqi Jews were brought to Israel.

The absorption of immigrants in the early years of statehood was astonishing in scope, not only in relative terms but in absolute numbers too: 102,000 in 1948, 240,000 in 1949, 164,000 in 1950, and 180,000 in 1951. By the end of 1951 there were more than 684,000 new immigrants in Israel – more than the size of the country's Jewish population when the state was established just three years before. Jewish immigration from Arab countries gradually dwindled. But the mass waves of immigration enhanced Zionist feeling in many countries, and Jews came to Israel from several North African countries. These included Libya and Tunisia, but by far the largest group – over 210,000 by 1963 – arrived from Morocco, primarily in 1955–56 and in 1957, on the eve of and immediately following Moroccan independence from France. The Jews left Morocco in a clandestine operation known as 'Operation Yakhin', organized by the Jewish Agency and the Israeli government, the Moroccan authorities closing one eye or the other.

Such massive immigration naturally raised many problems for the receptive society unable to accord the newcomers reasonable conditions, especially employment and housing. The first wave was housed, in part, in buildings abandoned or left vacant by Arabs during the War of Independence. In the second stage temporary camps were set up for the immigrants, where they lived in tents or huts. Over the years these camps, called *maabarot*, were incorporated into urban neighbourhoods or served as the nucleus for the development towns established in Israel in the late 1950s and early 1960s. Some of the new immigrants were sent to moshavim established for them, despite their lack of previous agricultural experience. The temporary camps remained temporary quarters for too long. Even the financial assistance of the Jewish people in the West was not enough to absorb the immigrants comfortably, and the fact that the 'absorbers' were mostly Ashkenazim while the 'absorbees' were mostly Sephardim left a mark on Israeli society that survives to this day.

The overall burden of absorption was huge. Israel in 1951 was, on average, less educated and less well-to-do than it had been in 1948. Many of the immigrants lived off welfare or earned a living from relief work, while most of the immigrant women were employed as domestic help by the Ashkenazi families in the nearby cities.

There was, however, virtually no expression of protest by the immigrants against this situation in the early 1950s, nor on the political level. Those from Arab lands had not been exposed to democratic political systems, and they tended to support Mapai, the ruling party led by the charismatic David Ben-Gurion, whom many viewed as a messianic figure, naming their sons after him.

The first outburst of violent protest occurred in Haifa in 1959, and there was another significant wave in the early 1970s under the leadership of a movement called the Black Panthers. The sense of discrimination was voiced politically by the second generation of immigrants – those who arrived in the country as children or who were born in Israel in the 1950s. The large wave of Soviet Jew immigrants (some 250,000 between the Six Day War of 1967 and the end of the 1970s) who received relatively better conditions of absorption because of the improved state of the Israeli economy at the time, led to a political shift to the right – the Likud – among Israelis stemming from the Arab countries. This was a belated protest against Mapai, the ruling party establishment, which was no longer headed by Ben-Gurion. This protest created a new voting pattern in Israel, with origin being the best indication of voting behaviour; about 70 per cent of Labour Alignment voters are Ashkenazi, and about 70 per cent of Likud voters are Sephardi.

One of the reasons why Israel could direct its attention to immigration immediately after the establishment of the state was the relatively light defence burden during those early years. The armistice agreements signed in 1949 with all the neighbouring Arab states were to be replaced with peace treaties. The feeling – at least in Israel – was that the armistice agreements were indeed just a step away from the desired peace. The United Nations established a special

Conciliation Commission which reported annually on progress towards peace treaties – albeit non-existent – but for many years the Arabs did not initiate a war. Security problems during Israel's first decade of independence stemmed from terrorist attacks and murders arising from infiltrations into Israel from territories controlled by Egypt or Jordan.

The Israeli response to these infiltrations in the early 1950s took the form of retaliatory attacks, in which the IDF struck military or civilian targets close to the sites of the Arab terrorist attacks in areas under Jordanian, Egyptian or Syrian control. With hindsight, we might question the wisdom of these retaliatory attacks which only contributed to the spiral of violence and counter-violence. For the IDF, however, limited in scope and equipment during those years, this was apparently the most reasonable answer to the infiltrations until the Sinai Campaign of 1956.

Developments in Egypt following the rise to power of Gamal Abdul Nasser led to the tightening of the Arab boycott, greater encouragement of infiltrators from the Gaza Strip into Israel, and most seriously, a naval blockade of the Eilat port, thus preventing navigation to and from Eilat via the Red Sea. The Sinai Campaign was designed to put an end to these developments. It was launched in November 1956 in coordination with an Anglo-French unsuccessful operation in response to Nasser's nationalization of the Suez Canal. Militarily, this was a highly successful operation which lasted only about 100 hours. The IDF gained control of the Gaza Strip and the Sinai Peninsula with only 172 casualties, while Egypt lost many hundreds, with 5,500 of its soldiers taken prisoner. Israel was pressured by the superpowers into withdrawing from the captured territories several months after the end of the campaign, but eleven years of security and freedom of navigation in the Red Sea was the major achievement.

The Six Day War broke out on 5 June 1967, again on Israel's initiative, following the closing of the Straits of Tiran two weeks earlier by Nasser and his expulsion of the UN forces from Sharm el Sheikh and from Gaza. Looking back, it becomes evident that the element most interested in instigating violence at the time was the Fatah organization affiliated with Syria. Terrorist actions and shooting incidents from across the Syrian border prompted Nasser's actions as well as the Jordanian–Egyptian cooperation agreement in the event of a war initiated by Israel. Nasser, whose army was involved in war in Yemen, was not prepared for war against Israel, and was apparently not interested in war at that time. Nor was King Hussein eager for battle. Israel had no interest in a third war with the Arab states, but events developed rapidly and, facing growing internal pressure to take pre-emptive action, the IDF launched an attack and found itself, six days later, occupying all of Sinai, the Golan Heights, the Gaza Strip, and the entire West Bank. Israeli losses numbered 803, while losses incurred by Syria, Egypt and Jordan are estimated in the tens of thousands.

This war, in which chance played a greater role than any other factor, significantly affected the future of Israel, altered national priorities, created a difficult demographic problem, and confronted Israeli society with new dilemmas. Should Israel agree to peace in return for territories? Should Israel establish settlements in the conquered territories? Should Israeli law be applied in the territories? And more. The outcome of the war altered Israel's international status and its image. The new, small, pioneering and egalitarian State of Israel, which arose out of the ashes of the Holocaust, became in the eyes of many a conquering state, ruling millions of Arabs to whom it was not prepared to accord full democratic rights. Israel, which had established close ties with Third World countries, was now seen by many as a colonialist state, and most later severed relations with Israel (especially after the Yom Kippur War in 1973).

After the first shock of defeat, anti-Israeli violence was resumed, both by Egypt and the Palestinians. Two weeks after the end of the war, Nasser declared in a speech that while he could not conquer Sinai, Egypt could wear down Israel's strength. For three years, a static war was waged between Israel and Egypt – the War of Attrition – in the course of which artillery battles were fought on both sides of the paralysed Suez Canal. This war reached its climax between March 1969 and August 1970 when, with American mediation, both sides agreed to a ceasefire. Artillery exchanges also took place with the Jordanian army, and similar though more limited exchanges took place between Israel and Syria. The major problem on the Jordanian front was the terrorist bases from which squads crossed the Jordan River to strike at targets inside Israel. The IDF conducted retaliatory raids inside Jordanian territory against the Fatah bases, and in the largest raid (the Karama Operation of 21 March 1968), the IDF lost about 30 of its soldiers. Terrorist activities on Jordanian soil ceased almost entirely after 'Black September' – September 1970 – when the Jordanian army took severe action against the terrorist concentrations in northern Jordan.

Between 1970 and 1973, the borders were quiet, but terrorist attacks against Israeli targets on a world scale increased – against Israeli diplomats, Israeli athletes (the 1972 Munich Olympics), and El-Al airline offices. The terrorists also hijacked planes flying to and from Israel.

If, immediately after the Six Day War, it had seemed that Israel would be able to reduce its defence burden, it soon became clear that the opposite was the case. Israel found itself ruling over a million more Arabs, and its borders had been greatly expanded. Defence expenditures grew from year to year, reserve duty became longer, and compulsory military service was extended from 26 months in 1966 to 36 months in the aftermath of the war. Israel became a different country, one which focused on security, invested in security, defended itself by ever newer methods. Security, in its various aspects, became the major, if not the only issue on the national agenda.

The chances of peace, which seemed so close immediately after the war, now appeared increasingly distant. Defence Minister Moshe Dayan, appointed during the tense days which preceded the war, announced that he was waiting for a phone call from King Hussein of Jordan. The Israeli government decided on 19 June 1967 secretly to make known Israel's readiness to negotiate peace treaties with Syria and Egypt on the basis of the international border. This decision met with no response other than the convening of the Khartoum Arab Summit Conference at the end of September of that year. This summit declared: no recognition of Israel, no negotiations with Israel, and no peace with Israel. On the other hand, when in 1971 the UN representative to the Middle East, Gunnar Jarring, put forward a proposal for a settlement with Egypt and Jordan, it was the Egyptians who responded favourably while Israel turned it down.

The Yom Kippur War, which surprised Israel in 1973, came in the wake of disappointment with the progress towards peace, relative calm along the borders, and ongoing terrorist activity. Ironically, Israel suffered a heavy and unexpected blow while it was in control of a territory several times its own size, on the holiest day in the Jewish calendar, when there is never any traffic on Israel's roads and the communications media are shut down. On 6 October 1973 Egypt and Syria launched an attack against Israel, with impressive initial results. With considerable difficulty the IDF succeeded in repelling the attack, even crossing to the western side of the Suez Canal. But the price paid by Israel in this war, which lasted until 24 October

1973, was very high: 2,569 dead, 7,500 wounded and 301 taken prisoner.

The Yom Kippur War was a traumatic event in Israeli history, both because of the extent of Israeli losses and because of the shock suffered by all those who, after the success of the Six Day War, had believed that Israel was invulnerable and that the Egyptians were incapable of crossing the Suez Canal. The war produced political changes, sharpened positions, and hastened the development of extra-parliamentary groups. The six years of euphoria – from 1967 to 1973 – were gone for ever.

Towards the end of the war the Geneva Conference was convened with the two superpowers, the United Nations, Israel, Egypt and Jordan as participating parties. The conference led to Israel's signing of two disengagement agreements: the first with Egypt in January 1974 and the second with Syria in May 1974. While the Geneva Conference was not resumed, US Secretary of State Henry Kissinger continued his efforts to widen the agreements achieved in 1974. Indeed, interim agreements between Israel and Egypt, as well as between Israel and Syria, were signed in September 1975, laying the foundations for President Sadat's historic visit to Jerusalem two years later.

When Anwar Sadat first assumed the position of President of Egypt, he was generally viewed as a weak and provisional leader, and his repeated declarations of a 'year of decision' were not treated with any great seriousness in Israel, nor elsewhere in the world. Sadat wanted to restore the Sinai Peninsula to Egypt, whether by peaceful means or through war, and when the former failed to produce results, he embarked on war. The Yom Kippur War restored Egypt's honour, but did not bring victory. However, in the wake of his partial military achievements and the interim agreement with Israel, Sadat found it easier to take a more far-reaching step – his visit to Jerusalem and his historic speech in the Knesset.

Sadat had decided in 1977 to act after the Israeli elections. Like many others, he was surprised at the electoral success of Menachem Begin. However, having consulted with the President of Romania Nicolae Ceaucescu, and following contacts between his Prime Minister Tohami and Begin's new Foreign Minister Moshe Dayan, Sadat decided to take the step which was to lead to negotiations with Israel, concluded in the United States, at Camp David, in September 1978.

The Camp David Accords constitute the basis for Israel's only peace treaty. Israel was to relinquish the entire Sinai Peninsula; all the Israeli settlements in Sinai as well as three modern airfields built there for the IDF were to be evacuated. With regard to the West Bank and Gaza district, it was agreed the establishment of a Palestinian administrative authority in the territories would be negotiated, though it would function as an autonomous area for five years. In the course of this period, negotiations on the future of the territories would proceed, with the participation of Egypt, the Palestinian administrative authority, Jordan and Israel.

After thirteen days in Camp David, the agreement was signed on 17 September 1978 and Menachem Begin returned to Israel, into the midst of a sharp debate. Within his own party, he was criticized for having agreed to relinquish the whole of Sinai and to abandon all the Israeli settlements there, as well as for accepting the idea of autonomy for the West Bank and Gaza, which meant either relinquishing or postponing the extension of Israeli law to these territories. Certain circles within the Labour party, especially those affiliated with the settlement movements, criticized him for his readiness to abandon the Israeli settlements in the Sinai, arguing moreover that his opposition to the principle of surrendering territory in the West Bank would lead him – through the autonomy plan – to a surrender of all the territories and to a process which would ultimately result in the establishment of a Palestinian state in all the territories conquered by Israel in the Six Day War.

Ultimately, following heated debate, the Knesset approved the Camp David Accords by a large majority. Menachem Begin's Herut party split, and a group of extremists from within it formed the Tehiya movement. Most Herut Knesset members did not support the agreements, and it was the Labour party which accorded them the overriding majority.

The agreement between Egypt and Israel was implemented: Israel withdrew in several stages from Sinai; the two countries exchanged ambassadors; and there was a partial normalization of relations between them. However, the autonomy talks between Israel and Egypt went in circles. It became increasingly difficult for Egypt to conduct such negotiations in the name of the Palestinians with no Palestinian or Arab backing, while Begin had no special interest in being forthcoming with regard to altering the status quo on the West Bank. The talks were not held in the countries' capitals, by Egyptian decision. But the moment that the Israeli delegation stipulated that the next meeting would be held only in Jerusalem, Israel knew that it was closing the door on the autonomy talks – as indeed was the case.

Begin took advantage of the time-lag between the appointment of the Egyptian ambassador to Israel and the last stage of the Israeli withdrawal from Sinai to annex the Golan Heights. He presumed – correctly from his standpoint – that Egypt would not recall its ambassador before the conclusion of the withdrawal, for in this case Israel would not have completed the withdrawal. In a rapid legislative process which lasted twelve hours, the Knesset – contrary to the position of most of the Labour MKs – decided to extend Israeli law and justice to the Golan Heights. Beyond international protests, this move produced no reaction. Israel's withdrawal from the Rafiah approaches was completed in April 1982, and two months later Israel launched the Lebanese War (officially called Operation Peace for Galilee).

This war, which was intended to last two days and to destroy the terrorist infrastructure in a range of 40 kilometres from the Israeli border, lasted three years; with 650 Israeli casualties, it also failed to realize the dream of some of its proponents – such as the then Defence Minister Ariel Sharon – of establishing a representative and pro-Israeli government in Lebanon. This was the first war which gave rise to controversy in Israeli public opinion, bringing 400,000 to the streets in September 1982 to demonstrate against it, following the massacre of Palestinians by Lebanese Christians in the Sabra and Shatilla refugee camps, under the noses of the IDF soldiers.

Only after the establishment of Israel's National Unity Government in January 1985 was the decision taken – contrary to the position of most of the Likud ministers – for a unilateral withdrawal from Lebanon and for the establishment of a security belt in which a limited number of IDF soldiers would continue to operate on a temporary basis alongside the local Christian militia, which maintained ties with Israel. This unilateral arrangement, which was carried out in June 1985, proved an optimal solution for ensuring the security of the Galilee residents. The withdrawal from Lebanon, the decision to transfer the border dispute between Israel and Egypt over the Taba area to international arbitration, and the return of the Egyptian ambassador to Tel-Aviv allowed the head of the National Unity Government, Shimon Peres, to examine the possibility of widening the circle of peace to Jordan and to seek a solution to the Palestinian problem.

In November 1984, two months after the establishment of the

National Unity Government, King Hussein appeared before the Palestine National Council in Amman and proposed that the Palestinian representatives participate as a joint Jordanian–Palestinian delegation within the framework of an international conference. Hussein's intention was that this delegation, which would discuss a political settlement with Israel through direct negotiations, would lead to a Jordanian–Palestinian federation.

The idea of an international conference did not meet with a positive response within the Israeli political system, which preferred direct negotiations. Yet memories of the Geneva Conference were not negative, and even the negotiations with Egypt in December 1977 had been held within the framework of a kind of international conference. It was Menachem Begin who had written about Israel's readiness to participate in an international conference in the guidelines of his first government (June 1977), but the preference for direct negotiations was clear. Probes carried out by the US showed that King Hussein saw the international conference as the only possibility for conducting direct negotiations with Israel, in which he and the Palestinians would receive less than their full demands. At this stage, Peres strove to ensure that the conference would not contain any element of coercion and would not have the power to veto any arrangement agreed upon on the bilateral level. A detailed agreement to this effect was achieved with the help of the US State Department between Peres – then serving as Vice Premier and Minister of Foreign Affairs – and King Hussein of Jordan in April 1987. However, this agreement was not approved by the Israeli cabinet because of the opposition of the Likud ministers, headed by Prime Minister Yitzhak Shamir, to any idea of an international conference.

If Israel had agreed to the convening of an international conference, would it have been possible to convene such a conference in the spring or summer of 1987? And, if so, would the uprising in the occupied territories have been avoided? The fact is that the April 1987 agreement was not approved, that the international conference was not convened, and that on 9 December of that year the uprising in the occupied territories began.

The uprising began, like similar events elsewhere in the world, as the result of a coincidence of circumstances, but it quickly became a way of expressing the deep and continuing frustration of the masses. On 8 December 1987 there was a traffic accident in the Gaza Strip; a collision between an Israeli lorry and another vehicle resulted in the deaths of four local residents. The residents saw this accident as a deliberate Israeli act designed to kill Palestinians, and rumours of the purported malicious act quickly spread. The following day the Gaza Strip and West Bank began to burn with the fire of hatred; there were demonstrations, stones were thrown at Israeli soldiers and civilians, and Molotov cocktails were launched as missiles. Rubber and plastic bullets, and tear gas formed the response.

The uprising – or, by its Arabic name, the 'intifada' – replaced terrorist actions in the territories with semi-violent protest, requiring Israel to send many soldiers to the occupied territories. Israel's international position was seriously damaged as the measures taken to halt the uprising were broadcast worldwide on the electronic media.

As a product of twenty-one years of frustration under Israeli rule with no hope for change, there are those who are surprised that the uprising did not occur earlier. It opened a new page in relations between Israelis and the Palestinians subject to their control, confronted Israeli society with a new challenge, and provided the background for the elections to the 12th Knesset on 1 November 1988.

The intifada did not pose an existential threat to Israel, but it constituted a continuing nuisance, aggravated the sense of personal insecurity and seriously harmed Israel's image in the world. All the feelings of frustration and hatred towards Israel which had been concealed for twenty years behind blank faces along the squalid roads of the Gaza Strip, in the crowded streets of Nablus, Hebron and East Jerusalem, in stairwells, in the back rooms of brightly lit restaurants, in the garbage trucks and on the scaffolds: all these feelings erupted when social and political hostility combined, bringing thousands into the streets to attack Israelis anywhere, be they IDF soldiers and civilians or Jewish settlers in the territories.

The government, which at first viewed the intifada as an outbreak of local 'disturbances' which could be put down in a matter of days, understood only weeks or months later that this was civil revolt. The revolt comprised a series of activities, the most characteristic being to throw stones at Israeli military and civilian vehicles travelling in the territories. Home-made Molotov cocktails were also sometimes thrown, and there were several waves of knifings of Israelis, as well as cases of the injury and even murder of employers of workers from the occupied territories by their own employees. The intifada was also expressed in a boycott of Israel – Israeli produce disappeared from the shelves of stores in the territories for an extended period. There were even attempts by local leaders to prevent residents of the territories from working in Israel, but the need to earn a living prevailed and this effort failed.

The many villages in the West Bank and Gaza began to be run by local committees. Every few weeks leaflets were published by anonymous groups which instructed the residents how to act. The leaflets determined when a general strike was to be called in the territories to mark the anniversary of various Palestinian events, and during what hours businesses were to open and shut. Those who did not comply with the instructions soon felt the brute force of the local masked youths, who used violence against them. Local residents in the police force were instructed to resign, and virtually all of them did, as did many of the employees of the civil administration. The latter were service workers employed in the areas of transportation, health, etc. who received their salaries from the civil administration in the territories, which was a military framework. Israel, for its part, closed the universities in the territories, claiming that they served as centres for incitement activities, and also closed the schools for several years. Most of the universities were reopened during 1991.

The IDF responded, at first, with the notion that forceful action would nip the outburst in the bud. A debate raged in Israel for many months on whether or not the Defence Minister had explicitly instructed the soldiers to break the arms and legs of the Palestinian demonstrators, but in any event this was what many officers and soldiers understood their duty to be; two or three Palestinians were killed almost daily, and many were wounded. Most of the wounded refused to be evacuated to hospitals in order not to incriminate themselves as having participated in violent demonstrations. Some of the dead were 'snatched' from the hospitals and were buried by their families. In the course of time the situation changed. The IDF reinforced its forces in the territories, issued strict orders on opening fire, and plastic and rubber bullets were used against the demonstrators and stone-throwers. The number of casualties caused by IDF soldiers was greatly reduced, although the masked youths, who in many places seized control of the Palestinian streets, killed anyone they considered a collaborator with the Israeli authorities. Hundreds of Palestinians were murdered, most of whom had absolute by nothing to do with the IDF authorities; this became the most salient mark of the intifada in its last years.

Young children, twelve or thirteen years old, standing by the roadside and throwing stones at army jeeps carrying armed soldiers, wearing full uniform and helmets; soldiers beating youths throwing stones and Molotov cocktails; masses of women going out into the streets and screaming at the soldiers; soldiers conducting surprise searches in Palestinian homes in the middle of the night, awakening the inhabitants and sending them all out to the village square for an identification parade; tens of thousands of people arrested – whether under administrative detention or after trial in improvised courts set up in tents in the Negev; the houses of people thus accused demolished or sealed by the IDF; the expulsion to Lebanon of dozens accused of incitement: all these were familiar sights of the intifada. The small, sophisticated, moral Israel of the 1950s and 1960s was transformed in the eyes of the young generation of television viewers from David into Goliath, while the stone-throwers became the modern-day Davids.

Israel found itself in a very complex situation. No new decision had been made nor any action taken to produce the wave of violent demonstrations. Israeli spokesmen interviewed on the Western television networks said – and justly so – 'They started it. If they won't throw stones, not a hair will be harmed on anyone's head.' There was no one who desired the end of the intifada or who sought answers to the intifada more than the Israelis, but the world was not satisfied with this. It was clear to many that the decades of Israeli rule in the occupied territories with no political light at the end of the tunnel would sooner or later have led to violence, and that one could not relate to the intifada simply in the context of 'who started it'.

After years of terrorist activity, which had made the Palestinian leadership anathema in Israel and the United States, the intifada, because of its popular nature and relatively low level of violence, won the Palestinians points. In Israel, it made it obvious that it is impossible to control 1.7 million Palestinians against their will – without an economic infrastructure of their own, without newspapers or means of self-expression, unable to organize themselves or to set up political frameworks, subject to severe administrative orders and norms of occupation which had extended far beyond the brief period for which they were intended. The sense of insecurity among Israelis grew, and non-essential outings or travel to the occupied territories ceased almost completely. Even East Jerusalem, to which Israeli law had been extended as early as June 1967, became a site for violent demonstrations, stone-throwing, Molotov cocktails and knives, and many Israelis stayed away. At the same time the kidnapping and murder of soldiers and knifings along the 1967 border and inside Israeli sovereign territory, including grenades thrown in Tel-Aviv and other cities, restored to public awareness the existence of the 'Green Line' – the 1967 border erased by government decision from almost all official maps of Israel a quarter of a century earlier – and dealt tourism a severe blow.

The intifada prompted the United States in 1988 to propose a new procedure for the political process, despite its being an election year (in both America and Israel) when the American administration does not as a rule raise political proposals. The initiative put forward in February by then Secretary of State George Shultz sought to overcome the long-standing dispute between Israel and the Palestinians on how to ensure that the proposed interim autonomy arrangement should not become a permanent settlement. The Likud-led Israeli government demanded that the autonomy talks be conducted separately, and that only towards the end of the autonomy period would negotiations begin on the final settlement, while the Palestinians proposed that the autonomy would be a first stage in the application of the final settlement, and that this settlement should be agreed upon before the implementation of autonomy. Shultz proposed the term 'interlock', based on the idea that autonomy talks would continue until a pre-determined date, after which negotiations on a permanent settlement would begin even if agreement had not yet been reached on the implementation of autonomy. He came to the Middle East, shuttled between Israel, Jordan and Syria, and established indirect contacts with the PLO. However, while no party rejected his proposal, neither did anyone endorse it, and the initiative expired with the conclusion of the Reagan administration.

About half a year after the establishment of the second National Unity Government, the Israeli government proposed a political plan of its own, based on elections in the occupied territories which would select a delegation to negotiate an interim settlement with Israel (the Camp David Accords spoke of elections to the autonomy admin-istration only after which all details of the autonomy arrangement for five years would be agreed upon). What remained unresolved was the determination of election procedures (who would be eligible to vote and who to be elected; whether or not the residents of East Jerusalem would be eligible to participate; how the election campaign would be conducted; what type of organization would be permitted in anticipation of the elections, etc.). Egyptian President Mubarak proposed an informal meeting between Palestinian and Israeli rep-resentatives in Cairo. The proposal, raised in the autumn of 1989, was brought before the Israeli inner cabinet, in which the Labour

Alignment and the Likud had equal representation. The Labour ministers approved the proposal, the Likud ministers opposed it, and thus it was defeated.

Following the defeat of the Mubarak proposal, which came in the wake of the Likud's thwarting of the agreement with Jordan and the Shultz initiative, pressure began building within the Labour Alignment to withdraw from the government. US Secretary of State James Baker then proposed a new procedure to determine the composition of the Palestinian delegation to the Cairo meeting. Although Foreign Minister Moshe Arens was involved in formulating the proposal (which included the participation of Palestinians living in East Jerusalem and of deportees whom Israel would be prepared to allow to return), Prime Minister Yitzhak Shamir rejected it, despite the risk of his government falling as a result. This in fact occurred on 15 March 1990.

As the intifada continued the situation steadily deteriorated. The United States did not put forward any new proposals, hinting that for its part both parties could continue to bleed if they did not want peace. The Secretary of State, testifying before Congress on the situation in the Middle East, went so far as to say that if the Israelis wanted to continue the political process, they should please telephone him, even providing the phone number of the White House in Washington. Relations between President Bush and Prime Minister Shamir cooled, and for a long time no meeting took place between the two heads of state – a departure from earlier Israeli–American relations.

The change came after the Iraqi invasion of Kuwait on 2 August 1990, and particularly with the approach of the Security Council ultimatum of 15 January 1991. It was clear that if war should erupt Israel would be involved, at least as one of Saddam Hussein's targets. This new situation led to a renewed understanding between Washington and Jerusalem. The United States, engaged in building its anti-Iraqi coalition, wanted Israel to refrain from dealing Iraq a preemptive blow, and even from responding to the launching of Iraqi missiles against Israel.

The shuttle diplomacy of the Secretary of State, James Baker, in the woke of the Gulf War led to the Madrid Conference on 31 October 1991 between Israel, a Jordanian–Palestinian delegation, Lebanon and Syria, under the chairmanship of the USA and USSR, and with the participation of the UN, Egypt and the European Community. This conference was followed by a series of bilateral meetings in Washington, and by a multilateral meeting in Moscow which dealt with economic projects in the Middle East once peace prevails. Whether the new process will bring about the change which would transform the Middle East into a peaceful region is still not known.

Political Milestones

The first parties to be organized with the renewal of Jewish settlement in Palestine were the labour parties. They vied against one another, they split, and they shaped the image of the Yishuv. The right-wing parties – the conservative party (the 'General Zionists') and the radical right party (the Revisionist Party) were founded in the 1920s, as was the Religious-Labour party.

With the establishment of the state, three major blocs took shape among the 120 Members of Knesset: the leftist bloc, the rightist bloc and the religious bloc. The political system was based on a dominant party – Mapai – which in the early decades, under the leadership of David Ben-Gurion, won about 45 seats and formed a coalition with parties on the left and right as well as with religious parties, on the basis of the principle laid down by Ben-Gurion: without Herut (the right-wing party which succeeded the Revisionists) and without the Communist Party. Thus, the size of the blocs had little significance as long as it was impossible to form a government without Mapai. Yet the blocs remained constant, with changes occurring mostly within the blocs, and very few shifts between them: between 1949 and 1969 the size of the leftist bloc varied from 66 to 71 seats, the size of the rightist bloc from 21 to 34, and the size of the religious bloc from 16 to 18. Thus, it was impossible to form a rightist-religious coalition against the left, a situation which lasted almost thirty years. The question in Israel on the eve of elections was not who would form the next government, but with whom Mapai would form the government. The last elections in which the left commanded an absolute majority were those held immediately after the Yom Kippur War on 31 December 1973. In these elections the entire left won 61 seats, the right won 39, and the religious parties only 15.

An historic change in the Israeli political system occurred in 1977 following the establishment of the Democratic Movement for Change, most of whose members and supporters stemmed from the Labour party. Lasting for only one parliamentary term, this party had an ephemeral existence; but it won 15 seats, which led to the crushing defeat of the Israeli left. In the 1977 elections the entire leftist bloc won only 41 seats, while the right won 46, the religious 17, and the DMC, with its 15 seats, joined the rightist-religious coalition. Menachem Begin, considered by many in Israel as the eternal oppositionist, became the first right-wing Prime Minister of Israel.

In 1981 the picture changed. The DMC collapsed and its members were scattered among other parties. The left- and right-wing blocs became more or less equal in size (53 and 54 seats respectively), and it was the religious parties (with 13 seats) which tipped the scales; as a group, they preferred the more traditional Likud, led by Begin. But in September 1983 Menachem Begin resigned with no explanation. Most commentators attributed his resignation to the failure of the Lebanese War and to his personal weakness. Yitzhak Shamir was elected as a compromise candidate to replace Begin, and he served as Prime Minister until early elections were called in July 1984. In these elections the leftist bloc won 59 seats, lacking only two mandates to block the establishment of a rightist-religious government. The right won 48 seats and the religious partis 13; since they supported the idea of a unity government, the National Unity Government was established.

The uniqueness of the National Unity Government lay not in the coalition between the two largest parties, for such a government had served for three years from the eve of the Six Day War until 1970 under the leadership of the Labour party, but rather in the equal representation between left and right, with the twenty-fifth minister in this government representing a religious party. In addition, for the first time in Israel, an inner cabinet was established; it was composed of ten ministers, five from each bloc, so equality enabled each side to block an initiative proposed by the other. Another innovation in this government was the rotation principle; during the first two years the government was headed by the Chairman of the Labour party, Shimon Peres, while Yitzhak Shamir served as Prime Minister for the latter two years.

The 1988 elections did not produce any more conclusive results. On the contrary, the two rival parties, working together with sharp differences, lost support, while the smaller parties with more clearly defined messages gained in strength. Labour, which stood for election without Mapam (whose six MKs had been elected in 1984 on the Labour list) lost five mandates, winning only 39 seats, while the Likud lost one mandate, winning 40. The entire left-wing bloc numbered

55 seats, the right-wing 47; the religious bloc with 18 was thus holding the balance.

Labour's attempts to establish a government with the religious parties failed. The President charged Yitzhak Shamir with forming a government, but he too encountered difficulties with the religious parties; he turned instead to the Labour Alignment to establish once again a National Unity Government. A sharp debate was held within the Labour Alignment on this proposal. Most of the 'doves' opposed renewed cooperation with the Likud on the grounds that it would prevent any progress towards a political process, with Labour serving as the fig leaf to conceal political paralysis. The 'hawks' argued, however, that slow progress in concert was preferable to Labour's remaining in opposition, where it would be unable to advance any political process. Ultimately, Shimon Peres and Yitzhak Rabin achieved a majority for their position. The Labour Alignment joined the government, waiving the demand for a rotation of the premiership.

The opposition of the Likud ministers to President Mubarak's proposal for an Israeli–Palestinian meeting in Cairo and the opposition of the Prime Minister to Secretary Baker's initiative combined to strengthen Labour's inclination to withdraw from the government in order to try and form a coalition with the religious parties. Following the vote by the Labour party's central committee to dissolve the National Unity Government, Yitzhak Shamir decided to dismiss his Vice-Premier and Minister of Finance Shimon Peres, taking advantage of a legal option which had been waived in the coalition agreement. All the Labour ministers resigned in protest against Peres's dismissal, and several days later, over the rejection of the Baker initiative, the Labour Alignment succeeded, with support from some of the religious parties, in bringing down the government in a vote of no-confidence – for the first time in Israeli history.

The President charged Peres with forming a government. Peres invited the Likud to join, but they refused to join a Labour-led government. Difficulties arose in negotiations with the religious parties, both because of the reservations expressed by their voters at a possible partnership with Labour, and because of the last-minute decision by several of their rabbinic mentors to prefer the Likud. Only one religious party ultimately joined Labour in its attempt to form a government, but, on the morning when Peres was to submit his government to the Knesset for its approval, two of its MKs announced that they would not support it, and the attempt failed.

Shamir was then asked to form a government, which he did in June 1990, joined by all the religious and right-wing parties.

This became a very fragile coalition, since the right opposed the peace process, based on autonomy in the West Bank and the Gaza Strip. When the Shamir Government felt that it could not let down the US President and agreed to take part in the International Conference in Madrid, and suggested the idea of autonomy for the Palestinians, the right withdrew from the Government and Shamir was left leading a minority government. In February 1992 the Knesset decided that the general election would take place in June 1992, instead of November.

Economic Milestones

The first immigrants to Palestine devoted themselves to agriculture. Farming, for them, signified the physical return to the land, a sense of renewed ownership of the ancient homeland, liberation from the trades which had characterized the Jews in the diaspora – small tradesmen, middlemen, etc. – and control over relatively broad tracts of land through their cultivation. Many of the leaders of the Yishuv expressed an unequivocal preference for agriculture over industry, which had begun its rapid development in Europe at the beginning of the twentieth century. The rebuilding of the 1920s included the industrial sector as well. Economic prosperity during this period was closely linked to the waves of immigration. The vicissitudes continued until the establishment of the state, in part because of the narrow economic base and a chronic lack of credit.

Paradoxically, it was during World War II that the economy in Palestine reached its high point. In the entire Middle East, Britain could rely only on Palestine as a supply and production centre. During this period the Palestinian economy exhausted the entire potential built up in the course of the 1930s, and factories worked on three shifts to provide the needs of the British army in food, clothing, ammunition and more. The war years, especially 1941–43, were a test of maturity for the local industries, demonstrating that they were not merely an auxiliary of agriculture.

The tremendous outlays incurred for security and for the absorption of the mass immigration caused the newly founded state economic hardship, leading to the inauguration of a strict rationing policy, in which products could be bought only with the appropriate coupons. This policy ended in the early 1950s, followed by rapid economic growth (an average of 11.4 per cent annually between 1950 and 1958), with the help of massive German aid ('Reparations').

In the mid-1950s, with the appointment of Pinhas Sapir as Minister of Trade and Industry, the government began to encourage industry, with emphasis on replacing imports with local manufacture, by allocating government budgets to selected localities and industries. During those years development towns were established far from the centre in an effort to reinforce the frontier areas and to achieve better population distribution. The government invested huge sums in infrastructure for these towns and in the accompanying industries, primarily food and textiles.

Rising inflation in the mid-1960s and a reduction in the German Reparations, combined with the slowing of immigration and the completion of several major national projects, such as the laying of a water pipe from the Galilee in the north to the Negev in the south, produced a severe recession in 1966 – reflected in unemployment, bankruptcies, and a dramatic reduction in construction. Public investment and increased immigration began to give the economy new direction one month before the outbreak of the Six Day War. This war, which changed the national priorities, also accorded the economy new momentum. The metal and electronic industries now assumed a central place, and investments in security were doubled; new and sophisticated equipment was purchased in order to maintain control in the occupied territories, and guard against terrorism. The country returned to full employment and rapid growth was resumed, but the distribution of income became less and less equal. The balance of payments showed a growing deficit, and inflation began to increase.

The Yom Kippur War of October 1973 cost Israel an entire year's gross national product (GNP). This war was undoubtedly a most significant and negative turning point in Israel's economic history. Professor Michael Bruno notes that for fifty years, from 1922 to 1972, when the country's population grew thirty-fold, the GNP increased by a factor of 250, while the GNP per person achieved a world record, increasing during this period from 15 to 50 per cent of the American level.

The growth in GNP during these years was the result of input of manpower, input of capital (30 per cent each) and a growth in productivity. After the Yom Kippur War economic growth virtually ceased, the new manpower added to the labour force turned to the public sector and not to the business sector, and productivity declined. The energy crisis dealt Israel a severe blow and, unlike the other countries affected by it, Israel found recovery difficult – primarily because both households and the public sector over-consumed.

The Israeli economy entered a spiral; there was a large budgetary deficit and inflation was rampant. The rapid increase in defence expenditures (about 11 per cent of the budget in 1967 increasing to an average of 22 per cent in the following years) prompted Israel to request American financial aid, making Israel dependent on the United States. It also led to an increase in the domestic national debt through the issue of bonds to the public, not in order to invest in the economy but in order to finance expenditures that had no economic yield. The government's massive entry into the capital market greatly reduced the ability of the private sector to use the capital market for investment.

The major factor fuelling inflation was the government deficit which, in the late 1970s and early 1980s, reached an annual rate of over 100 per cent – and by the mid-1980s exceeded 450 per cent. Foreign currency reserves declined alarmingly, and Israel's ability to borrow money abroad was steadily reduced. Thus, the promise by the Prime Minister of the new National Unity Government, Shimon Peres, to implement a far-reaching economic programme led to immediate American aid which halted the race to the last dollar.

The economic programme implemented in July 1985 – including a significant cut in the state budget (primarily in defence and subsidies), a large devaluation, a reduction of the civil service, a lowering of salaries and a price freeze – reduced inflation within a short space of time to an annual rate of 15–20 per cent, saving the Israeli economy. However, to date, economic growth has not returned to the high level it enjoyed in the period prior to 1972.

Half of the Israeli economy is engaged in 'traditional' industries, primarily textiles and food, which have a high labour input and relatively low wages. It is hard for Israel to compete in these areas (especially in textiles) with Third World countries which manufacture much cheaper products and where wages are very low. Israel's relative advantage lies in the know-how industries (such as software), in electronics, etc. Israel lacks natural resources, but it has skilled manpower, and the current immigration from the Soviet Union is serving to enhance its labour force with tens of thousands of engineers, technicians and other professionals. There is also a law encouraging capital investments which provides better conditions for the potential investor, especially in the peripheral areas.

The instability and insecurity of the region is essentially the reason why it is hard to attract foreign investments in Israel, and it is reasonable to assume that a change in Israel's political situation will lead to a readiness to invest in the country and, as a result, also in an increase in the scope of economic growth. The extensive government involvement in the economy is also burdensome. The state budget constitutes about 60 per cent of the GNP (the annual GNP is about $50 billion). There is today a trend towards reducing government involvement, apparent in the beginning of the privatization of government companies (there are in Israel some 150 such companies valued at about $8 billion) among others, but it is doubtful whether this trend will continue; the very large Soviet immigration will, after all, require considerable government involvement.

There is no doubt that Israel has long since removed itself from being classified as a developing country; indeed, on the basis of various indices, it can be included in the moderately developed category of the European Common Market countries. Were it not for its heavy defence burden, Israel could certainly join an even higher economic class.

The Israeli economy now requires about $30 billion to absorb current immigration from the Soviet Union, estimated at one million people, some 40 per cent of whom have already arrived. Israel's success in meeting this tremendous economic challenge will determine both the future of immigration to Israel and the fate of the country's economy.

3. The Structure of Israeli Government

Ottoman law prevailed in Palestine until its conquest by the British. On the eve of World War I, David Ben-Gurion – later Israel's first Prime Minister – and Yitzhak Ben-Zvi – later to become President of Israel – went to Constantinople to study law in order to understand the Turkish *majlis* and to be able to represent the affairs of the young Jewish community in Palestine. The war interrupted their studies, rendering them irrelevant. In the years that followed, the law of the land was to be British.

Article 46 of His Majesty's Order-in-Council of 1923 stated that the Ottoman laws which had existed in the country until the British conquest would continue unless specifically abrogated by order of the Mandate authorities. However, over the years, the High Commissioner issued many regulations which effectively replaced the Turkish laws. The judicial system in Palestine was very similar to the British system, and many local attorneys were educated in Britain. As a result, alongside a hostility to the British immigration policy, there developed an admiration for British government.

When the State of Israel was established it was decided that the existing laws would remain in effect, except for those changes necessitated by statehood. Thus, co-existing side by side in Israeli law were Ottoman law, the British mandatory ordinances, and legislation passed by the Israeli Knesset, with the latter growing proportionately with time. Only in 1980 was Article 46 of His Majesty's Order-in-Council abolished by the Knesset, thus preventing an appeal to British common law in the event of a lacuna. It was decided that Israeli legal norms were to be derived from the Knesset and from Supreme Court rulings and, in the event of a lacuna, that the courts were to rule on the basis of the 'principles of freedom, justice, integrity and peace inherent in the Jewish heritage'. In 1984 Ottoman law was completely abolished in Israel, but many British ordinances continue to occupy an important place in the Israeli law books.

When they discussed the question of an Israeli constitution, the Israeli law-makers were aware of Britain's lack of a constitution. The Declaration of Independence clearly states:

> 'We declare that, with effect from the moment of the termination of the Mandate, being tonight, the eve of Sabbath, the 6th Iyar, 5708 (15th May, 1948), until the establishment of the elected, regular authorities of the State in accordance with the Constitution which shall be adopted by the Elected Constituent Assembly not later than the 1st October, 1948, the People's Council shall act as a Provisional Council of State, and its executive organ, the People's Administration, shall be the Provisional Government of the Jewish State, to be called "Israel".'

This article of the Declaration of Independence was never implemented, and the Declaration itself became, in large measure, a partial alternative to a constitution on such questions as freedom of worship, equal rights, freedom of conscience, etc. Reservations regarding the idea of a constitution were raised in 1949–50 and, in a lengthy debate held on 13 June 1950, a compromise decision was passed in the Knesset by a majority of 50 against 38: 'The First Knesset resolves to impose upon the Constitution, Law and Justice Committee the task of preparing a draft constitution for the state. The Constitution will be built up chapter by chapter in such manner that each will constitute a Basic Law in itself.'

The opposition parties on both the right and the left called for a constitution, but the coalition composed of Mapai and the religious parties rejected their demand. Prime Minister David Ben-Gurion argued that it was impossible to write a constitution for Israel so long as most of the Jewish people were still living in the diaspora. In this, he expressed a feeling of transience: the Jewish people were in the midst of a great migration, and it was inconceivable that the minority already in Israel should decide on the way of life for the majority. The opposition of the religious parties undoubtedly played an important part in delaying the adoption of a constitution. A constitution that would have established full equality before the law would have posed serious problems for the religious community, which views Jewish religious law as its constitution. The British tradition, whereby norms are accorded greater importance than the constitution, and in which there is in fact no written constitution, was an important argument for those who opposed an Israeli constitution, claiming that the democratic tradition was more important than a constitution which would not be implemented.

Eight years passed between the decision to adopt a constitution by stages until the enactment of the first Basic Law (Basic Law: The Knesset). There are today nine Basic Laws, which are to be incorporated into the future constitution. Most of the Basic Laws are not proof against emergency regulations which can suspend them, nor against a simple majority in the Knesset which can abrogate them. It has been proposed to accord all the Basic Laws special status which would prevent their nullification by a simple majority, and to establish a constitutional court. Such a proposal – if accepted – will be an important step towards the adoption of an Israeli constitution and towards the severance from British norms.

The call for a constitution has been part of the Israeli political scene since the establishment of the state. The Civil Rights Movement established in 1973 espoused this as one of its basic principles. In 1987 a group of law professors in several Israeli universities launched an intensive campaign for an Israeli constitution, including the direct election of the prime minister and a change from proportional to regional elections. This group has attracted considerable attention both among the public and within the political leadership, and has succeeded in placing this issue once again on the national agenda. In January 1991 the majority in the Knesset opposed a private bill for the direct election of the Prime Minister.

The Separation of Powers in Israel

The separation of powers in the Israeli parliamentary regime is not as sharp as in the American presidential system, for example, in which each branch of government is elected separately by the people. However, each branch in Israel has a separate and well-defined role, which helps to balance the others. The existence of independent judicial review ensures – perhaps more than anything else in the Israeli government system – the principle underlying the separation of powers.

In practical terms, the cabinet retains most of the political power. Being always dependent upon the confidence of the Knesset, the situation which frequently arises in the United States, in which the executive faces an opposition Congress, is impossible in Israel. About

90 per cent of the legislative initiatives in the Knesset originate within the cabinet, and are brought before the Knesset by the cabinet. Private legislative initiatives by a Member of Knesset (MK) are usually doomed to failure, although there has been a definite increase in successful private member's bills.

Important decisions, both on the national level (war and peace) and in the public context (summer time) are taken by the Cabinet. The ratification of international agreements is also performed by the cabinet. The Knesset can at most voice its opinion through its members, but has no power of decision. When Menachem Begin brought the Camp David Accords to the Knesset for approval, he was making a parliamentary gesture not required by law; had he so wished, he could have brought them only before his cabinet.

On 19 May 1948 the Provisional State Council declared Israel to be in a state of emergency, a decision which has never been rescinded. As a result, cabinet ministers can apply emergency regulations which are renewed every few months, further strengthening the executive branch. These regulations deal with the supply of various services not related to the security-related state of emergency, but do not require Knesset approval for a limited period.

From the moment the government receives the vote of confidence from the Knesset, and provided the coalition is stable, the cabinet in effect has a green light to do as it wishes. No Knesset decision binds the cabinet, except for legislation, personal appointments or no-confidence motions. The initial vote of confidence grants the cabinet immeasurably greater power than any other branch of government in Israel. Even when the judicial branch – by means of the High Court of Justice – hands down a ruling on a particular appeal, in the absence of appropriate legislation, the cabinet can hasten to enact the relevant law. Thus, for example, when the High Court of Justice ruled in 1969 that the party finance law was illegal, in that it prejudiced the equal chances of the parties to win an election, and that the enactment of such a law, which constituted an amendment of a protected Basic Law, required an absolute majority of the Knesset, the cabinet hastened to have the law passed in the Knesset by the necessary majority.

A private bill submitted by an MK is subject to a month's delay, during which time the cabinet determines its position on the specific issue. Then, once the MK has overcome the hurdle of his own parliamentary faction – and, if he is a coalition member, that hurdle as well – he presents his bill for a preliminary reading. Only if he wins a majority is the bill submitted for the usual three readings. A cabinet bill, on the other hand, can be immediately submitted to the Knesset for the first reading and, if the cabinet feels that the law must be passed that same day, all stages of legislation are completed in a single day. Thus, for example, when Menachem Begin decided in December 1981 to extend Israeli law to the Golan Heights, he convened the cabinet in the morning, presented the bill to the Knesset in the afternoon, and completed the third reading by evening. Had an MK wished to enact such a law as a private member's bill, the process would have taken many months.

The cabinet determines its budget and, if necessary, requests an additional budget from the Knesset in the course of the year. The Knesset Finance Committee is the only committee which can prevent or approve government expenditure, but even it can wield only meagre tools against the cabinet. The Finance Ministry, with an extensive array of economists and economic experts, draws up a large and detailed budget, which is tabled in the Knesset at virtually the last moment. MKs lack professional assistance, and have minimal secretarial services, and legal and economic advice. Their ability to challenge the senior government cadres is very limited, according a clear advantage to the cabinet.

The proportional electoral system, in which the list of candidates is determined by the central committee of each party, accords a clear advantage to the well-behaved faction member. Dissenters, who vote contrary to their faction's decisions or behave in a manner which displeases the party's representatives in the cabinet, are in many cases shown the door in the internal party elections. This severely limits the individual coalition member's freedom of manoeuvre, and accords the party in government an automatic majority.

This state of affairs creates a certain disregard for the Knesset within the cabinet, especially if it rests on a stable majority. MKs often complain that the cabinet table in the Knesset plenum is empty, or that a minister is absent during a Knesset debate of issues within his jurisdiction. A duty roster of ministers, which is meant to ensure that at least two will be present at all Knesset sessions, is often not observed, and the Speaker sometimes halts a session because there is no representative of the cabinet present.

National agenda issues, which are debated in the cabinet and widely discussed by the media, reach the Knesset only at a later stage, when the debate has often become meaningless. The question of Israel's participation in an international peace conference, which raised a storm in the cabinet, and throughout the country and mass media, and which was a central issue in the 1988 election campaign, was debated in the Knesset only indirectly in October 1985, in the context of a no-confidence motion which was defeated. The Reagan initiative of 1982, which outlined principles for a solution of the Middle East conflict, was never debated by the Knesset. Neither was the 1988 Shultz initiative which outlined a procedure for a solution of the conflict.

The wider the coalition's base in the Knesset, the sharper the asymmetry in cabinet–Knesset relations. A narrow government, which enjoys a bare majority in the Knesset and a tenuous majority in its various committees, must arrive at certain agreements with the opposition (pairing of coalition and opposition MKs travelling abroad, for example) and take its MKs into consideration. Sometimes it must compromise with the opposition on bills which it brings to the Finance Committee in order that it should be allowed in turn to conduct the affairs of the various ministries undisturbed.

When the coalition is very broad, as it was in the National Unity Government of 1986–88 which rested on 98 MKs, the opposition loses its significance and the Knesset becomes a rubber stamp for cabinet decisions, except in the event of a 'revolt' by backbenchers who seek to demonstrate some measure of independence. The government can in effect do almost as it pleases, confident that the Knesset will approve every bill brought before it by any of the cabinet ministers.

According to the Knesset rules, 30 MKs can call for a special session of the Knesset. This rule was established in order to enable even a small opposition, comprising only a quarter of the Knesset, to make itself heard and to convene the Knesset even during a parliamentary recess. However, in the 11th Knesset the entire opposition numbered only 27 MKs. Had it not been for an amendment which allowed them to call the Knesset into special session, even this right would have been denied them. Clearly, in a situation where the government need not fear that the Knesset will refuse to approve or accept its actions, the Knesset loses its real ability to oversee the work of the government and ceases to be a deterrent factor serving as a check against the cabinet.

One of the means available to MKs to express their views on current issues is the urgent motion for the agenda. At the beginning of each week MKs can submit an urgent motion to the Knesset presidium, composed of the Knesset Speaker and his deputies, for approval. Dozens of such motions are submitted every week, most of them based on reports in the written and electronic media on various injustices or irregularities which call for a response from the minister concerned. The Knesset presidium weighs each motion and approves about five for debate that week. However, also present at the meeting of the Knesset presidium is a representative of the government – the cabinet secretary or a minister, or both – and they generally object to the urgent motions, many of which raise issues that may prove awkward or onerous to the minister concerned. They therefore often contend that a particular issue is not at all urgent or that another is unfounded, or that the report on which the MK has based his motion is inaccurate, and so on. Coalition members enjoy an advantage in the Knesset presidium, which is particularly attentive to the cabinet representatives at the meeting. Thus, even this opportunity available to MKs is quite limited, being in large measure dependent on the goodwill of the cabinet.

Closer and more comprehensive monitoring of the government is exerted by the Knesset through the State Comptroller, who in effect constitutes a fourth branch of government in Israel. The State Comptroller is elected by the Knesset Committee for a period of five years. He is empowered to inspect every government body as well as every institution which receives government funding, and submits an annual report of his findings to the Knesset. The Knesset State Control Committee conducts a regular follow-up of the government's implementation of the Comptroller's findings, and summons representatives of the government to report on the changes made in their ministries as a result of the Comptroller's criticism, on which it then reports to the Knesset.

The State Comptroller is responsible to the Knesset alone, and not to the cabinet. He may point to inefficiency and unfairness, as well as illegalities. Since 1971, the State Comptroller has also served as ombudsman, and as such submits an annual report on the various complaints received and on their merit.

There is in Israel an ongoing public debate on the powers of the State Comptroller. The Comptroller has no sanctions that he can apply to enforce his recommendations. Thus, the same criticism and the same recommendation are repeated frequently in the annual reports. Almost every year, with the publication of the report, there are those who propose to exact penalties from those responsible for the failure to implement the Comptroller's recommendations within a fixed period of time. Every State Comptroller so far has opposed such an amendment, out of a desire to refrain from becoming primarily responsible for ensuring implementation rather than simply submitting statements and recommendations. In my opinion, they are right. Their most important tool is the media, and when public institutions are involved one would be hard put to find a more effective sanction.

The Comptroller's findings – whether in the annual report or in a special report devoted to a particular body or institution – do indeed enjoy wide publicity. The government bodies and state-funded institutions criticized by the Comptroller, often headed by elected officials, do not want negative publicity, especially not from an authoritative source with whom they cannot argue. These bodies have therefore developed internal control systems through which attempts are made to forestall external criticism and to make the necessary corrections between one report and the next. Quite apart from the powers accorded to the State Comptroller, those who have filled the post have themselves been authoritative figures – leading lawyers or judges – without strong political leanings (except for the first Comptroller who was a member of a small liberal party). Their criticism has always been accepted as compelling and to the point. The current State Comptroller, Miriam Ben-Porat, a former chief justice, has become a leading public figure. Every report she issues receives sympathetic and prominent coverage by the media. Her major influence lies in the exposure of criticism without recourse to means of enforcement.

While the State Comptroller can be considered part of the legislative branch, it seems more and more to be becoming a separate – fourth – branch, distinct from the others, highly independent and divorced from political considerations. While the Comptroller officially reports to the Knesset, this fact is of only secondary importance.

A government branch much larger in scope, autonomous and very independent, is the judiciary. The judge is subject to the law alone, but the law is fairly open to interpretation. In this respect the judiciary fulfils a legislative role, even if the legislature sometimes appears to – and at times actually does – interfere by enacting laws which refute an earlier interpretation by the judge.

The decline in the prestige of the Israeli political system and politicians has been accompanied by an increase in that of the judiciary, which is generally perceived as being free from manipulation and which is accepted as the final arbiter. The political system itself requires more and more legal decisions. Indeed, politicians are often criticized for avoiding decisions by transferring the burden to the judges and legal advisers. The Attorney General, for example, generally appointed by the government from the academic or judicial spheres, has in recent years sat in on all cabinet meetings, whereas in the first decades of statehood, although consulted, he did not actually participate in the meetings.

Judicial committees of inquiry headed by a Supreme Court justice are appointed by the cabinet much more frequently than in the past, and they often deal with manifestly political issues. Thus, for example, a committee was appointed to study the collapse of the bank shares, and submitted a series of economic proposals to the cabinet. Another committee examined the Israeli health system. It is apparently more convenient for politicians to rely on the recommendations of a committee of inquiry than to decide for themselves and demand compliance with their decisions. They turn more and more often to the court to intervene in determining the legality of various Knesset decisions, and the court itself expresses greater willingness than in the past to intervene in the affairs of the legislative branch.

Politicians tend sometimes to adopt certain legislative decisions on the assumption that those who will be prejudiced by the legislation will appeal to the court, which will in turn invalidate the decision. For example, there were some MKs who, complying with party discipline, supported the principle of conversion according to Jewish religious law, hoping that those who would be harmed by the law would appeal to the courts, which would then annul the Knesset decision.

All judges in Israel are appointed by an appointments committee headed by the President of the Supreme Court and including the Minister of Justice and one other minister, two MKs elected by secret ballot in the plenum, two lawyers appointed by the Israel Bar Association, and two judges. Judges are appointed until the age of seventy, and although they may retire before then, such cases are very rare and are virtually unfeasible without their consent. The fact that the judges are not dependent on the political system to retain their position ensures their independence to a considerable degree, although their advancement from magistrate's court through district court to Supreme Court is dependent on the appointments committee, four members of which are clearly politicians.

The appointments system has on the whole proved itself. It is generally agreed that Israel's judges are of high calibre, and the judiciary is viewed as an island of honesty and professionalism. Although the appointments committee is undoubtedly subject to personal and political pressures, and there are undoubtedly some judges who are appointed because of their political ties, the majority of the judges rigorously uphold their apolitical identity.

The executive and legislative branches do not interfere in the considerations of the judiciary. Criticism of the judiciary by legislators – even if legitimate – is rare. The independence of the judiciary and the great prestige of the judges combine to create a situation in which judges are sought after – more so now than in the past – for non-judiciary roles in society. The National Unity Government, which in 1984–88 found it hard to put forward candidates not identified with one side or the other, and preferred to appoint district judges to the positions of both Attorney General and State Comptroller, further encouraged this trend. In 1988 a former Supreme Court justice was appointed to the latter position.

The role of the High Court of Justice has been greatly enhanced in recent years as part of the tendency to transfer responsibility from the political to the judicial level. The Supreme Court sitting as the High Court of Justice is, in effect, an administrative court, a constitutional court and a civil rights court. After the Six Day War, the High Court of Justice was also accorded authority to deal with infringements on the rights of the residents of the occupied territories, a function not prescribed by the Geneva Convention and constituting a precedent in international law.

The High Court of Justice has in recent years allowed itself to decide on procedural issues related to the work of the Knesset, an area in which it had declined to involve itself in the past. Two prominent cases followed the election of Meir Kahane to the Knesset in 1984. Kahane demanded to be allowed to present a no-confidence motion; the Knesset presidium ruled that a single member faction did not have this right, and Kahane appealed to the High Court of Justice which affirmed his right to submit the motion. The Knesset later disqualified a bill submitted by Kahane on the grounds of its racist nature; once again Kahane turned to the High Court, which overruled the Knesset's right to disqualify a bill because of its content. The Knesset rules have subsequently been amended, so that no bill of racist content can today be tabled in the Israeli parliament.

In 1986 the High Court of Justice was called upon to rule on the decision of the President of Israel to pardon the members of the General Security Services involved in the death of terrorists interrogated in the 'Route 300' affair. This was a special pardon, as it was given before indictments had been handed down. There was considerable tension throughout the country while the High Court considered the legality of the President's decision. The three justices were divided in their opinion, two ruling that the action was legal while the third, in a minority opinion, declared the President's action to be invalid. The seemingly natural intervention of the Court in the President's judgement, on a matter which is exclusively within his jurisdiction – the right to pardon – is further proof of the growing power of the High Court of Justice and of its accepted precedence over every other government body in Israel.

4. The Changing Agenda

The national agenda of the State of Israel can be likened to a long poem, comprising many stanzas but with a recurring refrain. This refrain is security-related tension on the one hand, and religious–secular tension on the other. Some of the issues related below were public knowledge, and can easily be found in the newspapers of the period. Others were less known, but no less important. One such example was the ambivalent attitude towards the East–West orientation of Israeli foreign policy in the early years of statehood. Ben-Gurion's original neutral viewpoint was quickly replaced by a pro-Western position, which found expression, *inter alia*, in Israel's stand in the Korean war.

The controversy surrounding the establishment of the nuclear research centre in the early 1960s was even less well known. The issue was whether the small State of Israel should enter this area of research, premised on its capabilities in the field of conventional weapons being likely always to remain quite limited in comparison to the strength wielded by the Arab states. A positive decision was eventually adopted by Ben-Gurion, at the urging of Deputy Defence Minister Shimon Peres.

Complex internal discussions were held in the 1950s and early 1960s on the scope of Israel's defence industries. It was ultimately the embargo on arms sales that forced Israel greatly to expand its own weapons industry, and in the course of the years arms sales came to be an important part of Israeli exports.

Israel's national agenda underwent a complete change following the Six Day War of June 1967. (We are justified, therefore, in dividing the period since the establishment of the state into the years which preceded this war, and those which followed.)

The two major controversies which arose in the course of Israel's War of Independence were the conquest of the West Bank and the incorporation of underground movements into the Israel Defence Forces. Ben-Gurion, who took responsibility for the defence portfolio throughout his years as Prime Minister, decided to refrain from any attempt to conquer all of western Palestine, lest the number of Arab residents in the territory under Israeli control should exceed the number of Jews. Yigal Allon, commander of the Palmach,* sharply criticized Ben-Gurion's decision as being, he felt, a golden opportunity missed. This criticism, coming from the left end of the political spectrum, was shared by the right-wing leader, Menachem Begin, who accused Ben-Gurion of conceding Israel's historic control over all of western Palestine with his very own hands. This debate subsided in the early 1950s, being superseded by *de facto* acceptance of the borders created by the War of Independence.

The controversy over the incorporation of the underground movements into a joint army was bitter and painful. The Hagannah, which constituted the largest and most significant military force before the establishment of the state, became the new national army, while the other underground movements preferred not to be assimilated into this force but rather to preserve their uniqueness. The Palmach wanted to ensure its own independent staff within the joint army but ultimately was forced to forgo this demand, not without a residue of deep bitterness among both the rank and file and the senior officers. They were apprehensive about the incorporation of an idealistic voluntary group, which preferred inner over formal discipline and abhorred all outward military symbols such as rank, into a regular army with compulsory service, hierarchy, uniforms and ranks.

The IZL (Irgun Zevai Leumi) at first asked to join the IDF as a distinct group, rather than being scattered among the various army units. Its request was denied. During the War of Independence (June 1948) the IZL, under the leadership of Menachem Begin, commissioned an arms ship, the *Altalena*, to supply the IZL troops in the IDF. Ben-Gurion decided to take action to prevent the partisan use of the weapons. After failing to convince the IZL commanders that the weapons be placed at the disposal of the entire army, the ship was attacked and prevented from reaching the Israeli shore. This

---

* The shock troops established by British initiative in 1942 in order to repel Rommel's army; they went underground after the conclusion of World War II as part of the Hagannah.

episode, in which several IZL members who chose not to abandon ship were wounded, left deep scars among members of the generation which took part in this 'civil war'. However, it unequivocally established the unified nature of the IDF and Ben-Gurion's authority. Lehi (*Lohamei Herut Israel* – Freedom Fighters of Israel), headed by Yitzhak Shamir, also found it hard to accept integration into a single military framework. Its leaders continued to operate underground even after the establishment of the state, and were consequently arrested by the Israeli authorities. They were released several months later, and hundreds of members of this small organization eventually joined the ranks of the army.

After the conclusion of the War of Independence, the major national effort was directed to immigrant absorption. While the refugees from Europe were a direct continuation of the veteran Israeli population as regards education, culture, behavioural norms and spoken language, the immigrants from the Arab countries represented a totally new phenomenon. To the elite which had settled in pre-state Israel, with an average level of education which was among the highest in the world, a new population was now added which had not been exposed to Western civilization. The absorption of this population, different in character, different in the darker hue of their skin, and different in dress, became the major issue among both the decision-makers and the public. The decision by the Israeli establishment, under the leadership of David Ben-Gurion, to bring to Israel entire Jewish communities from those Arab countries which so permitted, had a direct impact on Israeli demography, on the economy and the allocation of resources, and on the nature of Israeli democracy. It was to have far-reaching implications for Israel's political spectrum, as will be discussed below.

The issue of immigration appeared on the decision-makers' agenda in the form of selective immigration; namely, whether Israel should reconcile itself to the situation in which the older and weaker members of the diaspora communities automatically came to Israel, while some of the younger and stronger preferred to settle in other parts of the world (primarily North America, and some in France). The decision adopted was to accept this situation.

The education of the young immigrant generation was another issue. Although the majority of the new immigrants were religious, the secular Israeli establishment had no desire to strengthen the electoral power of the religious sector by directing hundreds of thousands of children to its schools. Mapai's attempt to establish a religious school system of its own proved unsuccessful, and some of the religious youths were sent to non-religious schools. This gave rise to a government crisis, leading to early elections in 1951.

Religion lay at the root of another matter which preoccupied the decision-makers in 1951: the conscription of women into the army. The ultra-Orthodox camp viewed this as a very serious matter, opening the door to dangers of sexual licentiousness and exposing the soldiers to temptation and moral decadence. The secular establishment, on the other hand, viewed the issue as an expression of the equality of women in the new Israeli society and rejected the demand that they be exempted from military service. The compromise solution permitting religious girls to perform national service (in hospitals, schools, etc. rather than in the army) failed to satisfy the ultra-Orthodox camp, and they consequently refrained from joining a Labour-led coalition until 1984.

While the major political crises focused on religious issues, the major concern of the public at large was immigrant absorption; they volunteered to teach Hebrew and to assist the new immigrants, while suffering themselves a sharp decline in their standard of living.

The political recruitment of the new immigrants, most of whom had never been exposed to a party system; the problem of providing employment for these immigrants (some were employed in public works, such as afforestation, etc.); the floods which in the winter of 1951 left many of the immigrants without a roof; the anger of the immigrants at the failure to move them to permanent housing and complaints of preference accorded to those with political connections; the problem of directing the immigrants to the peripheral areas against their wishes; the decision to send some of them directly to agricultural settlements despite their lack of agricultural experience: all of these were constant concerns to Israeli society during the years of mass immigration, 1949–56, and to a great extent afterwards as well.

In the economic sphere, rationing of basic commodities created a black market which aroused considerable criticism. On the one hand, the heavy burden of immigrant absorption and the low foreign currency reserves required belt-tightening and frugality; on the other, ration books created a solution and, to a limited extent, psychological pressure on the public (which had been accustomed to relative plenty even during such difficult times as World War II) made the pursuit of law-breakers futile. Moreover, it created a dispute between the socialist Mapai, which wished to continue the rationing system, and the

General Zionists, who, with a liberal approach, campaigned against continued rationing, presenting it not as a necessity but as part of an egalitarian ideology. The success of the General Zionists in the 1950 municipal elections and in the 1951 Knesset elections, based on the popular campaign against rationing, hastened the end of this policy.

Defence issues were conducted far from the public eye during this period. There was no television in Israel until 1968; the radio, which was run by the Prime Minister's office, for many years had only one station, whose character was in large measure determined by the government. Military censorship was extensive and the newspaper editors accepted self-imposed restrictions, establishing in 1953 an editors' committee which received current information from the state's leaders in exchange for which they agreed not to share this information with the public.

Debates on the scope and strength of the young army thus remained within circles close to the Prime Minister and Defence Minister. One such dispute led to the resignation of Yigael Yadin in 1952. Another centred on how to respond to infiltrators, mainly from Egypt and Jordan, who attacked border settlements, causing loss of life and property. The 1950s were characterized by a policy of retaliatory attacks, culminating in the 1956 Sinai Campaign, in effect the most extensive retaliatory action, which put an end to infiltrations.

The military government was an issue of broader public controversy, going beyond the question of security. For eighteen years after the establishment of the state, Arab citizens of Israel were subject to a military government, which meant obtaining special exit permits to leave their villages for the city, military governors, etc. Ben-Gurion was afraid to abolish military rule, while both the left and the right supported its abolition. Only the election of Levi Eshkol as Prime Minister led to a change of policy and the revocation of the military government, putting to rest an issue that had been a constant subject of debate in the press, the Knesset, and the public.

Israel's relations with Germany was a fixed issue on the national agenda from the establishment of the state. Israeli cinemas did not screen German-speaking films, the radio did not broadcast songs in German, and Wagner was not played in the concert halls. Many Israelis refrained – and continue to refrain – from purchasing German products.

In 1952 a public storm arose over Prime Minister David Ben-Gurion's intention to inaugurate negotiations with the West German authorities on the payment of reparations for material losses suffered by the Jewish people in the Holocaust. The pragmatic Ben-Gurion had concluded that German aid to Israel would facilitate the establishment of infrastructures for industry, transportation and energy. In January, during a Knesset debate on the issue, a mass demonstration was held at Zion Square in Jerusalem, at which Menachem Begin, head of the Herut movement, said: 'This will be a war of life or death ... Today I shall give the order: Blood!' At the conclusion of the demonstration, some of the participants approached the Knesset, threw stones and broke its windows. This was the sharpest confrontation between the public and the Knesset since the establishment of the state. Hundreds were arrested, Begin was barred from the Knesset for three months, and Ben-Gurion declared that the government would do everything to ensure Israeli democracy.

The issue of German reparations created a rare alliance between right and left, with the leftist Mapam party joining Herut in opposition to this issue. This unique alliance was to remain in effect for many years. In September 1952 the reparations agreement was signed with Germany, leading, in the course of twelve years, to an influx of goods valued at $750 million from Germany to Israel.

In March 1965 Israel accepted West Germany's proposal to establish diplomatic relations between the two states. The public debate which ensued raised the question of whether it was possible, in our generation, to open a new leaf in relations with Germany, and whether this was truly a different Germany. Herut demanded a referendum on the issue. The Knesset rejected this demand and approved the establishment of relations.

Formal relations did not bring about a clear change in the nature of these relations. Many Israelis continued to boycott Germany, refusing to travel to Germany either privately or officially, and when the Likud came to power in 1977 Menachem Begin found his new position as head of the government to be in direct conflict with his traditional stand. With Foreign Minister Moshe Arens' 1990 statement taking a favourable view of the unification of West and East Germany, the Likud party which he represents can be said to have adopted a pragmatic approach.

The Holocaust of European Jewry has remained in the background of Israel's development throughout the years. It was the Holocaust which hastened the establishment of the state and which prompted many countries to support it. Immediately after independence was declared, tens of thousands of refugees arrived from Europe. The most popular radio programme was that devoted to the search for relatives, with daily reports of citizens who had lost their families in the Holocaust and who were trying to locate them in Israel. The large number of people with numbers tattooed on their arms played a role in shaping the new Israeli society and left their mark on its daily life and culture. Yet, aside from the constant shadow of the Holocaust, specific issues related to the Holocaust appeared from time to time on the national agenda.

In June 1955 the country was convulsed by the slander suit conducted by the state against Malkiel Gruenwald, who had accused Israel Kasztner (a senior government official at the time who was the former head of the Zionist rescue committee in Hungary) of having entered into an agreement with the Nazis exchanging his cooperation for the safety of his family, ignoring the Nazis' intent to destroy half a million of Hungary's Jews. Gruenwald's defence counsel was one of the country's leading jurists Shmuel Tamir, and he succeeded in reversing the slander suit, in effect placing Kasztner himself on trial. In handing down his ruling acquitting Gruenwald, the presiding judge Dr Benjamin Halevi stated that Kasztner had 'sold his soul to the devil'.

Herut submitted a no-confidence motion against the government on the basis of the verdict, thus bringing into focus the political tensions behind the trial: Shmuel Tamir was a former IZL leader and a member of the Herut movement, while Israel Kasztner was a Mapai candidate to the Knesset, and Justice Benjamin Halevi was later to resign from the bench to join Herut as a Member of Knesset. Herut praised the impartiality of the court and accused the Mapai establishment of having backed Kasztner, while Mapai claimed that it was impossible to issue such a clear-cut judgement in an affair which had taken place in the context of the Holocaust and in such special circumstances.

The General Zionists, who were at the time part of the government coalition, abstained in the no-confidence vote, and, in response, Prime Minister Moshe Sharett announced the resignation of the government and established a new government without them. The Attorney General appealed Gruenwald's acquittal, and, in January 1958, the Supreme Court accepted the appeal and convicted Gruenwald of slander. Dr Kasztner was by then no longer alive; he was assassinated in March 1957 for his alleged collaboration with the Nazis.

On 31 December 1957 Ben-Gurion submitted his resignation from the government because of a leak about a forthcoming visit to

Germany by a senior Israeli official. The leftist factions in the coalition strongly objected to such a visit. Ben-Gurion was furious about the leak and at the opposition it aroused. In January 1958 Ben-Gurion established an identical coalition government, obligating the ministers to uphold government decisions in the Knesset.

In 1960 the Holocaust was once more centre stage when Adolf Eichmann, one of those responsible for masterminding the exter-mination of European Jewry, was abducted in Argentina and brought to Israel to stand trial. The Eichmann trial, which opened in Jerusalem less than a year later, was a public trial broadcast live on radio, photographed and recorded for posterity. Many survivors of the Holocaust testified in the course of the trial, relating personal stories which made the horrors perpetrated by the Nazis tangible to the Israeli public. The entire population was glued to the trial, whether through attendance, listening to the radio broadcasts, or reading the newspaper reports. At the end of 1961 Eichmann was sentenced to death, and in May 1962 was executed by hanging.

In 1962 a new security incident provoked another storm in the context of Israeli–German relations, that of the German scientists in Egypt. During that year, it was revealed that missiles had been developed in Egypt, with the help of hundreds of German scientists employed in several factories in Egypt, which had a range of 280 km and 560 km.

The Mossad, Israel's secret service, asked Prime Minister David Ben-Gurion to intervene with Chancellor Adenauer, requesting that he halt the employment of the German scientists in Egypt. Ben-Gurion refused, in order not to cast a shadow over the improving relations between the two countries. The Mossad decided to take independent action against the scientists in Egypt; a conversation with the daughter of one of the German scientists was even initiated, in an effort to convince her father to leave Egypt. The conversation took place in Switzerland. The daughter informed the Swiss authorities who arrested the Israeli agents, thus exposing the affair and raising a furore in Israel.

In an effort to obtain the release of its agents, the Mossad presented the new German threat in the Israeli press in all its gravity. The newspapers were flooded with information, creating hysteria in Israel combined with a sense of impending doom. Criticism was focused on Germany, on Israeli–German relations, and on the naivety of the belief that post-war Germany had indeed changed.

In March 1963, all factions in the Knesset united in a stormy debate, in which the Germans were accused of continuing to threaten the Jews with extermination. Many Members of the Knesset, headed by Menachem Begin, severely criticized the Prime Minister both for the alibi which he, as it were, accorded the Germans, and for his erroneous policy, which included shipments of Israeli 'Uzi' sub-machine-guns to Germany and the maintenance of diplomatic relations with that state.

Two schools of thought quickly emerged: one, led by the head of the Mossad, presented the developments in Egypt as disastrous for Israel; the other, headed by Ben-Gurion and his deputy Shimon Peres, maintained that the panic was unfounded and that the weapons which had been developed in Egypt were unusable. The Prime Minister asked the Mossad to stop spreading panic among the public, as the German scientists were not of the first order and had in fact unsuccessfully attempted to develop an old-model missile. The head of the Mossad disagreed with Ben-Gurion; he continued to maintain that this represented a dangerous phenomenon and that pressure should be brought to bear on the German government to stop it. His subsequent resignation made news around the world.

To return to religious issues: in May 1951, against the background of the conscription of women into the army, a radical religious underground group – Brit ha-Kanaim (covenant of the zealots) – was uncovered. This group had planned to throw a dummy bomb into the Knesset during the debate on female conscription in an attempt to use force to ensure the observance of the Sabbath and to prevent the conscription of women. The police discovered its weapons cache and arrested fifty of its members. The exposure of this underground organization marked a climax in religious–secular tensions in the early years of the state.

Towards the end of 1952 the conscription of women caused yet another stir, when notices appeared throughout the country calling on religious girls to choose imprisonment over conscription. The coalition between Mapai and the religious parties was dissolved, the latter joining the opposition. The Liberals (General Zionists) joined Ben-Gurion's government in their place.

In mid-1953 two radical religious youths were apprehended in Jerusalem as they prepared to blow up part of the Ministry of Education and Culture. Their planned action was in response to the enactment of the State Education Law which, it was feared, would infringe on the independence of the religious schools. In the end, the various religious school systems retained their independence, while the secular schools, which had previously been divided by political affiliation, were united into a single state education system.

In July of that year, another crisis arose, again on the question of the conscription of women. A split developed between the national religious and the non-Zionist ultra-religious camps, when the former agreed to the enactment of the National Service Law which allowed religious girls to serve the state outside the framework of the army, a law to which the latter strongly objected. In July 1953, when the bill came up for preliminary reading in the Knesset, a 10,000-strong demonstration was held, led by thousands of women, and there were clashes with the police. The pressure exerted by the ultra-Orthodox influenced the more moderate national relgious delegates, who did not vote in favour of the bill, although they were a part of the ruling coalition.

In 1957 a series of demonstrations were held by religious groups in protest against the operation of public transport before the end of the Sabbath. This issue and that of the use of private automobiles on the Sabbath would continue periodically over the years to arouse the anger of ultra-Orthodox circles to the point of violence (the stoning of cars travelling near religious neighbourhoods), followed by the restoration of calm.

In 1958 religious–secular relations were aggravated by the 'Who is a Jew?' issue. The Law of Return grants immediate Israeli citizenship to any Jew who immigrates to Israel. Since the enactment of this law in 1950, it had become customary to accept the statement by the immigrant that he was a Jew, unless it could be proven otherwise. In March 1958 Interior Minister Israel Bar-Yehudah (of the leftist Ahdut ha-Avodah) changed this custom into an official ruling. The religious parties demanded that only the Chief Rabbinate be authorized to determine whether an immigrant was a Jew, while the leftist factions called for the total omission of religion and nationality from Israeli identity cards. The affair gave rise to a stormy debate in the Knesset, and has since then repeatedly come to the fore on the public agenda.

Less than a month later another religious issue arose: the opening of a swimming pool in Jerusalem. Orthodox Judaism separates men from women: they are separated at public affairs; they pray in separate rooms. Thus, when it was learned that one of the Jerusalem hotels was planning to build a swimming pool in which men and women would bathe together, the ultra-Orthodox raised a hue and cry. Of course, there were already swimming pools in other parts of the country, but not in Jerusalem, and the idea of building a pool for mixed bathing in Jerusalem was to them revolutionary. The issue was discussed by the Jerusalem public and by the municipal council; later it became a national issue when it came up for discussion in the Knesset. A violent demonstration calling for bloodshed was held by ultra-Orthodox Jews in March 1958. Twenty citizens and three policemen were injured in the demonstration, after which the leader of the radical Neturei Karta sect Amram Blau and several of his followers were imprisoned for several months.

The 'Who is a Jew?' issue gave rise to another crisis at the end of June 1958, leading to the resignation of the National Religious Party (NRP) ministers from the government. Ben-Gurion declared that Israel was not a theocratic state, and that for the purposes of administrative registration, a person's Jewishness could not be determined by rabbinic criteria. Several months later he co-opted the Chief Rabbi of Tel-Aviv-Jaffa, who had no political affiliation, to his government as Minister of Religion.

In 1960 the abduction of the child Yosele Schumacher from his parents aroused public feeling; he became the most famous child in the country, rekindling the religious–secular debate. The child was eventually located in the United States, where he had been taken by his grandfather and uncle, and he was only returned in 1962. The grandfather admitted to having abducted him in order to ensure his proper religious education and to prevent his secular parents from educating him in accordance with their views. Both the grandfather and uncle were arrested and brought to trial. The Yosele Schumacher affair engaged the Israeli public for years.

The question of 'Who is a Jew?' was raised once again when Brother Daniel, a Carmelite priest, asked to be registered as a Jew under the Law of Return upon his arrival in Israel in 1958. Oswald Rufeisen was a Polish Jew who, having been captured and imprisoned by the Nazis during World War II, succeeded in escaping, and helped other Jews to elude the Nazis. He subsequently found refuge in a Carmelite monastery, and in 1942 converted. Rufeisen continued throughout the years to consider himself a Jew, and when his request to be registered as such was denied, he appealed to the Supreme Court. The ruling of the Supreme Court on the case at the end of 1962 decided that a distinction should be made between the religious and secular definition of a Jew. While Brother Daniel was perhaps still a Jew by religious law, having been born to a Jewish mother, in a secular sense, and in any rational sense, a Christian priest could not be considered a Jew. Brother Daniel's request that he be recognized as a Christian by religion and a Jew by nationality was eventually rejected by the Supreme Court, after a debate which had deeply engrossed the Israeli public.

A similar legal case served as a subject for debate in 1968–70. Benjamin Shalit submitted a request that his children be registered as Jews by nationality, despite the fact that his wife was not Jewish and hence, according to religious law, neither were his children. Shalit, like Brother Daniel, was asking to draw a distinction between religion and nationality, claiming that he and his family had no religion but demanding that they be registered as Jews by nationality. The court approved his appeal, and the nationality of his children was registered accordingly. In January 1970, several days after the court's ruling, the government adopted a decision granting the family of a Jew Israeli citizenship under the Law of Return, whether they be Jewish or not.

Despite these specific rulings, religion and nationality were never really separated in Israel, and whenever the issue was raised, a singular solution was found which prevented a serious explosion – as in the Shalit case. Another difficult case which aroused considerable public feeling and to which a specific solution was also found, was that of Hanoch and Miriam Langer, a brother and sister who were in 1955 declared by the court, in an internal ruling, to be unfit for marriage because they were bastards. The Langer children were begat by their mother's second husband while she was still married to her first husband, from whom she was divorced only several years after the children were born. Only in 1966, when the son Hanoch applied for permission to marry, did he learn that he was prohibited from doing so. He embarked on a legal and public campaign. For four years the children's case was argued in the regional and high courts of rabbinic law, which ultimately decided to uphold the original ruling which forbade them to wed. The affair threatened to bring about a government crisis. The Independent Liberals, a coalition party, were prepared to present a bill to the Knesset that would allow those who had been disqualified from marriage by the rabbinate to be wed in Israel outside the rabbinic framework. Such a bill would have opened the door to civil marriages in Israel, a situation which would have been unacceptable to the religious parties. Both Prime Minister Golda Meir and Defence Minister Moshe Dayan tried to intervene in the matter, as both brother and sister were serving at the time in the IDF. The affair was only resolved at the end of 1972 by a rabbinic tribunal presided over by the Chief Rabbi of Israel, Rabbi Shlomo Goren.

Chief Rabbi Goren revoked the designation of the brother and sister as bastards by casting doubt on the Jewishness of the mother's first husband who originally had been a Christian, but who immigrated to Israel with the children's mother, having undergone some process of conversion. Later, of course, he separated from her. If his conversion had in fact not been valid, neither was the mother's marriage to him. Since a bastard (*mamzer*) as defined by Jewish religious law is a child born to a married woman by a man other than her husband, if her first huband had indeed not been Jewish, then she had not legally been married to him. Thus, only her second marriage was valid, and her second husband was the legal father of her children.

Rabbi Goren's ruling saved the government, and won praise from Golda Meir, Moshe Dayan and others. The Independent Liberals shelved their bill. Extremist circles took a grave view of the ruling, however, and threatened the Chief Rabbi. The names of those who sat with him on the tribunal were not made public, for fear that they would come to harm.

This affair, which caused such ferment among the Israeli public, demonstrated that when the public could not accept a certain state of affairs – and it could not, in the latter third of the twentieth century, accept the total ban on the marriage of someone defined as a bastard – the religious establishment was forced to provide a practical solution, thus precluding the need for a more radical solution to the problem.

Four years later the Rabin government fell because of a crisis with religious origins. On 10 December 1976 an official reception was held at an air-force base in Israel to mark the arrival of the first three F–15 fighter planes from the United States. The planes arrived on a Friday afternoon, and a small ultra-religious faction (Poalei Agudat Israel) presented a no-confidence motion on the grounds that the reception had led to the desecration of the Sabbath. Part of the NRP faction, a coalition party, abstained in the vote, and the Rabin government decided to avail itself of its legal option and to remove the NRP from the government. The next day, Rabin presented the resignation of the entire government to the President, in order to call early elections. This event, later mockingly called 'the brilliant manoeuvre', did indeed bring about early elections – but also the painful defeat of the Labour Party which, having governed the country for an entire generation in the pre-state and state eras, was forced into opposition, and the Likud came to power. The removal of the NRP and the resignation of the government created a deep rift between the Labour Party and the religious parties, which many years later remains unmended.

The Likud governments had in large measure relied on the support of the religious parties. There were no government crises of a religious nature during these years, as the government yielded to pressures on various religious issues, the total cancellation of flights on the Sabbath by El Al (causing it significant financial losses) among them.

The amendment of the Law of Return, whereby only a Jew who has been converted in accordance with the norms of Orthodox Jewry may be registered as a Jew, from time to time was brought before the Knesset, but never received a majority. The question of immigrant registration occasionally arose, and cases in which Jews converted by Reform rabbis are registered as Jews did give rise to crises. These diminished, however, with the establishment of the National Unity Government, in which the religious parties no longer held the deciding vote. In this new political situation (1984–90), the religious parties maintained their position of importance because both major parties wanted to secure for themselves the option of establishing a narrow coalition with these parties.

When the Unity Government fell in a no-confidence vote, the ultra-religious parties assumed great importance since neither the left nor the right bloc could have formed a government without them. Eventually, the left failed and Shamir formed his narrow government with the Right and with the whole religious bloc, giving almost every religious member a function as a minister or deputy minister in the Government. After the 1992 election, the religious parties have become less important since Labour could have formed a government without them.

The security problems which characterized Israeli society both before and after the establishment of the state served as a unifying factor which generally supplanted other disputes. In contrast to the criticism it aroused among the other Western participants, the Suez war was not a controversial issue in Israel. The public debate began only when the superpowers presented Israel with an ultimatum to withdraw from Sinai. This brief war combined the French and British interest in opening the Suez Canal which had been nationalized by Egyptian President Gamal Abdel Nasser and in overthrowing his regime, with the Israeli interest in opening the Tiran Straits, which had also been closed by Nasser and which constituted Israel's door to the Red Sea and south-east Asia. The campaign was waged at a time when the USSR and the US seemed to be engaged in other matters (the Hungarian revolt against the Soviet Union and Gomulka's ascension to power in Poland) and would not interfere in the joint campaign. Fighting began on 29 October 1956 and was concluded a week later, Israel having taken control of the Gaza Strip and all of the Sinai peninsula. On 2 November the United Nations General Assembly called upon Israel to withdraw its forces from Egypt and when Israel failed to comply, the Soviet Union recalled its ambassador from Israel. The General Assembly adopted a resolution to dispatch a UN emergency force to the territories occupied by Israel, a resolution which Israel firmly opposed.

Ben-Gurion, appearing before the Knesset to explain his opposition to a withdrawal from Sinai and the stationing of a UN force, expressed his readiness to make peace with all Arab states. He was supported by all factions, from Herut – led by Begin – to Mapam, except for the Communist Party. One day later Ben-Gurion announced his readiness to accept an Israeli withdrawal from Sinai and the stationing of a UN force there; he had received two letters – one from the Soviet Prime Minister Marshal Nikolai Bulganin, and the other from US President Dwight Eisenhower – containing an unequivocal demand for an Israeli withdrawal.

Herut was strongly opposed to such a withdrawal, viewing it as tantamount to unconditional surrender. In the no-confidence motion presented to the Knesset Ben-Gurion received the support of the leftist coalition factions as well as non-coalition factions – the General Zionists and the ultra-Orthodox. But the controversy was further sharpened when it became apparent to Ben-Gurion that the international demand included withdrawal from the Gaza and not only from the Sinai peninsula.

The political debate over Gaza continued for several months, at which point Israel intimated that it would be prepared to withdraw from the Gaza Strip and to accept the stationing of UN forces. This time Ben-Gurion was opposed by both Herut and the leftist coalition parties – Ahdut ha-Avodah and Mapam – who resolved to vote against withdrawal in the vote to be held in the Knesset on 6 March 1957. Many participated in a mass demonstration against the surrender of Gaza, a move they viewed as a capitulation which could have been avoided. Ben-Gurion, however, was determined not to enter into sharp conflict with the superpowers. He salvaged his government by refraining from presenting a government motion on the issue of withdrawal, making do with the vote of all the coalition parties against the opposition motions.

While the Sinai Campaign did not develop into a government crisis despite public debate and differences of opinion within the coalition, the Lavon Affair created a real crisis, which was to cast a shadow over Israeli politics for many years – at first secretly and later openly – becoming known simply as 'The Affair'. Although it would explode only in 1960, its origins date back to 1954.

Negotiations were conducted between the United States – which supported the officers' junta in Egypt – and Britain, aimed at removing the 80,000 British soldiers stationed in the Suez Canal bases from Egypt. The US hoped that after the departure of the British it would be possible to add Egypt to the Middle East regional defence organization. Israel was apprehensive of the possible dangers posed by the departure of the British, and a group of senior officers, led by the head of IDF intelligence Colonel Benajmin Gibli, decided to carry out acts of provocation in Egypt. This operation was to be executed by two units trained in Israel, but sent to Egypt in order to launch attacks on the Egyptian rear in the event of an Israeli–Egyptian war. The targets were sites related to the Western states (consulates, libraries, cultural centres) in order to prove that the new Egyptian government was not in control of the situation, and that without a British military presence it would be impossible to guarantee the security of the Western diplomatic presence in Egypt.

In the spring of 1954, during which talks were held between the US and Britain on withdrawal from the canal zone, Moshe Sharett was Prime Minister of Israel, Pinhas Lavon was serving as Defence Minister, and Moshe Dayan was the IDF Chief-of-Staff. David Ben-Gurion, who was not in the government at the time, was living at Kibbutz Sde Boker of which he had become a member.

The idea of instigating anti-Western provocation was raised in talks between Benjamin Gibli and Pinhas Lavon. Lavon expressed his support for the idea in principle. No actual instruction – written or oral – was given by Lavon, a matter which later became a point of dispute, gaining momentum over the years.

On the orders of IDF intelligence (conveyed to the units by radio in the form of recipes for housewives), operations were carried out against targets in Egypt in two phases: the first on 14 July 1954 in Cairo and Alexandria, and the second on 23 July 1954, this time in cinemas and train stations, in the same cities. The first attacks did not cause any real damage and demonstrated the amateur nature of the entire operation. In the second phase, a member of one of the units was caught when a bomb exploded in his trousers. As a result, all eleven members of the ring were apprehended.

When the head of intelligence learned of the failure of the operation for which he had not received prior orders, he apparently decided to cover himself *ex post facto*. Without reporting to the Defence Minister that the operation had already been carried out and had failed, he requested permission to execute it. Permission was granted, thus making Lavon responsible for giving the order, a fact which he later denied. The Prime Minister, who knew nothing of the matter, asked whether there was any truth in the Egyptian claim that it had captured an Israeli spy ring. It was only several weeks after the group was captured that the Prime Minister was told of the affair.

Immediately after the failure of the operation, two parallel affairs evolved: the trial of the members of the ring in Egypt; and the question of who had given the order, Gibli himself, or Lavon. The trial opened on 11 December 1954, arousing media interest in Israel and worldwide. During the course of the trial two people related to the affair committed suicide – an Egyptian Jew by the name of Karmona and an intelligence officer Max Bennett. A third, Victorin Ninio attempted suicide. Pinhas Lavon, who learned during the trial that the operations in Egypt had been carried out prior to his approval, asked the Prime Minister to set up a committee of inquiry to determine when the order had been given.

Supreme Court Justice Yitzhak Olshan and Ya'akov Dori, first Chief-of-Staff of the Israel Defence Forces, were appointed by Sharett to study the matter. They were appointed in secret; even the government was not informed. Sharett himself was very tense about the outcome of their investigation, knowing that one possible conclusion might force him to dismiss the Defence Minister. Their conclusions, however, submitted on 13 January 1955, were not clear-cut. While they were not convinced that the head of intelligence had not received the order from Lavon, neither were they convinced that Lavon had given the order. These ambiguous conclusions angered Lavon, who threatened to request the establishment of a parliamentary committee of inquiry that would undoubtedly accord the entire affair wide publicity.

The leaders of Mapai met – Moshe Sharett, Golda Meir, Levi Eshkol, Zalman Aranne and Shaul Avigur, Sharett's brother-in-law and an unofficial leader – and recommended that Lavon be asked to resign and that Gibli be transferred to a different position. Sharett, a weak Prime Minister, could not remove and replace Lavon without the moral approval of Ben-Gurion, who was living in Sde Boker. At first Ben-Gurion was not inclined to call for Lavon's resignation, but after a series of consultations he agreed. When Lavon learned of this he resigned, retaining the right to expose the affair before the Labour Party institutions and before the Knesset Foreign Affairs and Security Committee.

Lavon did not carry out his threat. After his resignation in early February 1955, he appeared before the Knesset Foreign Affairs and Security Committee, where he explained that he had resigned over a difference of opinion on a restructuring of the Defence Ministry. David Ben-Gurion replaced him as Defence Minister, having been persuaded to return for this purpose from his kibbutz home.

While this dispute was raging in the upper political echelons, Israel strove to free its people apprehended in Egypt. It conducted a campaign in the Western capitals, explaining that these were innocent victims who had in fact been 'framed'. This effort failed, and at the end of January 1955 the verdict was given: Samuel Azaar and Moshe Marzouk were sentenced to death and six others to long prison terms, while two were released for lack of sufficient evidence.

An affair like this can occur only in the early years of statehood: the public did not know the truth, the Knesset did not know the truth, the Foreign Affairs and Security Committee did not know the truth, and even the government was not briefed. The entire Lavon–Gibli affair took place far from the spotlights of the media (which were subject to censorship), cut off from the outside world, in a totally informal framework. The Israeli public were indeed convinced that these were innocent Jews who had been caught by the officers' junta in Egypt, and sentenced in the face of world indifference. Lavon was powerless to fight the verdict passed against him, and nurtured a deep and long-lasting grievance, which was to re-emerge six years later.

In 1960 Pinhas Lavon was Secretary of the Histadrut (General Federation of Labour), Benjamin Gibli was serving as the IDF attaché in London, and David Ben-Gurion was again Prime Minister and Defence Minister, following elections in which his party achieved peak power. The 'Affair', which had faded for several years, reappeared on the national agenda like a thunderclap, bringing Lavon's political career to an end, leading to early elections, and producing a deep rift within Mapai. Paradoxically, it was none other than Pinhas Lavon himself who returned the affair to the public eye. It was he who asked the Prime Minister to initiate an examination of new findings, according to which documents had been forged by IDF intelligence in order to present Lavon as having given the order for the provocations in Egypt.

Ben-Gurion, who had not clashed personally with Lavon and who had even encouraged his election as Secretary of the Histadrut, was at the time on friendly terms with him and asked his military adjutant to look into the matter. Within two months the adjutant confirmed that changes had indeed been introduced into intelligence documents. On the basis of this and other findings discovered at the time, Ben-Gurion asked the Chief-of-Staff to establish a committee of inquiry. This committee was established, headed by Supreme Court Justice Haim Cohn and two army colonels. The role of the committee was to examine whether intelligence documents had been forged and whether there had been any instigation to false testimony before the Olshan-Dori board. On 25 September 1960 the matter became public in a headline in the daily *Ma'ariv*: 'Ben-Gurion ordered the reinvestigation of the testimony that led to Lavon's resignation from the government in 1955.' From this point on the affair became part of the public domain.

Lavon was not interested in the Cohn committee. For him, the fact that intelligence documents had been forged was enough to prove that he was not the one who ordered the operation in Egypt, and he expected Ben-Gurion to clear him of this charge. Ben-Gurion maintained that the findings were insufficient to clear Lavon without a thorough investigation. This marked the beginning of a sharp conflict between the two leaders.

The press, which knew of the conversation between them, demanded justice for Lavon, feeling that Ben-Gurion was showing indifference to the Histadrut Secretary's just demand. The matter soon became a major media issue, and Ben-Gurion found himself attacked by both the opposition-backed press and by other newspapers. Ben-Gurion, who had not been in the government at the time of the Egyptian operation and who valued Lavon highly, found himself drawn into the controversy in a manner not to his advantage. He now began a careful study of the entire affair, and at the end of the year formulated his position.

The public atmosphere became increasingly difficult for Ben-Gurion. The matter was raised by the opposition at several meetings of the Knesset Foreign Affairs and Security Committee. The friction between Ben-Gurion and Lavon became more and more pronounced, taking on a more personal character. The Prime Minister making it clear that it was not his role to clear Lavon's name, it was Lavon himself who exposed the entire affair – for the first time – before the Knesset Foreign Affairs and Security Committee. He claimed that he had not given the order but rather had fallen victim to a trap as a result of a series of forgeries. He also rejected Ben-Gurion's contention that only a judicial committee could clear him. Ben-Gurion, for his part, accepted the findings of Haim Cohn's committee that intelligence documents had been forged, and handed them over to the Attorney General. On the latter's recommendation, Ben-Gurion decided to dismiss Benjamin Gibli from the army.

It was during this period that military censorship in Israel began to be relaxed. The deliberations of the Foreign Affairs and Security Committee were no longer totally classified as they had been in the 1950s, and matters raised there were leaked to the press. Thus, the Lavon Affair became the central issue on Israel's agenda, although some facts remained undisclosed until 1972, when the prisoners were released in Egypt and arrived in Israel.

The Prime Minister was incensed at Lavon's audacity in exposing state secrets and criticizing the army before a Knesset committee in which opposition parties had notable representation. After a careful study of the events of 1954, he gradually became – almost against his will – Lavon's greatest enemy. The other Mapai leaders understood that this clash over an historical event which had no direct bearing on the present was liable to produce an avalanche of national proportions and an irreparable rift in the ruling party; they made a supreme effort to bring the crisis to an end, realizing that a judicial commission of inquiry would cause a protracted crisis and open a Pandora's box. They proposed the establishment of a ministerial committee that would study the material and decide on the necessary steps. This proposal was brought before the government. Ben-Gurion did not object, and the ministerial committee – known as the 'committee of seven' and headed by Justice Minister Pinhas Rosen – was established. Its deliberations continued for a month and a half towards the end of 1960. However, instead of proposing a course of action, and without hearing any testimony, it unanimously decided that Lavon had not issued the order, and that the acts of provocation carried out in Egypt in 1954 were carried out without his knowledge.

The government endorsed the decisions of the 'committee of seven' by a majority vote, and Ben-Gurion resigned as Prime Minister and Defence Minister. The Mapai leaders tried repeatedly to convince Ben-Gurion to retract his resignation, but to no avail. They concluded that the only way to convince the Prime Minister to resume his post was to oust Lavon from his position as Secretary of the Histadrut, despite the conclusions of the ministerial committee. Four days after Ben-Gurion's resignation, the Mapai Central Committee convened on the initiative of Levi Eshkol, without Ben-Gurion, and decided to dismiss Lavon. The decision was approved, by secret ballot, by a vote of 159 to 96, with the strong objection of Moshe Sharett.

Although Ben-Gurion was appeased, the coalition partners were not. They refused to join a government headed by Ben-Gurion in the light of his position *vis-à-vis* the conclusions of the 'committee of seven'. While a government might have been formed with Levi Eshkol as Prime Minister, all preferred that Ben-Gurion head the government. It was decided to call an early election, two years before the scheduled date. With Mapai losing five mandates, Ben-Gurion succeeded in forming his last government in November 1961.

This narrow coalition, put together with great difficulty, lasted only two years. Ben-Gurion himself was a frustrated Prime Minister, widely criticized for his behaviour towards Lavon. Yet he continued to be engrossed by the 'Affair'. In June 1963 Ben-Gurion resigned 'for personal reasons'. In fact, according to his later published memoirs, the repercussions of the Lavon Affair were at the root of his resignation, particularly his inability to reconcile himself to the establishment of the 'committee of seven' and the adoption of its conclusions.

Immediately after his resignation, Ben-Gurion sought to reopen the investigation of the Lavon Affair. This time material prepared for him by the journalist Hagai Eshed, showing that Pinhas Lavon had given the order for the 1954 Egyptian operation, was in his possession. The new Prime Minister Levi Eshkol had no interest in pursuing this painful matter further, and even sought to conciliate Lavon and restore him to public life. Ben-Gurion, who viewed Eshkol as his natural heir, summoned him to a private talk at which he asked him to set up a committee of inquiry into Lavon's behaviour before the Knesset Foreign Affairs and Security Committee. Eshkol declined, viewing the entire matter as a terrible and superfluous burden. Thus began a thorny hostile relationship between the former Prime Minister and the new Prime Minister.

In May 1964 Levi Eshkol and several other Mapai leaders wrote to Pinhas Lavon asking him to return to party activity, making it clear that his earlier dismissal no longer held any significance. Ben-Gurion decided at precisely that time to intensify his involvement in the Lavon Affair; he enlisted the help of two important jurists to prepare a file on the affair and to present it to the Attorney General with a demand for a comprehensive investigation. The Mapai leaders begged him to drop the matter and to leave it to history, but Ben-Gurion viewed this as his primary mission during the remainder of his life. The Attorney General was greatly impressed by the material he received from Ben-Gurion, and the Justice Minister decided to recommend the opening of an investigation.

Eshkol hesitated about whether or not to accept this recommendation. The matter had developed into a sharp internal party debate between those local branches that supported Ben-Gurion and those that supported Eshkol. On the eve of the discussion in the Mapai Central Committee on whether or not to establish a committee of inquiry, with Eshkol fearing that he could not command a majority in his own party, he decided to resign the premiership, thus postponing the decision in the Central Committee. It became apparent to the Mapai leaders that, should Ben-Gurion achieve his objective as regards the committee of inquiry, Eshkol would no longer lead the party, and then the party was likely to fall from power.

The Mapai party institutions called upon Eshkol to reform his government, and voted by an overwhelming majority against the establishment of the committee of inquiry. The issue was not even raised by the newly formed government.

At the Mapai party convention held in February 1965, the Lavon Affair appeared once again on the agenda. The dying Moshe Sharett, who had served as Prime Minister in 1954, made an emotional speech; he argued that Ben-Gurion was forcing the party to deal with a matter of which the public wished to hear no more. He questioned the right of a retired leader to decide that this was the most important issue on the public agenda. Unlike other issues which arose in the course of Israel's history, the question now was whether this was an issue which at all justified public discussion. A secret ballot was held at the conclusion of the convention on Ben-Gurion's motion to bring the 1954 affair before the state's judicial institutions. Only 40 per cent (841 votes) supported the ageing leader's motion, while 60 per cent (1,226 votes) opposed it.

Ben-Gurion refused to accept the decision of the party convention. He embarked on a crusade against Levi Eshkol, asserting that he was not fit to head the Israeli government. Prior to the 1965 elections, Ben-Gurion's candidacy for the premiership was once again raised. The Mapai Central Committee, which convened without his participation, gave Ben-Gurion only 36.5 per cent of the vote, while Levi

Eshkol received 63 per cent. Ben-Gurion again refused to accept the party's verdict, and forced his intimates to split from Mapai and found a new party, Rafi (Reshimat Po'alei Israel – the Israel Labour List), which sought to rival the mother party. Rafi ultimately received only ten mandates, while the Ma'arach (alignment of Mapai and Ahdut ha-Avodah) received forty-five. Rafi remained in opposition for almost two and a half years, and on the eve of the Six Day War in 1967 joined the National Unity Government, with Moshe Dayan being appointed Defence Minister, a position which was to identify him more than anyone else with Israel's great victory.

The Lavon Affair waned from the national agenda, and the Six Day War brought with it new issues and a new spirit. The unification of the Labour movement was accelerated, and in 1968 the Israel Labour Party was established, uniting three parties – Mapai, Ahdut ha-Avodah and Rafi. Ben-Gurion continued his private war. He did not join the Labour Party, instead heading the Statist List which won only four mandates in the Knesset elections. In 1970 he resigned from the Knesset and from public life.

Nevertheless, the Lavon Affair left a deep imprint on Israeli political culture. It created many precedents. It exposed the work of Israel's secret service whose failing had been publicly revealed, thus damaging its myth. It also exposed the working relations between the Defence Minister and the entire military establishment, demonstrating that such relations should be overseen – an area into which no one had previously dared to enter. The dismissal of Lavon to satisfy Ben-Gurion was a trauma which precluded repetition in any later context. The 'Affair' led to Lavon's resignation in 1955 and his replacement by Ben-Gurion; prompted early elections in 1961; was one of the factors leading to Ben-Gurion's resignation in 1963; brought down the Eshkol government in 1965; and, that same year, produced a split in Mapai and prompted the formation of Rafi. The Lavon Affair engrossed Israeli media and literature, and enriched the Israeli political lexicon with code words dictated by the constraints of censorship ('the mishap', 'the senior officer', 'the third man'). But, above all, the 'Affair' drew red lines: it defined new norms of behaviour throughout the military establishment (much more rigorous authorization of orders), the political leadership (showing that even charismatic leaders cannot impose unilateral and arbitrary decisions on their party), the legislature (which learned that it could play a more important role in the decision-making process), and the media (which discovered its power and influence, and demonstrated its ability to bypass censorship and to reach the public through allusions and codes).

No other affair so engaged the public as the Lavon Affair did, and all subsequent affairs were measured against it. An incident reminiscent of the Lavon Affair was that of the General Security Services (GSS). In April 1984 four terrorists hijacked a bus on Route 300 in southern Israel. The security forces succeeded in overpowering the terrorists and released the passengers. Two terrorists were apprehended and two killed. The matter might have rested at that, had not an alert photographer recorded the event on film, showing the two terrorists later killed alive and well, cuffed to two security personnel.

On the suspicion that the two terrorists had been beaten to death during their interrogation following the release of the passengers, Prime Minister Yitzhak Shamir decided to establish a committee of inquiry headed by Major-General (Res.) Meir Zorea. The committee heard testimony from members of the army and the General Security Services, with the representative of the GSS Yossi Genossar serving as adviser to the committee. It concluded that the injuries to the two terrorists had been inflicted as the passengers were freed and not during their interrogation. The impression given was that the IDF had severely beaten the terrorists while the GSS emerged as blameless.

The conclusions of the Zorea committee might have closed the matter, if it had not been for the presentation of a totally different version of the affair by a senior GSS officer Reuven Hazak and two of his colleagues before Prime Minister Shimon Peres two years later. According to them, it was the head of the GSS Avraham Shalom who had given the order to kill the two terrorists after their interrogation, and that Yossi Genossar had been posted to the Zorea committee to keep the heads of the GSS informed and to coordinate the false testimony of GSS officers. The Prime Minister refused to believe this accusation, viewing it as an attempt by Hazak to depose the head of the GSS, for whom Peres had the greatest respect, so that he might be appointed in his stead.

But Hazak's version also reached the ears of Attorney General Yitzhak Zamir, on the eve of his resignation. Zamir called for an investigation or, alternately, the dismissal of the head of the GSS and of those involved in the affair.

As the Lavon Affair had been, so the current affair was two-dimensional: first, there was the illegal order to kill the terrorists at the conclusion of the interrogation; and secondly there was the interference in the investigation of the Zorea committee. Senior GSS officers strongly objected to a deal by which the top echelons of the service would resign, on the contention that such deeds had been common practice in the GSS for years, causing a serious shock to the entire organization. On the other hand, they opposed a judicial inquiry which would have exposed the actions of the organization which, by their nature were clandestine, forcing them to admit to the use of false testimony with the full knowledge of the heads of the GSS, perhaps even those to whom the heads of the GSS are answerable – Israel's Prime Ministers.

During the early months of 1986 the affair remained under wraps in the bureaux of the Prime Minister and the Attorney General; it erupted in the headlines and in parliamentary and public debate in the middle of the year. Just as the Lavon Affair broke the taboo surrounding the Mossad, so the current crisis broke the taboo surrounding the GSS, an organization whose very existence had always been concealed as part of the military establishment and the identity of whose leaders and employees had always been classified. The name of the head of the GSS Avraham Shalom was published, and the question of security versus the law was debated in the press. The 'Prime Ministers' Forum' (comprising the three Israeli premiers, past and present, serving in the National Unity Government – Shimon Peres, Yitzhak Shamir and Yitzhak Rabin) represented the security approach which accorded the fullest confidence to the nameless soldiers of the GSS, while the Attorney General rejected the idea of any contradiction between the two, maintaining that miscarriage of justice and interference in the legal process would ultimately also be damaging to national security. Zamir's position enjoyed support within the government, where several left-wing ministers also urged an investigation of the heads of the GSS.

The Israeli establishment generally viewed the exposure of the GSS to police investigation as a grave error, and had the deepest respect for its operations which, under immense pressure, succeeded in foiling many terrorist activities. It therefore viewed the Attorney General's insistence on Avraham Shalom's resignation or, alternatively, a state investigation, as sheer obstinacy and blind adherence to the letter of the law, with no consideration for Israel's special situation and the constant threat to its security. In the course of the discussions on the GSS affair, and after Zamir recommended the opening of a police investigation against the heads of the GSS, the Attorney General was replaced by district judge Yosef Harish. Harish found himself a partner to the deliberations of the Security Cabinet (composed of five ministers from the left and five from the right). The Cabinet decided to make an exceptional appeal to the President, requesting that he pardon the head of the GSS and ten other senior GSS officers. The singularity of the appeal lay in the fact that the pardon was to be granted before the commencement of legal proceedings, and not as a consequence of the verdict. On 25 June 1986 the President granted the Cabinet's request. The heads of the GSS immediately resigned and were replaced by a new leadership cadre.

The Route 300 affair produced a public uproar, and proved damaging to all concerned: the GSS was exposed, and a considerable portion of its activities became public knowledge; the Attorney General, who had been willing to continue in his post, was forced to step down; the new Attorney General was obliged to support an irregular procedure, while the President was obliged to execute it. The GSS suffered a heavy blow, both to its image and to its freedom of manoeuvre, with the disclosure that it had for years accorded legitimacy to false testimony to cover the use of violence during the interrogation of witnesses.

However, unlike the Lavon Affair, this affair did not leave a deep imprint on the public, primarily because it was exposed during a period of National Unity Government. The treatment of the affair enjoyed relative consensus among the various parties and could not be used as a weapon against any one member of the coalition, while the opposition was too small to cause ferment. Had either the Labour Alignment or the Likud headed the coalition on their own, this serious incident might well have become a stormy and lengthy affair that could have brought down the government and led to early elections.

One of the effects of the Route 300 affair was to revive the Nafsu case, which also involved false testimony by the GSS. Izat Nafsu, an army lieutenant of Circassian origin, was accused in 1982, during the Lebanon War, of treason, espionage and assistance to the enemy in time of war, and of supplying armaments for terrorist attacks from Lebanon against Israel. He was sentenced to eighteen years' imprisonment and discharged from the army. Although Nafsu confessed under interrogation to the charges against him, in the course of the trial he maintained that the confession had been obtained by force (he was kicked and slapped, placed under cold showers, not allowed to sleep, etc.). A mini-trial was held to test his claim, at which GSS interrogators testified under oath that no violence had been used in his interrogation. The military court accepted the interrogators' testimony and condemned Nafsu, primarily on the basis of his confession.

The Route 300 affair two years later aroused suspicion within the GSS that Nafsu had been unjustly condemned and that his interrogators had borne false witness. When, at this time, the Nafsu family learned that the same person (Yossi Genossar) who had been responsible for subverting the legal process in the Zorea committee had also been involved in Nafsu's interrogation, they demanded a retrial. Ultimately the Supreme Court dismissed the military court's verdict and sentenced Nafsu to twenty-four months' imprisonment (which he had already served) and demoted him from lieutenant to company sergeant major.

This affair, coming so soon after the Route 300 affair, continued to focus public attention on the GSS; debate on whether, in a democratic state proud of its rule of law, there can be a contradiction between security and justice recurred. As a result, the Landau Committee was established in June 1987 to examine both the methods and interrogation procedures used by the GSS in cases of hostile terrorist activity and also GSS procedures with regard to court testimony on these interrogations. The committee, headed by a retired Supreme Court justice, was asked to recommend procedures of interrogation, taking into consideration the special needs of anti-terrorist activity. Four months later the committee submitted its recommendations, some of which were made public while others remained classified. This broke yet another taboo in Israeli society, in exposing and sharply criticizing many of the GSS methods.

The Landau Committee stated that in most security cases, unlike police interrogation, the testimony of the accused is the only incriminating evidence, as other evidence is generally classified. Until 1971 trials of terrorists had been prosecuted by the police. Subsequently, defence counsel began to demand that the GSS interrogators appear in court to testify that the terrorists' confessions had not been obtained by improper means. Truthful testimony would have exposed the interrogation methods used by the GSS and jeopardized the chances of convicting suspected terrorists. In many cases, therefore, the GSS interrogators lied to the court, in contravention of the law and their written instructions. The interrogators found it relatively easy to lie, convinced as they were of the guilt of the terrorists.

While the Route 300 and Nafsu affairs exposed specific cases of perjury by GSS interrogators, the Landau Committee exposed a method employed for sixteen years during which many were sentenced to prison as a result of such false testimony. The committee accused the heads of the GSS, particularly Avraham Shalom, of having known of the method and even actively having encouraged it, alongside the GSS legal advisers who should have advised against it. The findings of the committee were shocking, and indeed engaged both the media and the public. But these findings, too, would probably have aroused much more controversy had there been a significant opposition when they were published. The fact that a National Unity Government was in power at the time was the major factor preventing the development of a real crisis.

While crises of a socio-cultural nature did not bring down governments in Israel, they undoubtedly had a decisive effect on long-term political processes. The first public storm arose following the Wadi Salib disturbances. The whole incident began as a result of a police mishap: on 8 July 1959 police encountered a drunkard, Yaakov Akiva Elkarib, in the Wadi Salib quarter of Haifa, a neighbourhood of abandoned Arab houses inhabited by new immigrants who had arrived from Morocco in the mid-1950s. The police ordered him to halt. When he failed to do so, they fired 'into the air', but the man was wounded in the leg and taken to hospital. This incident aroused sharp ethnic antagonism, giving rise to a wave of violence which spread throughout the country. Rumours were circulated in Wadi Salib that Elkarib had died of his wounds in hospital, and a spontaneous demonstration was organized by David Ben-Harush. Marching on the police station, the demonstrators carried three banners – one black, and two Israeli flags dipped in blood. The police tried to convince the demonstrators that Elkarib was alive, but to no avail. They stoned police and private vehicles, broke into the local Histadrut and Mapai clubs, and set fire to cars. The demonstrators did not confine themselves to the boundaries of their own neighbourhood but also rioted in the Hadar Hacarmel quarter of Haifa, smashing display windows, and forcing merchants and customers alike to flee for their lives. Thirteen policemen were injured in the riots, and dozens of demonstrators were arrested. The disturbances spread to other parts of the country, such as Beersheba and Acre, prompted by the sharp sense of ethnic discrimination experienced by the Moroccan immigrants.

The commander of the northern police district Superintendant Avraham Zelinger appointed a police investigation committee, which concluded that the use of firearms against Elkarib had been a mistake. It was, however, clear to everybody that the Wadi Salib riots went far beyond citizen response to a police error. The failure fully to integrate the immigrants from North Africa became more than a public issue; it became a central media issue. Public figures visited Wadi Salib, displayed interest, talked with the residents, and promised to improve conditions in the neighbourhood. The government eventually decided to set up a committee of inquiry (headed by district judge Moshe Etzioni) to study the Wadi Salib disturbances and their implications. The committee recommended the establishment of a public authority that would oversee the integration process, although this recommendation, like many others, was not implemented. David Ben-Harush became a momentary hero, and made an unsuccessful bid to run for the Knesset. The riots became a symbol of Israel's social time bomb, which would explode once again with a loud bang some twelve years later.

At the beginning of 1971 news of an organization of Jerusalem youths filtered through to the Israeli press. This group, which fashioned itself after the Black Panthers in the United States, decided to challenge the Ashkenazi (European) establishment for its discrimination against the Sephardi Jews of North African and Asian origin. It was several months after the ceasefire which ended the War of Attrition between Israel and Egypt along the Suez Canal; after a long period of security tension, the national agenda was free to deal with social issues. The hardships of those living in the city slums were clear when compared with the relatively comfortable conditions being provided to new immigrants from the Soviet Union. The feeling of those living in the disadvantaged neighbourhoods was that the new immigrants were receiving preferential treatments as regards housing, tax exemptions, etc., and they demanded that these gaps be bridged. The establishment's explanations on the need to accord the immigrants special conditions did not satisfy the immigrants of the 1950s, whose sons now raised the banner of discrimination.

Israel's Black Panthers mainly came from large families living in Morasha, a poor Jerusalem neighbourhood; they had generally dropped out of school after less than eight years' study and had spent a large part of their lives in institutions for juvenile delinquents. They formed street gangs, and the city workers who dealt with them became their go-betweens with the media, drawing them towards political activity. In early March 1971 the police carried out a series of preventive arrests among the Black Panthers in order to prevent them from holding a demonstration opposite the Jerusalem municipality, a demonstration for which they had not received a permit.

The demonstration nevertheless took place, with the participation of hundreds of youths – Morasha residents and students – and aroused a public storm. The Knesset debated the problems of the disadvantaged youth as opposed to those of the new immigrants, and the media gave wide coverage to the newly founded movement and to its leaders. Prime Minister Golda Meir met with the leaders of the Black Panthers, although after the meeting she was to remark: 'They're not nice', which was a phrase that would haunt her for the rest of her life. She established a public committee for distressed youth, whose recommendations would later be reflected in the enactment of the State Welfare Insurance Law.

The movement was encouraged by this broad public response. Many young residents of Morasha joined up, and branches were opened in other towns and cities. Other organizations of Sephardi youths were founded to protest against discrimination. During 1971 the Black Panthers held a large demonstration about once a month, some of which became violent. The group was quite creative in its activities: they held a procession of coffins, for example, symbolizing the death of social equality; changed the name of Jerusalem's Zion Square to Sephardic Jewry Square; stole milk bottles from well-to-do neighbourhoods in Jerusalem and distributed them in disadvantaged areas – to name only a few.

The movement began to be institutionalized; it was officially registered as an association, issued membership cards, etc. Soon afterwards, however, it experienced a series of internal conflicts, quarrels and ruptures. In September 1973 the movement stood for election to the Histadrut convention and won a notable number of seats. It tried to ride the wave of success in the subsequent Knesset elections. But because they were held in the aftermath of the Yom Kippur War, the major issue of these elections was security. The Panthers, who had been identified with the Israeli left, now found their way to the extreme left-wing camp – Rakah and Sheli – and two of its members entered the Knesset on these lists.

The years which followed the Yom Kippur War were characterized by a series of economic scandals involving several senior members of the Labour Party, probably hastening its electoral defeat. The progression of white-collar crimes began in the summer of 1974 with the collapse of the Israel–British Bank and the indictment of its director-general Yehoshua Bension, a leading figure in Israel's economic life, who was sentenced to fourteen years' imprisonment. This was followed by the arrest of another leading figure, Michael Tzur, director-general of the Israel Corporation and former director-general of the Ministry of Trade and Industry, and Pinhas Sapir's right-hand man. He was accused of having embezzled millions of dollars from the corporation, and was sentenced to fifteen years' imprisonment. Directors of several large Histadrut-owned corporations were linked with corruption scandals under investigation. Although in some cases sufficient grounds were not found to place them on trial, their reputations were tarnished. Major contractors were tried for corrupt activities in the construction of the large defence fortifications in the Sinai peninsula. Famous names burst onto the front pages and the public agenda. Prime Minister Yitzhak Rabin and Justice Minister Haim Zadok did not try to conceal the affairs nor to grant anyone immunity. Nevertheless, the opposition parties on the right and the left chose to present these disclosures as typical of the decadence of the Labour government.

In September 1976, following government approval of Asher Yadlin's appointment as Governor of the Bank of Israel, charges were filed against him and the police opened an investigation. Yadlin, then chairman of the Histadrut's Kupat Holim (health fund), had previously served as secretary of Hevrat Ovdim (the umbrella organization of all Histadrut-owned enterprises) and was one of Pinhas Sapir's closest associates. The opening of the police investigation was a shock to the public. Yadlin, who was to have assumed his prestigious post on 1 November, was suspected of having taken bribes from go-betweens in land deals involving Kupat Holim. The police hastened their investigation in order to be able to recommend to the government whether to cancel his new appointment before it took effect. The opposition Likud party accused Prime Minister Rabin and several Labour ministers of having known of the suspicions prior to Yadlin's appointment – an accusation which was promptly denied.

This was the only issue on Israeli society's agenda in the course of these months. The Attorney General, the young and determined Aharon Barak, together with superintendant Ya'acov Kedmi, head of police investigations, were the heroes of the day. The various stages of the investigation were extensively reported in the media; the press eagerly devoured the leaks from the investigation as well as the stories about Yadlin, the wife from whom he was separated, his young girlfriend and his previous mistress. Yadlin himself was questioned but, as an important personality, not placed under arrest, and was interviewed frequently by the electronic and written media, furnishing daily news stories. He denied the charges against him, and succeeded in altering his image as a manipulator of the Israeli economy to that of the underdog, arousing a certain degree of sympathy.

On 14 October Attorney General Barak completed his initial report, and, on the basis of its findings, he recommended that the police continue its investigation. This meant that Yadlin would not be able to assume the post of Governor of the Bank of Israel. Several days later Yadlin was arrested, despite the reservations of the Prime Minister, who felt that the economic scandals being uncovered were the work of internal party sabotage designed to hurt him and his associates. On 24 October, just one week before the new Governor was to have assumed his responsibilities, the government hastily appointed Arnon Gafni, the director-general of the Finance Ministry, to the position due to be taken by Yadlin.

Shortly after this appointment the Rabin government resigned and early elections were called. The Yadlin affair became increasingly political in nature. Yadlin himself announced that the funds which he received had been intended for political purposes, while the leaders of the Likud declared that the deal which Yadlin ultimately made with the prosecution had been designed to conceal serious information regarding the Labour Party. About two and a half months before the elections, Asher Yadlin, the most senior Israeli official convicted of a white-collar crime to date, was sentenced to five years' imprisonment on charges of bribery. But another incident overshadowed even this event – the suicide of Housing Minister Avraham Ofer – a close childhood friend of Asher Yadlin – who had for many years managed the Histadrut construction company, Shikun Ovdim.

During the Yadlin affair, information was published on various illegal deals between Kupat Holim (managed by Yadlin) and Shikun Ovdim (managed by Avraham Ofer). It was also reported that Shikun Ovdim had sold an apartment to Ofer's confidants, contravening procedures and without linkage to the index. A journalist filed a complaint with the police on these and other accusations, and the police opened a special investigation. This was the first time in the history of the state that the police were to investigate a government minister. The media devoted all their attention to the new affair, while the investigation of the Governor-designate of the Bank of Israel continued in the background. The position of Attorney General Aharon Barak was unshakable, and all the ministers, with the Prime Minister at their head, were uncomfortable in his presence. Head of police investigations Ya'acov Kedmi and head of fraud investigations Benjamin Ziegler formed, with him, a trio which shattered Israeli myths to the applause and admiration of the media, and, to a large extent, of the public.

Rabin asked Barak to expedite Ofer's investigation, but he refused to set a timetable. The investigation continued, casting a shadow on the day-to-day work of the government. In December 1976, during the investigation, Prime Minister Rabin resigned. The Rabin government became a transitional government from which ministers could not resign, and Ofer found himself 'trapped' in his ministerial position.

With the approaching elections, these two scandals became a major political asset for the Likud, and the investigation of Ofer was raised by Likud representatives in the Knesset. Ofer, who had not at that stage been questioned, felt the noose was tightening around his neck, and saw that his fellow ministers had no desire to help free him. Rabin wanted to issue an official statement, based on what the Attorney General had told him, that most of the charges filed against Ofer were unfounded, but Barak forbade him from issuing such a statement. On 3 January 1977 the Housing Minister shot and killed himself, before he had even been summoned by the police to respond to the charges against him. With his death, the investigation of the affair was closed. The question of whether Ofer committed suicide because he feared the disclosure of serious wrongdoings, or because he could not bear the strain of an investigation being conducted without his involvement, with his fellow ministers having turned their backs on him, remained unanswered. The suicide of a government minister, the first police investigation of a government minister; these combined to create a temporary climax in the series of scandals characterizing these years.

The next scandal penetrated the home of the Prime Minister himself; it was probably the straw that broke the back of the Labour Party – just one month before the fateful 1977 elections and less than two months after Rabin's close victory over Peres at the Labour Party convention. Rabin, as Israeli Ambassador to the United States, had been entitled to maintain an ordinary current account with an American bank. However, after his return to Israel in 1974, he was once more subject to the law which prohibits all Israeli citizens from holding such accounts, and he should have exchanged the foreign currency in his possession into Israeli currency. An Israeli journalist in Washington discovered that three years after his return to Israel, the Prime Minister and his wife still maintained savings and current accounts in Washington to the value of over $20,000.

Having consulted with Attorney General Aharon Barak, Rabin decided to suspend himself from the premiership (as Prime Minister of a transitional government he was prevented by law from resigning), and to hand over the conduct of government meetings to Shimon Peres. Rabin's wife admitted to maintaining the two bank accounts and was tried by the Tel-Aviv district court.

But even this was not to be the end of the scandals. Shortly before the elections it was reported that former Foreign Minister Abba Eban also maintained a foreign currency account for the royalties received on his book, without having received the necessary permission from the Finance Ministry. A thorough check was undertaken by the Finance Ministry who found no evidence that such permission had been granted. The affair came to an end only several months after the elections. Attorney General Barak decided to halt the investigation, having concluded that Eban was indeed convinced that he had received permission.

No single reason can be given for the severe defeat suffered by the Labour Alignment in 1977. Personally, I share the view that the 1977 vote was a delayed reaction on the part of the Israeli voters to the Yom Kippur War. However, no Israeli historian can ignore the economic scandals of 1976–77 which all involved senior Labour personalities. These, rightly or wrongly, produced a tarnished portrait of a movement which, after governing the State of Israel for twenty-nine years – and many more in the pre-state period – had become corrupted. The public was confronted with a domino effect: Solel Boneh, Kupat Holim, Shikun Ovdim, the abortive appointment of the governor of the Bank of Israel, the suicide of a government minister, the Prime Minister himself – the public were more pre-occupied by all these issues during these years than anything else. The Likud made clever use of these scandals in its election campaign; newspaper advertisements, for example, presented photographs of the Labour figures involved.

Further corruption scandals continued to engage the public in the years that followed, setting yet more new precedents. In July 1978 the Knesset was asked to lift the immunity of Shmuel Rechtman, a Member of Knesset for the Likud and the Mayor of Rehovot, in order to prosecute him for the receipt of bribes from a contractor in exchange for a building extension permit. Rechtman's immunity was revoked and he stood trial. He was sentenced to three and a half years' imprisonment; this was the first conviction of a Member of Knesset.

The next precedent was the passing of a prison sentence on an Israeli government minister. The Minister of Religion, Aharon Abuhatzeira, of the NRP, was in 1981 acquitted of charges of accepting bribes. One year later he was charged with having made personal use of money from a charitable fund named after his father, prior to his ministerial appointment. The court imposed a three-month sentence which he discharged through public work. The son of a Moroccan Jewish family identified with the religious leadership of this community, Abuhatzeira was tried to the accompaniment of sharp ethnic feelings and loud assertions that the Ashkenazi establishment was trying to dislodge a member of the Sephardi community who had made good – too good for their taste. It is interesting to note that despite Abuhatzeira's conviction and prison sentence, he did not retire from political life, and instead acquired the reputation of a machinator and a survivor. He stood for the Knesset in the 1981 elections at the head of a Sephardi list and won three seats. After his conviction he resigned his ministerial post and since then he has not returned to government; but he has not resigned from the Knesset (according to law, only a prison sentence of one year or more requires the resignation of a Member of Knesset). He stood for election again in 1984, winning a single mandate. In the 1988 elections he joined the Likud and was elected to the Knesset on its list.

In 1990 a police investigation was opened against Interior Minister Aryeh Deri on the suspicion that he exploited his position to transfer funds to his political associates, and even to members of his family. This is, to a certain extent, a repetition of the Abuhatzeira affair. The initial reaction to the publication of the investigation was a feeling of solidarity amongst the Sephardi community and notices in the press which portrayed the young Deri as a victim of the Ashkenazi establishment which was seeking to hurt the rising Sephardi star. At the time of writing the affair has yet to run its course, and it is hard to say where it will lead. But if legal proceedings are begun, it will undoubtedly be presented to the public as a serious blow to the law and to the norms of proper government. Conversely, it will also be argued that this is no new phenomenon, but rather one that is acceptable so long as it is carried out by Ashkenazim. Thus, the affair clearly embodies the potential for a revival in ethnic tension.

The collapse of the bank shares was the most important single economic affair in Israeli history. It sent shock waves right through Israel's banking system and, quite apart from the great interest it aroused, it directly affected many households, impoverishing many and hurting others. In the late 1970s and early 1980s, the major Israeli banks encouraged their customers to purchase the shares issued by the banks. The shares rose steadily during those years and were very popular. Many people who had never invested on the stock exchange or who had invested only in government bonds, now purchased bank shares which were considered very safe, as it was assumed that the government would back the banks. Most of these shares carried no voting rights, and the controlling vote remained almost exclusively in the hands of the founders of the major banks.

The banks, at the height of their success at that stage, made a great effort to assure a high return on their shares, and were prepared to pick up shares on the market at any cost. In order to bear this burden, they coordinated their actions and took out very large loans abroad. The Finance Ministry and Bank of Israel understood what was happening; they continued to encourage the public to purchase and hold bank shares, however, even when it became apparent to everybody that the value of the shares exceeded by more than three times the value of the banks themselves.

The bubble burst at the beginning of 1983. The banks were no longer able to pick up available shares with foreign currency, thus putting an end to their articifial regulation of the shares. The Tel-Aviv stock exchange was closed for many days, and the heads of the banks opened talks with the Finance Ministry and the Bank of Israel, finally agreeing on an arrangement for the bank shares. The government eventually decided to stand behind the banks and did not allow them to collapse. At a cost of some $8 billion, the government provided guarantees that those holding bank shares would be assured of their real market value or their value prior to the cessation of regulation, linked to the dollar and with low interest, on condition that they continued to hold the shares for at least five years.

The collapse of the bank shares was a shock to the Israeli economy, dealing a heavy blow to both commercial enterprises and private households, and shaking the public's confidence in a system which they had believed to be invulnerable. Only two years later, public and parliamentary pressure led to the establishment of a state committee of inquiry into the bank shares affair, headed by Justice Moshe Beisky. The committee's conclusions, published in April 1986, were far-reaching. They led to the replacement of the management of four of Israel's major banks, and the ousting of the Governor of the Bank of Israel. The committee made no recommendations regarding the personal future of Yoram Aridor, Finance Minister at the time of the collapse, because he no longer held any government post.

Various events related to the bank shares affair remained on the national agenda for a relatively long time. With the government's assumption of the banks' obligations, Israel's banks were in effect nationalized. However, the government has never sought to realize this nationalization, and the management of the banks remains firmly in the hands of their boards of directors. A government company has been established to sell the banks and hand over the revenues to the government, but at the time of writing this process only proceeds slowly. But the Israeli banking system will never regain its earlier status.

In 1973 the public was made painfully aware that the Israel Defence Forces were not omnipotent; in the course of the 1970s it learned that the political system was not free from corruption. The 1980s revealed the weakness of a banking system which had been perceived as 'the oxygen of the state', to quote an advertising campaign of one of the banks in its 'golden era'. In a sense, this was another example of the maturation of Israeli society which now abandoned its economic innocence as well. The price of the maturity thus attained, however, was very costly, contributing further to the rampant inflation of the early 1980s.

The weather forecast is rarely a subject which engages Israeli society; it is almost never the opening item on news broadcasts. Israeli summers are hot, and last from May to November. Israeli winters are rainy but with little snow and not too cold, lasting from December to April. Floods, earthquakes and snowstorms occur rarely in Israel. Rain is not expected in summer. It is a climate with few surprises, and is rarely of special interest to the public. The English custom of beginning a conversation with a reference to the weather cannot be applied in Israel. Other issues, such as fires or acts of violence, also rarely reach the headlines or the national agenda. Similarly, sports news almost always remains marginal. Only when Israel wins important international competitions does sport attract public attention. Even when the leading Israeli basketball team, Maccabi Tel-Aviv, won the European cup in 1977 – the most important sports event in Israel's history – a political news item removed it from its deserved place: on the day of this victory, Prime Minister Yitzhak Rabin announced his resignation over his foreign currency account in the US.

Ecological issues, which have been known to make and break European governments, only rarely appear on the Israeli national agenda. The environmental issue which came closest to crisis dimensions was the construction of the Reading 4 power plant in Tel-Aviv. The Israeli electric company wanted to replace the old plants which had been operating in Tel-Aviv since the early 1960s, building a power plant that would produce half a million kilowatts of electricity. The new plant was to have emitted about eighty tons of sulphuric dioxide and three tons of soot daily. The Tel-Aviv workers' council exerted pressure on the mayor and government ministers to agree to build the plant so that the electric company would continue to employ workers in Tel-Aviv. Pressure was also brought to bear on several members of Knesset to oppose the construction of the plant in order to prevent carcinogenic pollution, or at least to install a device that would absorb the poisonous pollutants, adding 15 per cent to the entire cost of the project.

The controversy over the building of the plant took place in the mid-1960s, and came to a head in 1967. The opposition parties, led by MK Yosef Tamir, opposed its construction, while most of the coalition members supported it. The parliamentary debate was supported publicly by the council for the prevention of poisonous and pollutant substances, which was accorded expression in the media.

The coalition was uncomfortable in this controversy and was not sure that it would command a majority to defeat Tamir's motion for the agenda. However, once again, in the most important public debate on an environmental issue, security affairs succeeded in pushing ecology aside. The Six Day War was on the doorstep, and the discussion of Tamir's motion to remove the plant from Tel-Aviv was the last item on the Knesset's agenda before war broke out.

In light of public criticism and uncertainty as to whether the plant met the criteria of the Planning and Construction Law enacted two years earlier (1965), the government decided to take blunt action by the enactment of a special law, the Tel-Aviv Power Plant Law, which was submitted to the Knesset for a preliminary reading two months after the Six Day War. The bill was supported by 32 MKs, while 28 opposed. The government, fearing the loss of its scant majority in the subsequent readings, employed steamroller tactics, obliging all coalition members to vote in favour. Within six days the bill became law, after its second and third readings.

The Knesset decision did not provoke mass demonstrations. Neither did the issue play a part in the Knesset elections held two years later. The most important ecological controversy in Israel had thus, once again, been overshadowed by existential problems. The committee established by the residents of north Tel-Aviv for the removal of the Reading 4 plant published several advertisements in the press following the Knesset decision, accusing the coalition parties of having accorded preference to the narrow interests of the electric company at the expense of the residents' health. With this, the affair was in effect closed.

Existential security issues have always been the major items on the agenda of Israeli society, however, and no other issue could rival them. A review of the Israeli press since the establishment of the state reveals clearly that over 80 per cent of the headlines have dealt with national security issues: threats by Arab leaders, Arab aggression against Israel, terrorist actions against Israeli targets at home and abroad, Israeli military operations and war.

5. The Arab–Israeli Conflict

It is impossible to understand Israeli society without a grasp of the ongoing conflict between Jews and Arabs in the country. This conflict was not 'planned'. The leaders of the Zionist movement concerned themselves with such issues as how to obtain an international concession for Palestine, the nature of the new Jewish society there – whether religious or modern – and much more, but the problem of the existence of an Arab community in the country was relegated to the sidelines. They did not ignore it completely, but the rural Arab population and the Bedouins were viewed more as part of the pastoral landscape than as a problem.

Theodor Herzl wrote his visionary book *Altneuland* at the end of the nineteenth century; in it he described in idyllic terms the new society in Palestine, but he did not neglect the Jewish–Arab problem. Rashid Bey, the Arab protagonist in the book, is a warm, positive Oriental type. When a Jew says to him: 'We brought civilization here', Rashid replies: 'Excuse me, my friend, but civilization has existed here before – my father planted many orange trees here.' Thus, while Herzl was not unaware of the problem, the slogan of 'a land without a nation for a nation without a land' was as relevant to him as to the other Zionists.

The truth is that Palestine was not objectively attractive at the end of the nineteenth century. For thousands of years it had not been ruled by its residents, but had been successively conquered by various outside forces who left behind ruin and destruction. The Crusaders who conquered the land in the eleventh and twelfth centuries were in turn defeated by Saladin. Next came the Mongols, followed by the Mamelukes, who were later vanquished by the returning Mongols. In 1516 Palestine was conquered by the Turks, who held it for four hundred years, interrupted only by temporary conquests of the land by Napoleon and Ibrahim Pasha.

In 1862 a very distinguished visitor came to Palestine. The Prince of Wales, later to become King Edward VII was accompanied by A.P. Stanley, who described this visit in his book *Sinai and Palestine*:

> Above all other countries in the world, it is a Land of Ruins ... There is no country in which they are so numerous, none in which they bear so large a proportion to the villages and towns still in existence. In Judaea it is hardly an exaggeration to say that whilst for miles and miles there is no appearance of present life or habitation, except the occasional goat-herd on the hillside, or gathering of women at the wells, there is yet hardly a hill-top of the many within sight, which is not covered by the vestiges of some fortress or city of former ages.

The strong earthquake which struck Palestine in 1837, combined with a series of epidemics and famines, had led to mass emigration. Thousands of Egyptians arrived in the wake of Mohammed Ali to replace these mid-nineteenth century refugees and they settled in various parts of the country. Several years after France had conquered Algeria, refugees from that country also arrived in Palestine, followed later by Circassians and Turkoman nomads. In 1800 the ratio between Jews and non-Jews in Palestine had been 1 to 40 (6,700 Jews to some 260,000 non-Jews), yet even when the number of Jews reached 50,000 and the number of non-Jews 500,000, the Arabs of Palestine displayed no concern when they learned that the First Zionist Congress had convened in Basle with the aim of establishing a national homeland for the Jews in Palestine.

At the Seventh Congress, held in 1905, one year after Herzl's death, the issue was raised in all its poignancy by Yitzhak Epstein, a teacher and farmer from Rosh Pina. In his speech Epstein warned of a national awakening amongst Arabs against Jewish settlement and he called upon the Jews to establish good ties with them in order to forestall this. Two years later the speech was published as 'The Hidden Question'.

The Jewish agricultural settlements attracted labourers from various parts of Palestine, as well as from Egypt, Syria and other neighbouring states. Rishon Lezion, Nes Ziona, Rehovot, Gedera and Ekron relied upon Arab labour, and the number of Arabs in these settlements exceeded the number of Jewish settlers. There is no doubt that Jewish immigration raised the standard of living for the Palestinian Arabs; it provided them with jobs, accorded them higher wages, created a market for their agricultural produce, and increased the price of land. This was a loveless convergence of interests. The Jewish settlers needed the workers, and the local *fellahin* (Arab peasants) needed the work. The farmers exploited their workers, who undertook hard labour for a pittance. When the Jewish immigrants arrived they were not hired, because they were not prepared to work for Arab wages. In 1908 the Young Turks revolution altered the situation, and the anticipated confrontation between the new Jewish settlers and the fellahin and Bedouin in Palestine began to take on an ideological character. The basis of the Arab–Israeli conflict, as defined by Yosef Gorni, was moulded during these years: the doubt over the national identity of the Arabs of Palestine versus the doubt over the right of the Jewish people to live there.

Surprisingly, it was easier for the right to recognize Arab nationalism. They argued that because the Jews had only one country while the Arabs had many, the Arabs would have to surrender their national rights in Palestine and agree to live there as a minority. According to the leader of the Revisionist movement, Ze'ev Jabotinsky, the Arabs would accept this only when they came up against the 'iron wall', namely Jewish power. Only this would persuade them that they could never hope to vanquish the Jewish state but would have to accept it.

The Israeli left has been debating the question of the Palestinian Arab national identity for over eighty years. To define the Arabs living in Palestine – and later Israel – as a nation leads to the necessary conclusion that they deserve the same right of self-determination demanded and received by the Jews. Only by defining them as an entity which does not constitute a nation can one explain why they are not entitled to self-determination. Ber Borochov, one of the most important thinkers of socialist Zionism in Russia, distinguished between a 'people' – a group objectively distinct from its surroundings – and a 'nation' – the same group after it achieves self-awareness. He recognized the Arabs of Palestine as a people but not as a nation; they were therefore in his opinion not entitled to realize their unique national character.

Another Labour Zionist Moshe Beilinson, a doctor by profession and a journalist by trade, differentiated between a 'people' and 'fragments of a people'. According to his analysis, the Arabs of the Middle East are a people entitled to national expression, while the Arabs of Palestine are 'fragments of a people' who comprise a part of the larger Arab people and are therefore not entitled to separate national expression.

The fundamental difference between left and right in Palestine during those years was very similar to the difference which prevailed in the democratic world at the time; it was based on such issues as the right to strike, a planned economy versus a free economy, etc. Politically, there was basic agreement between them on the need to establish a Jewish state within the borders of Biblical Israel, on both sides of the Jordan, in which a Jewish majority would be guaranteed and the Arab minority would enjoy equal civil rights. However, the left found it very hard to accept that the land to which they were coming was not a *tabula rasa*, but a place where another people lived, with rights of their own. Jewish labour versus the Arabs' right to work, joint Jewish–Arab representation in trade unions, or such a fundamental question as the rights of the Arab fellahin to the lands purchased from the tenant farmers and deeded to the Zionist movement: all these deeply troubled the left, and continue to do so to this day, in one way or another. When Prime Minister Golda Meir declared in the early 1970s that she was a Palestinian, many considered this a ludicrous statement – and rightly so. But she herself resorted to this absurd argument because she understood that to admit the separate existence of a Palestinian entity in Israel was to recognize its national rights. The statement was anyway based on the fact that during the mandate period she, like all those living in the country, carried identification as a resident of Palestine.

On 4 June 1918 a meeting took place north of Aqaba between the Arab and Zionist leaderships. Chaim Weizmann, who arrived from London as part of the Zionist delegation (a delegation of world Jewry to the British military administration), reached a measure of understanding with Emir Faisal, the son of Sharif Hussein, leader of the Arab revolt. Faisal, who was on his way to Syria, dreamt of an Arab kingdom in the north and, in order to receive the support of the Jews, he was prepared to accept the existence of a Jewish entity in Palestine. This understanding accorded with the Balfour Declaration given to the Jews, as well as with the promises made to Sharif Hussein and his son for the leadership of an independent state outside Palestine.

Seven months later Weizmann and Faisal signed what was then considered an historic agreement, but which over the years proved no more than a fleeting episode. Vaguely worded, it promised 'the closest possible collaboration in the development of the Arab State and Palestine', the acceptance of the Balfour Declaration, and the encouragement of large-scale immigration of Jews to Palestine and their rapid settlement on the land. The Arab fellahin and tenant farmers were promised protection of their rights and assistance in their economic development. The agreement did not mention the Jewish state, nor the rights of the Palestinian Arabs. Faisal made his commitment conditional on the complete fulfilment of the demands for Arab independence, as outlined in his memorandum to the peace conference.

The agreement delighted the Jews of Palestine, but aroused both opposition in the Arab world and sharp criticism of Faisal. The Emir was forced to qualify the interpretation of the agreement, claiming, for example, to have agreed to the immigration of only 1,500 Jews per year. He was deeply disappointed when the kingdom he founded in Syria lasted no more than several months, and the mandate for Syria was given to France rather than to Britain. Faisal was forced to leave Syria for Iraq, and his agreement with Weizmann came to nought.

The Arabs were bitterly disappointed by the League of Nations' wording of the British mandate over Palestine, which was even more far-reaching than the Balfour Declaration. Indeed, they refused to cooperate with the British. The League of Nations, which in effect established the British mandatory regime, accorded international recognition to both national movements. But while the Jews of Palestine viewed this as another step forward, the Arabs viewed it as a step backwards, and the Palestinian–Arab Executive Committee, founded in December 1920, began to formulate the Palestinian argument. That same year, Hajj Amin al-Husseini was sentenced to ten years' imprisonment for his role in the incitement of anti-Jewish riots in Jerusalem. However, in May 1921 he was released by the British and appointed Mufti of Jerusalem. One year later he headed the Supreme Muslim Council. Husseini was considered the most prominent Arab leader, a kind of unofficial prime minister of the Palestinian Arabs. The anti-Jewish riots which took place in several locations in Palestine in 1929 were for him a major success: he helped to nurture Arab animosity towards Zionism and played an important part in transforming the conflict into a no-win situation. He succeeded in influencing the intellectuals and uneducated alike with his opposition to Zionism and, through his extremism, drew the Arab states into the Palestinian conflict, for only their power could accord credibility to such an all-out struggle.

Hostility towards both Zionism and the Jewish attempt to change the status quo in the Middle East became a major factor in the organization of the Palestinian Arabs, who lagged behind politically, economically and socially. It helped to foster the demand for a promise that Palestine would be given to its Arab residents. The Palestinian movement was not born because of Jewish immigration; indeed, among the ideas which were raised during its early years was one forming a part of the Syrian Hashemite kingdom to be established in 1920. But it was the Zionist movement which reinforced the idea of an Arab state in Palestine.

The Zionist leaders were prepared to make two compromises with the Arabs of Palestine. Even after eastern Palestine (Transjordan) was removed from the mandate and given to Emir Abdullah (who founded present-day Jordan), most Zionists were willing to accept territorial compromise in western Palestine, although they preferred to postpone the decision until a Jewish majority had been attained. The Zionist movement's mistake was that it was not made clear to the Arabs that there was no desire to do them any harm nor to drive them out of their homes, nor was it obvious that they were prepared to sit down and talk with any Arab party. The dialogue between Jews and Arabs in Palestine was not conducted directly, but rather through the British. The Jews demanded free immigration while the Arabs demanded a halt to Jewish immigration and a ban on further sales of land to Jews.

The year 1936 marked a significant turning point. Protest riots by the Palestinian Arabs spread throughout the country; they were no longer limited to isolated locations. Faced with this development, the Jewish underground organization, the Haganah, was transformed from a group of people charged with protecting Jews against local outbreaks of violence into a military organization with national commanders and a permanent staff. The Palestinians quickly realized that they themselves would not be able to take the Jewish community by force, and appealed to the leaders of the Arab states for assistance. Not all the Arab leaders responded enthusiastically, but in the course of time they began to understand the advantage of involving themselves in the Palestinian Arab problem: this was a pan-Arab challenge of unparalleled unifying potential.

There were now about 400,000 Jews in western Palestine, as opposed to 800,000 Arabs. Two well-established national movements confronted one another, each demanding the entire territory for a state of its own. Both understood that the balance of forces was temporary, and – with the steady arrival of Jews from Europe – that it would increasingly shift in favour of the Jews. Calling a general strike in April 1936, the Arabs demanded that a representative government be elected by the residents of Palestine which would reflect the proportions of the existing population. They also demanded of course that the British should impose an immediate halt to Jewish immigration and a ban on the sale of land to Jews.

When the intifada began in the occupied territories in December 1987, it reminded many of the riots of 1936–37. During both periods, the Arabs boycotted Jewish goods, established autonomous authority, and sharply escalated their violent attacks against Jews in various parts of the country. These years, which helped to consolidate the military force of the Jewish community, greatly sharpened the split between the two communities' economies in Palestine, increased the involvement of the Arab states in the conflict, and made it increasingly hard for the British to govern the country and to fulfil their contradictory promises.

The Peel Commission, which was established at the onset of the riots and which published its conclusions in 1937, proposed the establishment of two states in western Palestine – Arab and Jewish – for the first time since the beginning of the British mandate. Each was to have a national majority and both were to be very small in size, and Jerusalem was to be an international city. The Jewish Agency, after a bitter debate, viewed it as a basis for deliberation and consideration. The Arabs rejected the proposal. The British themselves decided not to adopt the commission's recommendations at this stage.

In February 1939, several months before the outbreak of World War II, Britain convened the Round Table Conference at St James. Three delegations were sent from Palestine: one Jewish, and two Palestinian – one in the name of the Mufti Hajj Amin al-Husseini and the other in the name of his opponents. Arab delegations came from Iraq, Saudi Arabia, Egypt, Transjordan and Yemen. This was the first international event at which Britain on the one hand and the Zionist movement on the other accorded legitimacy to the transformation of the Jewish–Arab conflict in Palestine into a Middle Eastern issue. The Zionist leadership believed at the time that the involvement of the Arab states in the conflict would serve as a moderating factor on the Palestinian Arabs, but in this they were proved wrong. The Jews proposed the establishment of a Jewish state that would be part of an Arab federation. The Arabs demanded once again the establishment of an Arab-dominated state in which the Jews would constitute a minority, and reiterated their demand for a halt to Jewish immigration. Britain, for its part, could not tolerate a continued Arab revolt with war imminent in Europe; announcing the establishment of an Arab state within a ten-year period and restrictions on Jewish immigration, in effect it went back on the Balfour Declaration.

The Jewish–Arab conflict was eclipsed by World War II. Hajj Amin al-Husseini allied himself publicly with Hitler, while the Jewish community totally identified with the Allies; they enlisted in local brigades operated at first by the British (the Palmach) and also in various units of the British army. The Holocaust of European Jewry increased international legitimacy for the establishment of a Jewish state that would be a haven for all Jewish refugees, and consequently the Arabs of Palestine intensified their pressure against it.

The Arab League was founded in 1945. Convening in Cairo shortly afterwards, it decided to demand independence for Palestine and yet again a halt to Jewish immigration. The pan-Arab movements which developed during this period (such as the Ba'ath party) viewed Palestine as a central issue which could serve as a common denominator for the unification of the Arab world, and they encouraged the Arabs to espouse it. The readiness of the Jewish Agency in 1946 to return to the 1937 partition idea did not help the British in their search for a solution to a conflict into which they had been unwillingly thrust. Unable to overcome the impasse alone, they passed the problem to the United Nations. A Special Committee on Palestine appointed by the UN to study the problem submitted its proposal for a solution – partition, once again. At the historic vote held on 29 November 1947, the proposal won more than the requisite two-thirds support of the General Assembly. The Arab states, which had themselves recently won independence, voted against it while the British abstained.

In hindsight, the Palestinian decision to reject United Nations General Assembly Resolution 181 on the partition of Palestine was perhaps their biggest mistake. Had they accepted it – even after the Arab states had voted against it – they could have been living for the past forty years and more in their own independent state alongside the State of Israel, thus sparing the thousands of lives lost and the hundreds of thousands of people injured and disabled. Moreover, the trillions of dollars used to purchase arms could have been used instead to develop the region and to alleviate poverty in the Middle East. But the clocks of history cannot be turned back. Thus, when Yasser Arafat spoke at the end of 1988 of the Palestinians' readiness to accept UN Resolution 181, when Israeli law today prevails in 80 per cent of western Palestine and Israel controls all of western Palestine, many saw this as a proposal which was too little and too late.

The partition of Palestine in 1947 was also debated within the Jewish community. The right, led by Menachem Begin, rejected the

United Nations decision, arguing that the Jews of Palestine did not have the right to accept in the name of the entire Jewish people only 54 per cent of the land. The Zionist left also opposed partition, preferring a bi-national state in which the national aspirations of both peoples would find expression without an artificial division of the country. But the centre, headed by Ben-Gurion, produced a majority in favour of partition, and on 15 May 1948 it was decided that the independent Jewish state would be established.

Violent civil war erupted in Palestine between Jews and Arabs. At first, during the early months of 1948, the Arabs displayed surprising strength, but the Jews quickly recovered, purchased weapons in Eastern Europe, and proved to be a much better organized, more experienced and stronger force. The Palestinian Arabs appealed to the Arab states for help. As soon as the State of Israel was established, seven Arab armies invaded it, firmly convinced that the young state would not be able to withstand such a combined force. From this moment, the fate of the Palestinians was placed in the hands of the Arab states. The Arabs of Palestine were in effect an irrelevant force in the conduct of the war, while Abdullah's Hashemite kingdom, with its professional and experienced army, was the major player on the field.

The Arabs were greatly surprised by Israel's strength. Israel, with a very small population, succeeded in recruiting a larger fighting force than the Arab states whose population numbered 30 million. The Israeli people, inspired in part by the sense that this was a war of survival, produced a brilliant Israeli victory, helped by Arab under-estimation of Israel's ability and contrary to all expectations. The territory of the stillborn Palestinian state was divided among Israel, Jordan and Egypt.

Many books have been written about the Palestinian refugee problem created in 1948. In this Rashumon-like tale, each side presents its own truth. Nevertheless, with the passing of the years, the picture has become clearer, and to a certain extent the numbers also. Of the Arabs who had until 15 May 1948 been living in the territory which was to become the State of Israel, about 600,000 became refugees and only 150,000 remained under Israeli rule. Of these refugees, 200,000 settled on the West Bank. The West Bank was annexed to Jordan two years later, and they became Jordanian citizens. Another 100,000 crossed to Transjordan, on the east bank of the Jordan River. The 200,000 Palestinian Arabs who fled to the Egyptian-controlled Gaza Strip were not granted citizenship, and the remaining 100,000 went to Syria, Lebanon and other Arab states. The latter, also denied citizenship, were placed under the care of the United Nations Relief and Rehabilitation Agency (UNRRA) and have since been used by the Arab states as ready ammunition against Israel. About half of the refugees fled Palestine in response to a call by the Arab leaders, who promised that they would return with the victorious army that would destroy the Zionist entity. The other half were expelled by Israel under the cover of war. For over forty years Palestinian propaganda has tried to prove that all the refugees were expelled by Israel, while Israel has tried to prove that they all left of their own accord. These efforts will probably continue even after a peaceful solution is found to the Israeli–Palestinian conflict.

The feeling which prevailed immediately after the war in 1949 was that, in light of Israel's clear victory, a peaceful settlement was very near. Indeed, the armistice agreements signed in the post-war shock explicitly stated that the next stage would be peace. The May 1949 Lausanne Conference, at which Israel, Egypt, Lebanon, Jordan and Syria participated in negotiations, raised many hopes. Israel made a significant gesture, agreeing in advance to accept 100,000 Arab refugees, but the conference ended in disappointment and the gesture was never fulfilled. The next round of talks, this time held in Rhodes, again failed to produce peace. A ray of hope came from Jordan, and towards the end of 1949 a peace agreement was reached with Abdullah, the Jordanian ruler, promising permanent borders and a solution to the refugee problem. This agreement was never implemented, however, and Abdullah himself was assassinated in 1951 on the steps of the al-Aqsa mosque in Jerusalem because of this understanding with Israel. Nearby stood his young grandson, Hussein, who was several years later to succeed him; undoubtedly he learned a lesson that day on the price of moderation.

The 1949 hopes for peace were replaced by frustration. Israel transferred the seat of the Knesset to Jerusalem and established Jerusalem as its capital, although to this day few states recognize it as such. All embassies are located in Tel-Aviv, and all Israel's efforts to change this situation have proven futile. The Arab boycott declared in 1946 was escalated; focusing at first on Israeli goods, it was later extended to include any company that traded with Israel. Ships and planes visiting Israeli ports were and are denied service in Arab facilities. More and more countries found themselves cooperating with the boycott (by supplying formal assurances that a company had no commercial ties with Israel, for example), although this often ran counter to their economic policies. Only a few states passed legislation against compliance with the Arab boycott, and most simply tried to circumvent it by establishing fictitious companies which maintain close ties with Israel in the name of large companies which thus technically abide by the boycott. During this period Egypt denied Israel passage through the Suez Canal, thus restricting its access to the east. An opportunity to achieve peace with Syria in 1949 disappeared when Hosni Zaim was assassinated in August 1949.

The Palestinian Arabs began to become accustomed to their new status as protégés of their host countries. In Israel they were granted citizenship, but for eighteen years lived under a military administration which restricted their movement. In September 1948 the Palestinians in Gaza established the Government of All Palestine, in the hope of being granted authority throughout western Palestine. Four years later, the Arab League abolished the government, asserting that the Arab states would from now on represent the Palestinians. The aim of the Arab states during these years was to push Israel back to the partition plan borders which they had previously rejected, while the Palestinian issues occupied only secondary importance. The Arab–Israeli disputes of the 1950s mostly focused on border issues, because of the ambiguity regarding the demilitarized zones created by the armistice agreements. Other sources of friction were the incursions of Palestinian refugees from Jordan, Syria and the Gaza Strip, and disputes over water sources. The infiltrations into Israel from the neighbouring states were at first for purposes of theft or smuggling, and Israel responded with retaliatory actions. Over the years, however, there was an increase in the number of infiltrations perpetrated for spying, sabotage and murder; while Jordan tried to prevent them, these were given encouragement by Syria and Egypt.

The Egyptian officers' revolt of 1952 and Nasser's assumption of power in 1954 aroused Israeli hopes of a more pragmatic government in Egypt after the corrupt monarchy. But these hopes were short-lived: the young, charismatic leader viewed the Arab–Israeli conflict as a means to strengthen his own leadership position, and it was he who was largely responsible for converting the conflict once again into a no-win game.

The large arms deal signed between Nasser and the Soviet Union in 1955 added to his self-confidence and caused deep concern in Israel. In July 1956 Nasser nationalized the Suez Canal and closed the Tiran Straits, which had provided access for Israeli ships from the Eilat port to the Far East. France and Britain went to war against

Egypt as the major shareholders of the Suez Canal, while Israel fought for its freedom of navigation and for a halt to the infiltrations, winning over ten years of tranquillity. Nevertheless, Nasser was not weakened by defeat. He now sought to transform the Arab–Israeli conflict from a dispute over the fate of the refugees and permanent borders into an existential conflict, which placed the existence of Israel in contraposition to pan-Arabism, both geographically and conceptually.

The generation of young Palestinians living in the Arab countries were much less prepared than their parents to accept their situation, and they sought to push the Arab states into war with Israel, a war which would restore the land to the Arabs and allow the refugees to return to their homes. Under Syrian patronage, Yasser Arafat founded the Fatah organization; as a counterweight, in 1964 Egypt established the PLO as its puppet organization, headed by Ahmad Shukeiri. The Palestinian organizations began to engage in organized terrorism and pressed for war. The most likely pretext for war seemed to be the water dispute between Israel and Syria, and the building of the Israeli national water carrier, by which Israel transported water from the Sea of Galilee to the Negev.

The Six Day War was not carefully planned by Nasser. Rather, it was the result of the dynamics of events which began with Nasser's belief that Israel was about to attack Syria in mid-May 1967. Once again, Nasser closed the Straits of Tiran, while his Foreign Minister demanded from the United Nations Secretary General that the UN forces be removed from Sharm a-Sheikh and Gaza. In the last week of May, Nasser returned to the Palestinian issue and spoke of the right of the Palestinians to fight for their homeland.

The Six Day War, in which Israel defeated Egypt, Jordan and Syria in less than a week, and which placed under Israeli control an area three times larger than its original territory and a population of about one million Palestinians in addition to the 300,000 Arab citizens of Israel, restored to Israeli control the many refugees who had left it during the War of Independence. It produced a widespread state of shock in the Arab states, and demonstrated to the Palestinians that it would not be at all easy for the Arab states to do their work for them. The Palestinian leadership, located in Jordan, now became a central factor in the Arab–Israeli conflict; without it no agreement could be reached. King Hussein, the host of the Palestinian leadership, became a much more welcome figure in the Arab world and the major spokesman of the Arab cause in the West. Immediately after the Six

Day War, terrorist activity originating in Jordanian territory, and under the leadership of Yasser Arafat, commenced, killing and injuring Israeli civilians. The IDF launched attacks against the refugee camps located along the Jordan valley, forcing the terrorists to seek refuge inside Jordan itself; there they in effect set up a state within a state. In 1969 Fatah seized control of the virtually defunct PLO framework and transformed it into a coalition of Palestinian organizations, enjoying an independent territorial base in Jordan. In its amended 1968 Covenant, the PLO emphasized its intention to establish an Arab Palestinian state in the entire area of greater Palestine. It received financial support from Arab states and transformed the Palestinian problem into a prominent international issue, presenting the Palestinians as a people cruelly uprooted who wished to return to their land.

In 1970 King Hussein decided that he was no longer willing to accept Palestinian autonomy in his country and, in a bloody battle known as Black September, he expelled the Palestinians from Jordan. The PLO began to create a new base in Lebanon and concentrated their efforts on flagrant and brutal terrorist attacks against Israelis.

The failure once again of the Arab states to win territory from Israel in the 1973 Yom Kippur War further strengthened the PLO. One year later, at the Rabat Conference, the Arab states decided that the PLO was to be the Palestinians' sole legitimate representative, thus delegitimizing Jordan's claim to represent its Palestinian citizens living on the West Bank. The PLO was from then on to be solely responsible for defining the rights of the Palestinians and how they were to be achieved.

All efforts to reach a political settlement between 1967 and 1973 failed. While Israel at first expressed willingness to reach a settlement, the Arab summit at Khartoum decided that there would be no peace, no recognition and no negotiations between the Arabs and Israel. When, as mentioned above, United Nations envoy Gunnar Jarring proposed a political settlement between Israel and Egypt in 1971, the new Egyptian President Sadat accepted the plan, but Israel rejected it. In 1972 Jordan proposed a plan for a federation between the east and west banks, but this plan came to nought too, although Israel has throughout preferred a Jordanian–Palestinian solution over a separate agreement with the Palestinians.

The transfer of responsibility for Palestinian representation to the PLO served the interests of the confrontation states bordering on Israel, guaranteeing the perpetuation of the conflict. They knew that as long as the PLO continued to fan the flames of the conflict, they would continue to receive special financial support from the oil-producing states. The PLO also enjoyed a new status: immediately after the Six Day War, the Palestinian problem was recognized as a political issue, and in UN Security Council Resolution 242 it is only mentioned as such. During the years that followed, the problem was increasingly viewed as nationalist, and after the Yom Kippur War the PLO became a central factor in a nationalist issue which attracted worldwide attention. The PLO was accepted in international organizations; Yasser Arafat appeared at the United Nations; and the self-determination of the Palestinian people became an accepted principle. The PLO posted ambassadors and diplomatic representatives in many more countries than those in which Israel was represented, while Israel was unjustly portrayed as a conquering and racist state; following the Six Day War its diplomatic ties with all the East European countries (with the exception of Rumania) had been lost, and after the Yom Kippur War with all the African states as well. The climax came with the 1975 United Nations decision defining Zionism as a racist movement. There could hardly have been a greater injustice done to the Jewish people, just thirty years after the Holocaust, but the world, identifying with the underdog, was not prepared to accept the new Israel and took the side of the Palestinians, even if their actions were not worthy of world approval. Only in 1991 was this UN resolution erased.

The question of Palestinian representation became the most insoluble issue in all efforts to achieve a political settlement. Israel maintained that it would not negotiate with the PLO, a terrorist organization whose National Covenant calls for the annihilation of Israel; to negotiate with it would signify agreement to the establishment of a Palestinian state. The Likud unconditionally rejected negotiations with the PLO, while the Labour Alignment has hinted that changes in the PLO's position might facilitate dialogue. In practice, the result is the absence of any parley. The 1973 Geneva Conference, at which the Palestinians themselves were not represented, was to have decided at its first session who would represent them. Nothing was resolved, and the conference has never been reconvened.

Of the many attempts made since 1973 to reconvene the Geneva Conference, the most serious occurred in 1977 following the joint American–Soviet declaration issued by Jimmy Carter and Leonid Brezhnev calling for the reconvening of the conference together with representatives of the Palestinian people. The new Israeli Foreign

Minister, Moshe Dayan, who was in the United States to hold talks with President Carter, agreed with him on a joint working paper which proposed a joint Arab delegation to the conference, the Palestinians being represented by individuals not known to be leading PLO members.

One month later, the greatest breakthrough in the history of the Arab–Israeli conflict occurred when President Sadat arrived in Jerusalem. The Cairo Conference held in December 1977 was regarded as a preparatory meeting for the reconvening of the Geneva Conference. Although the PLO was invited, it did not attend. Only Israel, Egypt, the United States and a representative of the United Nations took part in the talks, and again they failed to produce another Geneva meeting.

It is hard to determine whether Sadat truly wanted to solve the Palestinian problem, or whether he was merely paying lip-service to it. In any event, during the negotiations he insisted on several formulae which Menachem Begin found problematic. One of them, drafted in December 1977 at the Ismailiya talks, was the solution of the Palestinian problem 'in all its aspects'. I recall that at a meeting of the Labour Party's political committee, Golda Meir sharply opposed this formula which, in her opinion, portended a Palestinian state. Ultimately, Menachem Begin accepted the formula within the framework of the Camp David Accords. These accords contained several new and surprising definitions regarding the Palestinians (such as recognition of the legitimate rights of the Palestinian people), but they did not provide a solution to the problem. Even the talks conducted between Egypt and Israel, in the absence of the leading player on autonomy for the Palestinians of the West Bank and Gaza, were halted in 1982 when they reached an impasse. The first – and to date last – peace between Israel and an Arab state in effect side-stepped the Palestinian problem, and the Palestinians felt betrayed and used.

Meanwhile, the PLO stronghold in Lebanon – the soft underbelly of the Middle East – grew in strength. During the 1970s an enclave known as the Fatah-land was established, which served as a base for the launching of terrorist attacks and Katyusha rockets against Israel. Lebanon, where the delicate balance between Christians and Muslims had been upset, and which had become a state of militias, accepted the Palestinian militia with no real protest. The headquarters of the various Palestinian organizations were established within the Palestinian refugee camps, making the camps a reservoir for military recruitment to the PLO as well as the target of Israeli counterattacks.

The Israeli strike against southern Lebanon in July 1978 which was aimed at removing the Palestinian organizations from the area, did not produce real results, and attacks from Lebanon continued. The summer of 1981 was marked by particularly heavy Katyusha attacks from southern Lebanon against Israel's northern settlements. President Reagan sent his special envoy, Philip Habib, to the region. Through shuttle diplomacy, he achieved a ceasefire in the region, but not an explicit halt to attacks against Israeli targets throughout the world. In the meantime, Israel, under its new Defence Minister Ariel Sharon, was preparing for war in Lebanon; the aim, according to the minimalists, was to completely destroy the PLO's military infrastructure or, according to the maximalists to take over Lebanon and establish a new leadership that was friendly to Israel. For several months, Sharon sought a detonator for an Israeli attack; it was provided in early June 1982, when a Palestinian organization opposed to the PLO leadership made an attempt on the life of Shlomo Argov, Israeli Ambassador to London. After eleven months of a strictly maintained ceasefire between Israel and the PLO, based on an indirect agreement whose existence Israel has never admitted, Israel launched an air attack against Palestinian targets in Lebanon. The Palestinians responded with artillery fire against Israeli settlements in the Galilee, and Israel embarked on an attack which Prime Minister Menachem Begin named Operation Peace for Galilee.

Militarily, this was not a difficult confrontation for Israel. Its forces were far superior to those it encountered, and the IDF relatively quickly reached targets not defined in advance. But the Lebanese windfall proved to be a quagmire for which Israel would pay a heavy price. Israel became embroiled in internal Lebanese politics, and Bashir Jemayel, whom it tried to designate as President, was assassinated shortly afterwards. It was held responsible for the massacre of the Palestinians by Christians in the Sabra and Shatilla refugee camps because the IDF did nothing to stop it although it took place under their very noses. This episode was the nadir of Israel's involvement in Lebanon.

Beginning as a surgical, brief and efficient operation to remove the Katyusha launchers from its northern border, the Lebanon War became a prolonged campaign lasting three years, in which some 650 Israeli soldiers who did not know exactly what they were doing there lost their lives. The peace agreement signed between Israel and Lebanon on 17 May 1983 became a farce and was quickly suspended by Amin Jemayel, the new Lebanese President and brother of the late Bashir Jemayel. Syria steadily extended its control over Lebanon, while in the south the religious extremist pro-Iranian militia – the Hezbollah – gained strength, carrying out frequent fatal attacks on IDF soldiers.

President Reagan tried to make the best of a bad affair, and on 1 September 1982 put forward the Reagan Plan, which provided an outline for a solution to the conflict in the Middle East. In effect, the United States reverted here to old ideas: an Israeli withdrawal from most of the occupied territories and their transfer to a Jordanian–Palestinian framework, along with a rejection of a separate Palestinian state and support for a united Jerusalem. The Begin government immediately rejected the plan, while the Labour Alignment, headed by Peres, was prepared to view it as a basis for negotiations. The Arab states refrained from endorsing the plan, and it was shelved.

The PLO leadership was forced to leave Lebanon, and chose Tunis as its new centre, and to a certain extent Baghdad. Arafat resumed his ties with Egypt, forming a close relationship with President Mubarak. In 1984, fourteen years after Black September, he returned to Amman, the capital of Jordan, where he convened the Palestine National Council under the auspices of his bitter enemy King Hussein. It was at this forum that Hussein first raised the idea of solving the Arab–Israeli conflict within an international conference framework, not only the United States and the Soviet Union, but also the other three permanent members of the Security Council, participating. The Palestinians were to be represented by a joint Jordanian–Palestinian delegation.

For two and a half years, laborious and informal negotiations were conducted between Israel and Jordan through American offices, culminating in the so-called London Agreement of April 1987. This agreement provided for the opening of negotiations between Israel and the Arab states in the framework of an international conference; the five permanent members of the Security Council would participate but they would not be able to impose any settlement on the parties or to veto any agreement reached between them in bilateral negotiations. It was also agreed that a joint Jordanian–Palestinian delegation be formed, whose members would promise to renounce terrorism and to recognize Security Council Resolutions 242 and 338. The agreement was rejected by Israel, having not been submitted to the inner cabinet for approval, and Jordan began once again to distance itself from the political process. Among the Palestinians, increasingly disappointed with the political option, extremist elements grew in strength, and so the intifada began on 9 December that year.

The political initiative put forward by Secretary of State George Schultz in early 1988 (which very much resembled the London Agreement of April 1987) was not rejected by either side, but neither was it endorsed by anyone. The intifada in the occupied territories was escalated and passed into Jordan as well, where Palestinian unrest was directed against King Hussein. On the last day of July 1988 Hussein appeared in a television address to the nation and solemnly announced that he was severing himself from the West Bank. Jordan made it clear that it would no longer pay salaries to former Jordanian civil servants, would no longer provide the residents of the West Bank with Jordanian passports, and would not participate in any political negotiations on the future of the West Bank, leaving the field solely to the PLO. Palestinian prominence was thus restored: they are responsible for their own fate, while the Arab states identify with them but do not speak on their behalf. At the end of that year Yasser Arafat announced the PLO's recognition of Israel, its acceptance of the Security Council resolutions, and its readiness to renounce terrorism. In response, the United States declared itself prepared to enter into a dialogue with the PLO in Tunis on the diplomatic level. All this occurred in December, taking advantage of the transition period between American administrations, and the PLO, which had for many years sought American recognition, considered this an important achievement.

The dialogue between the US and the PLO was used to test that organization's reaction to Israel's May 1989 initiative. This initiative proposed the holding of elections in the occupied territories to choose the delegation for talks with Israel on both the interim agreement and permanent settlement. The PLO conveyed to the Americans its consent to a delegation of residents of the territories, who were to meet with an Israeli delegation in Cairo to determine the specifics of the elections. However, Israel objected to the inclusion of East Jerusalem residents in the delegation. This issue brought down the National Unity Government, and this plan, too, was shelved.

Though seemingly closer than ever, the historic meeting between Israelis and Palestinians did not take place, and frustration once again increased. When, during the summer of that year, there was an attempted terrorist attack on Israel's beaches, Arafat refused to condemn it, and the American government decided to suspend its dialogue with the PLO. Secretary of State James Baker appeared in the Congress, pulled out a Washington telephone number, and declared that when Israel was interested in pursuing the political process, they should call that number.

The year 1990 was one in which threads were undone, and it seemed as though the chances for political negotiations would be postponed for a long time to come. Paradoxically, it was Saddam Hussein's invasion of Kuwait on 2 August which once again placed the Middle East on the international agenda. The Iraqi President found it convenient to tie his aggression to the Palestinian problem, and he demanded a linkage between the solution of the problems of Kuwait and Palestine. Although the PLO and Jordan were among his only supporters in the Gulf War, American efforts to achieve a peaceful settlement in the Middle East could not ignore them, neither in the Madrid Conference nor in the Washington bilateral talks.

The attempt to solve the Palestinian problem by the Arab states alone will fail, as would an attempt by Israel to achieve peace with the Arab states solely through the Palestinians. Only a combined effort can solve a conflict which began with growing friction between the new Jewish immigrants and the Arab felaheen living in Palestine, and which grew by geometric progression into civil war on Israeli soil, a pan-Arab problem, and, in recent decades, an international diplomatic issue.

6. Political Culture in Israel

Symbols, Myths, Rituals and Taboos

The most important symbol in the political culture of Jewish Palestine since the beginning of the century has been that of the *halutz* (pioneer). At first the term referred to the vanguard – those who preceded their comrades, not really knowing what to expect: those who prepared the groundwork for those who would follow. Over the years the term was used with increasing frequency and gradually became institutionalized. In 1918 the Hehalutz movement was founded, and pioneering qualities were attributed to a variety of concepts; there was a pioneering mission, a pioneering movement, a pioneering youth movement, a youth and pioneer department in the Jewish Agency, and more. The pioneer appearing in leaflets and pictures was a young muscular man, wearing a hat against the sun and with a hoe in his hand, looking upwards, towards the future.

This symbol, of which much has been written, combines incipience with self-sacrifice. These two aspects accorded the *halutz* special status, which superseded majority–minority relations: the *halutz* did not need to be elected, he was above the common people; he renounced many of the pleasures of life and was deserving of the people's support. Combining yearning with fulfilment, he differed from both the fathers of Zionism who remained in Europe awaiting an official concession to bring the Jewish people to Palestine, and the immigrants of the First Aliya who quickly became landlords and exploited the labour of others.

The *halutz* is identified primarily with the Second Aliya. He asked the minimum for himself and gave the maximum to society. He was prepared to live on bread and water in order to advance the realization of the Zionist dream, and only he, in his view, could bring this dream to fruition. Only those prepared for the same high degree of sacrifice were willing to perform the most exhausting tasks (smashing stones into gravel to pave roads), and the most dangerous (draining swamps, and exposing themselves to mosquitoes whose sting was often fatal), necessary to create the dream.

Roberto Michles claims that every nation has an origin myth and a mission myth. The origin myth of the Zionist movement is undoubtedly anti-Semitism and the deep sense of rejection of the Jews by the gentiles. It was this that led Herzl and his colleagues to their far-reaching conclusions. The mission myth is more complex, and varies to a large extent from one group to another. The common denominator, however, is the Zionist belief that only in the land of Israel can the Jewish people survive in a way that will preserve its values. The mission of Zionism, then, is the Jewish survival of the Jewish people.

Aliya is sacred in Israeli society, excluding ultra-Orthodox Jews and the Arab sector. Even within ultra-Orthodox circles there has been a change in recent years, and the greater the role they play in Israeli society, the closer they approach the national consensus on this issue. The fact that a representative of ultra-Orthodox Jewry has been serving as Minister of Absorption since 1988 at a time when immigration occupies a central place in Israeli life helps to explain the change which has occurred within this sector of the population. Opposition to immigration for economic reasons and because of the burden it places on the less well-to-do strata in Israeli society, and talk of 'selective immigration' – allowing only the younger and better educated to immigrate – are definitely taboo in Israeli society. The term *aliya* itself is highly symbolic, very different from the neutral term for migration. *Aliya* is derived from *aliya le-regel*, meaning pilgrimage, and explicitly refers to the advantage inherent in immigration to Israel, in direct contrast to *yerida*, meaning descent, which signifies emigration from Israel.

During the early waves of immigration, many more immigrants left the country than remained. When Yitzhak Rabin, as Prime Minister, called the emigrants 'weakling drop-outs', his words were received with understanding. Israeli emigrants abroad tend to describe their stay there as temporary, saying that they are actually on their way back to Israel, that they will return after they finish their studies or complete certain business transactions.

The Zionist movement is identified with an array of symbols that link the Jews returning to Israel to certain periods in the life of the Jewish people. While throughout the two thousand years of exile special emphasis was placed on the study of the Talmud which, written after the Bible, established the rules of religious behaviour derived from the Bible, the leaders of the Zionist movement sought to pass over the later oral teachings, and especially the Talmud which was written in exile. They attempted to return to the source – to the Torah and the prophets – thus defining Zionist settlement as a direct continuation of the Biblical period. The agricultural holidays were restored to their natural environment – the prayers for rain, for dew and the harvest – while the holidays established later, relating to the revolt of the Hasmoneans and their struggle against Hellenistic and later Roman rule, received greater emphasis than they had ever been accorded in the long years of exile.

The Zionist ethos tried to erase the period of exile from Jewish history. The 'negation of the exile' became an accepted value. The First Temple period, and even more so the Second Temple period, assumed a central place in Jewish history, with a special emphasis on the struggle against foreign rule. The Zionist movement, in all its component parts, created for itself a worldview which in effect erased an entire chapter of Jewish history; it presented the Jews once again as a normal people with a common language and territorial centre, who identified with the post-Biblical stories of heroism.

The life of the Jews in exile was viewed as something to be despised. Only later, in the 1960s, did the term 'diaspora' penetrate into the legitimate lexicon. The term 'exile' took on a cynical meaning, so that when an Israeli would return from a trip abroad, for example, he would be asked, 'how was it in the accursed exile?' In other words, even after the term exile had clearly lost its earlier significance, the linguistic habit continued.

In the diaspora acceptance of the existing government was one of the foundations of Jewish survival, including prayers for the well-being of the Kaiser, the Tsar or the head of state wherever Jews lived. Opposition to provocation against non-Jews was another basic principle. The situation in Palestine was just the reverse. Here non-acceptance of foreign government became a legitimate principle; here revolt against the gentiles became a norm of behaviour, even if it did not bring victory. The Bar Kokhba revolt against the Romans, which was doomed from the outset and which ultimately proved catastrophic for the Jews of the country, suddenly became an ideal. Poems were written about this eccentric man, and the Lag Ba-Omer holiday, the origins of which are not clear but which is related in some way to Bar Kokhba, became one of the more important holidays in the secular–traditional ritual.

The saga of Masada became a vibrant example of the supreme readiness of Jew for self-sacrifice: Jews assembled in Herod's isolated fortress and committed collective suicide in order not to fall into the hands of the Romans. Jewish groups who had engaged in violence in the late Second Temple period kindled the imaginations of the right-wing Jews of contemporary Palestine; adopting their names, they modelled themselves on them (Brit HaBiryonim, Covenant of Outlaws, and the Sicarii). The revolt of the Jews against the Romans became the banner of the right. It is not by chance that Menachem Begin entitled his history of the Jewish underground in the pre-state period *The Revolt*.

The Hasmoneans who had rebelled against the Greeks were very popular. Streets were named after them in the new cities and towns. Their motto Maccabee, representing the initials of 'Who is like You, O Lord, among the mighty' and used to recruit the young men who were willing to join the dangerous challenge of rebelling against the Greeks, became the name of a sports association, a health fund, and was even adopted as a surname.

The Second Temple motto 'In fire and blood Judah fell, in fire and blood shall Judah arise' was adopted not only by the extreme right-wing elements within the Yishuv, but also became the motto of the left. Members of the Poalei Zion party who joined the Jewish legions in World War I hung the motto in huge letters in their encampments.

The leaders of the early waves of immigration certainly devoted great time and effort to the development of symbols and rituals. The new world of symbols was to take the place of religion, viewed as characteristic of the diaspora and usually abandoned there. A religious Jew who prays 'next year in Jerusalem', comes to Jerusalem and weeps for its destruction; the secular Jew coming to Jerusalem needed an explanation. The Zionist explanation was, in effect, continuity ; a line was drawn between a certain segment of Jewish history and the 'new Jew', who was coming to build a new life, a new world, a new order in his ancient homeland. Instead of the old religion, he was given a new religion. A.D. Gordon, one of the leaders of the Second Aliya and a member of the non-Socialist labour stream, called this the 'religion of labour'.

The *halutzim*, who fostered the barefoot myth and who were proud of their poverty and the serious illnesses they suffered, were prepared to view themselves as the 'generation of the wilderness' – another Biblical term which took on new meaning. The Bible speaks of the generation who went out of Egypt and whom God led for forty years in the wilderness in order that those born in Egypt should not reach the land of Israel, but only their sons. The *halutzim* were prepared to fulfil the thankless role of such a generation; they would suffer in order to prepare the ground for those who would follow. Only their sons or successors would enjoy well-being. This concept served those immigrants who, encountering difficulty in learning the language and in finding work in their professions, reconciled themselves to the fact that only their children would live full lives. It still maintains this function.

This cheerless myth was accompanied, however, by another, much more optimistic, of messianism and redemption. This was a romantic myth in which the relationship between the Jewish people and the land of Israel is likened to that between a woman and her lover who has been kept away, but who now returns to reconquer her from her unlawful master, liberating and redeeming her. These concepts were expressed in the purchase of the land from the Arabs, the effort to take over the task of guarding the settlements from the Arabs, and the attempt to replace the Arab labourers in the Jewish settlements with Jewish labourers. In the first thirty years of this century the redemption of the land, the conquest of labour and the conquest of guard duty were all common idioms.

While the myth maintains that the Zionists succeeded in redeeming the land, conquering the wilderness and taking over the task of defence with the establishment of the state, the reality was different. By 1948, Jews had purchased no more than 8 per cent of the area of Israel. Work on the agricultural settlements – and not only there – remained largely in Arab hands, particularly because Jews preferred different employment. A greater measure of success was achieved in defence. As relations between Jews and Arabs worsened, it became increasingly hard for the Jews to entrust the guarding of their fields to the Arabs.

The greatest success of Zionism, through, was the revival of the Hebrew language. The first immigrants understood that language would prove critical in this special attempt to restore a dispersed people to its land after an interval of almost two thousand years. Jews throughout the world spoke at least seventy different languages, and the perpetuation of this medley of tongues in Palestine would be liable to create a new Tower of Babel. In order to prevent this, at least two measures were required: firstly the modernization of the language, adding words which had not existed when it ceased to serve as a spoken language – from train, through electricity, to plane, missile and spaceship; secondly, all the immigrants would be obliged to learn and speak the language. The first task was complex, but relatively easy. The reviver of the Hebrew language was Eliezer Ben-Yehuda, who immigrated to Palestine in 1881. He added many words to the language, and contributed more than anyone else to its adaption to the new reality.

But the immigrants were not easily convinced that Hebrew could or should in fact become the spoken language, and certainly not the language of study. At the end of the nineteenth century and at the beginning of the twentieth, French was the major language of instruction. Hebrew was spoken in several kindergartens and in the girls' school in Jaffa, but other languages were used in the rest of the primary and secondary schools: the Alliance Israelite Universelle founded a network of schools in which French was taught and spoken; the Anglo-Jewish Association established English-speaking schools; in the Ezra schools of the German-Jewish Hilfsverein some subjects were taught in German; while the ultra-Orthodox Jews taught their children in Yiddish, viewing Hebrew as a sacred language to be used only for prayer and not for secular purposes. The first secondary school to implement Hebrew as the language of instruction was the Gymnasia Herzlia, founded in 1906 and named after Theodor Herzl, the father of the Jewish state. Its students played an important role in the 'language war' which was waged in the country in the early twentieth century. The students would appear at every function conducted in Yiddish – lectures, debates and the theatre – where they tried, with some measure of success, to break them up by interjections and by creating a general commotion.

In 1913 the Ezra Association, funded by German Jewry, decided to establish two centres for technological studies in Haifa – the Reali Secondary School and the Technion – where the language of instruction would be German. The Herzlia students led students from other schools in a struggle to ensure that Hebrew would be used at these two important institutions. They succeeded in bringing about a strike of students and teachers in the various Ezra schools. The German donors arrived in the country and tried to put an end to the strike with the help of the German consul in Palestine, but to no avail. They were ultimately forced to yield, agreeing that classes in the two new institutions would be taught in Hebrew.

Ten years later, in 1923, a legion of 'defenders of the language' was founded, parallel to the Jewish legions and the labour legion. It was quite natural that a group which wished to ensure the use of the Hebrew language should function as a 'legion' with strict discipline. At the outset it comprised students from several secondary schools in Tel-Aviv as well as the women students at the teachers' seminary, who used to march through the streets of the city every Friday, singing 'Jews speak Hebrew'. They would accost passers by speaking foreign languages, handing them a note which read 'Jews speak Hebrew'. Later the language legion was institutionalized and its goals were clarified: the publication of Hebrew books, the distribution of leaflets and propaganda promoting the Hebrew language, the disruption of gatherings held in foreign languages, and the removal of foreign language signs from shop-fronts. The legion established branches in Palestine and abroad, becoming so zealous over the years that even some of its greatest supporters – the national poet Chaim Nahman Bialik among them – came to criticize it.

The campaign to replace typically diaspora names with Hebrew names was part of the stubborn war for the Hebrew language. The decision to change one's family name was a kind of sacrifice, which sometimes served to blur the past in a new environment, attached as people were to their family name. But in this case, it constituted sacrifice for the sake of an ideology which sought completely to sever the Jewish people in Palestine from the Jewish life in exile, and to reintegrate them into an ancient history that had been interrupted. Eliezer Ben-Yehuda provided the first example, and he was followed by the leaders of the labour movement: Ben-Gurion (Gruen), Ben-Zvi (Shimshelevich), and many others. Choosing a new name became a ritual, and the social pressure to do so was considerable. A new name signified total separation from the past and the turning over of a new leaf for a new life in Palestine. There were various fashions in new name selection, and people who changed their names during the same period often found themselves with similar names. There were leaders who vehemently insisted on the substitution of foreign names, and who were unwilling to accept any excuse. Most intransigent in this regard was David Ben-Gurion, but there were others as well, such as Moshe Sharett and the future Minister of Education, Zalman Aranne. When the Israel Defence Forces were established, the senior officers were asked to change their names; and no one in the Israeli foreign service is sent to represent the state abroad unless he adopts a Hebrew name.

The Holocaust of European Jewry altered matters in this regard. Hatred and negation of Jewish life in the diaspora could no longer persist in the same degree, when Jewish life in Europe had been destroyed and no longer existed. Many did not wish now to relinquish their original names as they were the last members of their families alive. Israel had become an irrefutable fact, while at the same time a return to Europe had become unrealistic. Organizations like the legion of the defenders of the language disappeared from the scene, at least in part because they had won their battle.

The intensity of the struggle for the supremacy of Hebrew declined with the passing of the years. Many shops in Tel-Aviv and other cities boast English and French names, and Yiddish theatre has been revived, catering mostly to new immigrants from the Soviet Union. The passion for the Hebraization of names has passed, and there has even emerged an opposite trend; some people who adopted Hebrew surnames have later reverted to their original ones. There are some Israeli diplomats who choose a Hebrew name to go abroad, and return it to its packing-case upon their return home.

From time to time a bellicose editorial appears against the trend towards Americanization, against the neon lights bearing foreign names, against the use of non-Hebrew names by leading figures. But the number of people who fear the assimilation of the Hebrew language into other languages in Israel is steadily decreasing, and anyone who walks the streets of an Israeli city today and hears the heavy Russian accent of the new Hebrew speakers understands that Hebrew has without doubt emerged victorious.

National security casts a huge shadow over every other walk of life. It is therefore not surprising that some of the most powerful symbols and the severest taboos are to be found in this area. Many Israelis have served in two, three and four of the five wars in which participants have been decorated. Many families suffered bereavement. Military service is still the high point in the lives of Israeli youths; when parents are asked how many children they have, they often reply: 'We are raising three soldiers.' A citizen's military rank is always noted on his curriculum vitae. When the demands of a particular sector are not met by farmers, residents of outlying areas, or workers, they are threatened with the return of their army reserve service books. Israeli culture is intertwined with admiration for the military and for those who serve in it. Army troupes have filled an important place in Israeli entertainment, and most of Israel's stars were once members of these troupes. Those who do not serve in the army carry a stigma. They encounter difficulties finding employment, and if they become public figures, the media repeatedly reminds them of their failing.

Several months after my recruitment into the army, on the eve of the Passover holiday, I was informed that I was to remain on duty in my unit for the holiday. This was the first time that I was to be away from home for this special evening, symbolized by the family gathered around the table. When I told my mother that I would not be able to be home for the holiday, I expected her to say 'Don't worry', or 'Next year we'll be together', but instead she said spontaneously, 'I'm so proud that on this particular evening you will be in the army protecting us.' I did not engage in battle that night, and I was not stationed anywhere near the border. I simply remained on duty in my unit. But for my mother this was enough, for there is no function more important in Israel than defence.

Compulsory military service in the IDF originally lasted two and a half years. In the mid-1960s, in light of the reduced security tension, service was reduced to two years and two months, but shortly afterwards it was restored to the original term, and after the Six Day War was extended to three years, the maximum age for reserve duty being raised from forty-nine to fifty-five. At the time this change was considered temporary, but the limit remains to this day.

The sense that the entire people – men and women, young and old – serves in the army, the sense of an army made up of the entire people, of a 'nation in uniform', creates a situation in which there is no professional army with sectorial interests differing from the national interests. But it also creates a situation in which the army is viewed as taboo, in which any criticism of it is considered irresponsible and unnationalistic. There is an instinctive recoiling in Israel from criticism of the IDF, even when many agree that in certain cases such criticism is in order. This is primarily because the army – unlike the other security arms – is a body in which one's husband and brother, one's son and daughter, serve, and to criticize it is to criticize oneself.

Nevertheless, this taboo has not remained constant over the years. After the establishment of the state, the young army was viewed as a kind of marvel, and criticism of it was very rare. Another peak occurred during the years between the Six Day War of 1967 and the Yom Kippur War of 1973. During this period it seemed to many that Israel had become a military power, that the IDF had performed a miracle and was invincible. The surprise attack of 1973 and the

large number of casualties suffered seriously damaged this myth
and accorded legitimacy to criticism. This was reflected in both the
Agranat Commission of 1974 and the Kahan Commission in 1982. –
A state commission of inquiry established to investigate the failings
at the beginning of the Yom Kippur War, the Agranat Commission
led to the resignation, among others, of the Chief-of-Staff. The Kahan
Commission, a state commission of inquiry established following the
massacre of Muslims by Christians in Sabra and Shatilla in September
1982, led to the removal of the Defence Minister from his post and
the dismissal of very senior IDF officers.

The intifada has also damaged this myth to a certain extent. The
ongoing confrontation between West Bank and Gazan residents and
IDF soldiers imposes an impossible police role on the army; they find
themselves caught between the hammer (the threat to their lives) and
the sickle (injury to unarmed civilians). The trials of officers and
soldiers conducted in the past few years have exposed a different kind
of military weakness which also, to a certain extent, undermines the
myth.

The military parades which used to characterize Israel's Independence Day from the establishment of the state until the early
1970s are no longer held. It was suddenly discovered that tank tracks
damage roads, and that the whole affair was too expensive for a
country spending such a large part of its budget on defence. During
the 1970s there were still debates on whether or not to hold the
annual parade, a debate which arose again as preparations for the
40th anniversary of the state were being made. The matter was tossed
back and forth between a ministerial committee and the cabinet,
but ultimately it was decided not to hold the parade, primarily for
economic reasons. Every few years each army corps holds a special
'corps day'. On armoured corps day, tanks are stationed in the heart
of the cities and children are allowed to climb over and inside them;
on air force day there is a special flyover in the country's skies; and
on Independence Day many army camps are open to the public and
families come to view military installations first-hand.

The provisional government which operated from the establishment of the state in May 1948 until after the elections to the
Knesset in January 1949, considered that Israel was in a state of
emergency, and issued an official declaration to that effect. This
declaration has never been revoked, allowing the government to apply
emergency regulations in order to maintain vital services, even when
no security threat against Israel is involved. Democratic norms have

to date prevented all Israeli governments from taking advantage of this in such a way as to harm the democratic character of the state, but the very fact that no government has ever decided to lift the state of emergency, even after the peace treaty with Egypt, says something about Israeli society's self-image; it is a state under siege, with emergency its natural state.

It is perhaps easier in this context to understand the existence (since 1953) of the committee of editors of Israel's daily newspapers, in which the editors periodically receive confidential information from defence authorities, on the understanding that it will not be published. There is nothing more secret than a 'military secret', and nothing that silences tongues more than 'security consideration'. Such claims have undoubtedly been used by the establishment over the years to evade unpleasant questions and embarrassing situations.

The myth of Israeli security, apart from the links established between the identities of the people and the army, is founded on the principles of defence, voluntarism, self-sacrifice, the quest for peace, and the 'purity of arms' – the use of arms solely for the legitimate purpose of self-defence. The defence element is especially important, and has been part and parcel of the security myth since the beginning of the century. This is reflected, among others, in the names given to the various quasi-military organizations established since that time. The purpose of HaShomer – 'The Guard' – established in 1909, was to guard the fields of the Jewish farmers, not to attack Arabs. The Haganah, which succeeded HaShomer, defined its objective in its name – 'defence'. The policy it pursued in the difficult years of the 1930s, when the Palestinian Arabs attacked Jewish targets, was called by its opponents a policy of 'restraint'. The IDF, based primarily on the Haganah, also defined its goal in its name – the Israel Defence Forces. The 'secessionist' groups presented themselves differently. The Irgun Z'vai Leumi (IZL) 'National Military Organization' – which seceded from the Haganah, placed greater emphasis on the military and national aspects, while the name chosen by the IZL's splinter group Lohamei Herut Israel (Lehi) – 'Freedom Fighters of Israel' – clearly stresses combat. But these exceptions only serve to reinforce the fact that there was actually a broad consensus among those who perceived themselves as engaged in self-defence against Arab attack.

The myth of Trumpeldor, a one-armed Russian Jewish officer who was killed together with his seven comrades in 1920, while defending their small settlement in northern Palestine is a defence myth *par excellence.* This was not a band of soldiers embarking on a dangerous military operation and killed in the course of action, but rather a group of people engaged in collective farming along the frontier, defending themselves against Arab rioters at a time when there was friction between the French and the British over the borders in the Middle East, in the aftermath of World War I. The day on which the eight were killed became a national memorial day, and the famous statue of a lion was erected at Tel-Hai where they lived, becoming the site of an annual pilgrimage of school children from all over Israel. Part of the Tel-Hai myth is contained in Trumpeldor's words before his death: 'It is good to die for our country' although, over the years, certain doubts have surfaced as to whether he actually said this. Although Trumpeldor belonged to the labour movement, he became a hero of consensus, and Tel-Hai was adopted as the motto of the Revisionists. The Revisionist youth movement is also named after him.

'Purity of arms', which is something of an oxymoron, is an integral part of the concept of self-defence, of the view of war and weapons as a necessary evil which must not be employed for anything beyond the protection of life. 'Purity of arms' means that weapons are not to be used for torture, that innocent people are not to be harmed, that weapons are reserved solely for those who try to harm you. Israeli control over the Palestinians since 1967 has produced many deviations from this principle: the 'Route 300' incident was one, together with the treatment of civilians during the intifada. One of the recurring debates in Israel involves the army instructions on opening fire: is it permissible to use live ammunition against stones, against an incited, unarmed crowd, etc? I doubt whether any army can boast that its weapons are indeed used only out of necessity. I doubt whether the IDF can make this claim, but nevertheless this is one of the myths by which Israeli society lives.

Voluntarism is one of the basic elements of the security myth. Until the establishment of the state, security-related activity was generally voluntary, apart from recruitment into the Turkish army in World War I: Bar-Giora, the first guard group, HaShomer, the Haganah, the Palmach, the IZL and Lehi, and even voluntary recruitment into the Jewish Legions of the British army in World War I and into the Jewish Brigade of the British army in World War II.

A glance at the figures alone does not seem to indicate a particularly high rate of voluntarism. On the eve of the establishment of the state the Haganah had about 20,000 members, the IZL 3,000, and Lehi several hundred, out of a population of some 630,000. But the prevailing feeling was that the entire nation had in effect been mobilized. Even when the Israel Defence Forces were established, it was viewed as a volunteer army, although military service was compulsory for men and women alike. Within the IDF there is still a tradition which allows someone to volunteer for certain units composed solely of volunteers (such as the paratroopers), and the number of volunteers wishing to serve in these units always exceeds the quota.

Most Israelis are convinced that Israel has always extended its hand in peace, and that this hand has repeatedly been rejected by its enemies. When each new Israeli government is presented, the Prime Minister calls upon the leaders of the Arab states to sit down and negotiate peace – at any time and any place. Even the most extremist political movements claim that their goal is really to achieve peace, and that their solution will also benefit the Arabs. The most cynical use of the peace myth was that of former Prime Minister Menachem Begin, when he called the 1982 Lebanon war the 'Peace for Galilee' war.

Pacifism does not enjoy legitimacy in Israel. There are soldiers who refuse to serve in the occupied territories, and there are some who are prepared to spend a considerable part of their army service in prison for this reason, but there are virtually none who refuse to serve in the army on pacifism grounds. Even the most prominent 'doves' in Israeli politics like to stress their military service and rank, both to accord validity to their positions and to make it clear that the moderate positions they are adopting are not chosen out of weakness.

Army commanders are taught to lead their soldiers, and to endanger their own lives before endangering the lives of their soldiers; 'after me' is characteristic of the Israeli army. Living conditions for the officers do not differ much from those of the soldiers, and reserve duty for officers is half again as long (45 days) as that demanded of regular soldiers; serving as an example to the soldiers is an important element in the Israeli security myth. The principle that the wounded are never left on the battlefield is also crucial. Even when the danger is great, the time short, and the wounds fatal, soldiers are required to risk their own lives in order not to leave the wounded behind. While this is indeed observed in many battles, there have been occasions, which are always viewed as serious deviations from the norm, when the wounded have not been rescued. These two concepts have parallels in Israeli politics: the leaders are expected to provide an example in their behaviour for the public at large, and several

extreme examples of this can be cited. In the early 1950s one of the
leaders of Mapai was removed from the party ranks simply because
he built a house for himself at a time when the party leadership felt
it was not proper for one of their colleagues to enjoy such a standard
of living. In retrospect, this incident has been seen to exemplify
unnecessary and narrow-minded extremism. At the end of 1984 when
the National Unity Government was established, Minister of Labour
and Welfare Moshe Katzav decided to devote his Wednesdays to
working in a production plant. Every week he worked, as a labourer,
in a different factory, motivated by the 'after me' principle, but several
months after he began this experiment, reality got the better of him
and he stopped.

The most important and moving day in modern Israel is the memorial day for fallen IDF soldiers. The official figure published in April
1991, on the eve of Independence Day, counts 17,150 IDF dead and
56,272 disabled since the establishment of the state. There is a siren
at eleven o'clock on Memorial Day; for two minutes all traffic in the
country comes to a halt – people on the streets, and cars on the
roads – in memory of the fallen. All places of entertainment and
restaurants are closed the previous evening, and there are memorial
services held in all the country's cemeteries, attended by bereaved
families and government representatives alike. During the year separate memorial services are held for the different army corps, and
each such ceremony expresses the unity of the people and their respect
for those who have fallen for them. The large number of bereaved
families in Israel represent the greatest taboo. This is the Israeli 'holy
of holies', the most sensitive spot in Israeli society. In contrast to the
practice in other countries, the bodies of the fallen soldiers are not
shown on Israeli television, and great care is taken – even by the
opposition – not to refer to any military exercise as unnecessary, in
order that the bereaved families should not feel that their sons fell in
vain. Israeli bereavement is not exposed. Television interviews with
the parents of a fallen soldier on the day after his death are non-
existent. The writings of fallen soldiers – poems, stories, letters left
behind – have been published since the War of Independence in
volumes entitled *Parchments of Fire*; these parchments grow thicker
from war to war.

Most Israeli citizens are not religious, but the lack of separation
between religion and state and the fact that Israel is a Jewish state
make religion one of the most central issues in Israeli myths and
symbols. One of the questions which preoccupied Israelis during the

early years of statehood was whether they were Israelis first, or Jews first. Although it is hard to define the realistic implications of such a decision, David Ben-Gurion would always note that he was first and foremost a Jew. There was also a group of Jews formed in the early 1940s, whose members were called 'Canaanites'; they sought to distinguish between those Jews who settled in Israel or were born there and the Jews of the diaspora, claiming that those living in Palestine must be integrated into the Middle East alongside the Arabs of the neighbouring countries.

Israel is a secular state with a dominant Jewish set of symbols. The day of rest is the Sabbath, when all businesses are closed, as they are on the the Jewish holidays, which are also national holidays. On the holiest day in the Jewish calendar – the fast day of Yom Kippur – no vehicles are seen on the country's roads and no food is displayed in public. During the week of Passover, when *matza*, or unleavened bread, is eaten, no bread is sold. According to a relatively new law, restaurants are also forbidden to serve *pitta* (round flat Arab bread) even to those who wish. On the eve of Passover, the State of Israel 'sells' everything it owns that contains the forbidden leaven to a non-Jewish citizen for a symbolic sum. The heads of state, especially the President and Prime Minister, refrain from travelling on the Sabbath, although all those who have filled these positions to date had previously been accustomed to travelling on that day. On the important holidays – Rosh HaShannah, Yom Kippur, and the first night of Passover – the media announce where the President and Prime Minister will be attending synagogue services. On the first night of Passover at one of its bases, the IDF holds a central *seder*, the ceremonial meal conducted in every Jewish home on Passover eve; it is presided over by the Chief-of-Staff.

The Hebrew calendar reckons the years from the creation of the world. The Jewish year is lunar; it begins in September or early October, and every two or three years contains thirteen months instead of twelve. According to the Jewish reckoning, the year 1992 is the year 5752 after the Creation. There are few people in Israel who use the Hebrew calendar, or who remember the Hebrew month and the day of the month, but in every official publication, in every newspaper, in every government letter, both dates – Hebrew and Gregorian – are noted. The Hebrew date also continues to be observed in schools, but the attempt to conduct daily life in Israel solely on the basis of the Hebrew calendar has clearly failed.

While, in the past, the ultra-religious parties were satisfied to receive their part of the national pie, enabling them to serve their public and, most importantly, to reinforce their special school system, in recent years they have displayed a growing desire to influence the overall Jewish character of the state. The law banning the sale of leavened bread during Passover is part of this trend. Another is the law banning the sale of pork in Israel, and another the law banning advertisements displaying women in immodest dress on the streets or elsewhere. These small parties thus use their political power to influence Israeli lifestyle and symbols.

The collective self-image is composed primarily of two seemingly contradictory elements: isolation and choice. The late Prime Minister Levi Eshkol used a Yiddish phrase to describe this: '*Shimshon der nebekhdiker*' – Samson the wretched. The terms stressing the concept of choice, which appeared in the speeches of the state's first leaders and which continued to crop up in later speeches and articles as well, were the 'chosen people', 'You have chosen us from all the nations', and 'a light unto the nations' – all terms taken from the Bible. Their usage denotes, to a certain degree, part of the return to Biblical times, in a historical leap over the long years of exile. A return to the time when the Jewish people lived in its own land is thus also perceived as a return to the special status accorded it by God.

'A nation that dwells alone' is also a Biblical concept, and is one of the most commonly used to stress Israel's isolation, alongside such terms as 'a nation under siege'. Israel's existence as a lone Jewish state in a hostile Arab world is of course the basis for this feeling, which even the peace with Egypt has not yet altered significantly. Israel views itself as small and just, confronting a self-righteous and hypocritical world. Israel is always David, and the Arabs – or the rest of the world – are Goliath. This feeling remains unchanged. Even after 1967, when Israel gained control of an area three times its size, David remained young, agile and clever, destined to vanquish the clumsy giant facing him.

Jewish collective responsibility is expressed in the oft-repeated phrase, 'All Jews are responsible for one another'. This phrase embodies the mutual responsibility not only of Israeli citizens for one another, but also of Israel *vis-à-vis* the diaspora and vice versa. The Israeli government uses the foundation of this saying to demand the moral, political and financial support of diaspora Jewry, even when they do not always accept its policies. It is also used to justify the very high price paid to free Israeli prisoners of war, or hostages in a terrorist attack. The underlying concept is that the Jews are a small, oppressed people, and its handful of members have a special obligation to ensure the well-being of one another.

To the old concept of the 'people of the Book' was added in Israel's new self-image the concept of the book and the sword. The people of the Book is the nation that received the Bible – the Book of Books – from God. The later use of this term refers to the Jewish love of books; and indeed Israel does hold the record for the number of books read per person. The addition of the sword to the book signifies the need of the people of the Book to defend itself. This symbol expresses the fact that Israel, which had been prepared to live only by the Book, is capable at this stage in its history of succeeding in an area in which it had not proved itself throughout the years of exile.

Another term which characterizes the self-image of the young Israel is the 'sabra'. This appellation, given to those born in the country, has become a standard term, having years ago lost its humorous quality. The sabra – a type of cactus fruit very common in Israel – is prickly on the outside and sweet inside. This semi-complimentary image was accorded to native-born Israelis by their parents' generation as a reflection of what they saw as an exterior characterized by imperfect manners and rough behaviour and speech, but which, once penetrated, revealed many good qualities.

Political norms in Israel are in part borrowed from similar political frameworks elsewhere in the world, and in part represent original Israeli inventions. Israeli society is much more party-oriented than other democratic societies in the world. The left-wing parties established at the beginning of the century were originally frameworks which provided their young members with a variety of services, and which were expanded over the years. Political scientists have defined these services as those accompanying the individual from cradle to grave (hospital, kindergarten, school, youth movement, medical services, housing, employment, banking, newspapers, theatre, social security, old age home, and so on). The right-wing parties, which generally follow the pattern of skeleton parties, imitated the example set by the left and founded extensive frameworks of their own. Yet, there are few terms more offensive in Israel than 'party', even more so when used as an attribute. Thus, many parties founded after the establishment of the state call themselves 'movements' rather than parties, although there is no distinction between them. While the older parties (Poalei Zion, HaPoel HaZair, Mapai, the United Workers' Party, and the National Religious Party) were not deterred by the word 'party', the later parties (the Herut movement, the Poalei

Israel List, the Citizens' Rights Movement, the Democratic Movement for Change, the Tehiya Movement, the Tsomet Movement, the Movement for Change, the Moledet Movement, and more) preferred the term 'list' or 'movement', ostensibly implying a less binding, less institutionalized and more open structure.

In the past, the right–left dichotomy in Israel was more extreme in character. The right-wing party activists dressed in suits, and many were attorneys or businessmen. The left-wing party workers wore open-necked shirts and sometimes shorts, and prided themselves on their agricultural past, albeit very brief. In leftist circles, people address each other to this day as 'comrade', a term also used in correspondence and in the labour-affiliated newspapers. When former Chief-of-Staff Haim Bar-Lev was elected Secretary General of the Labour Party, he had notices pasted on all the walls of the Labour Party headquarters, saying: 'Call your comrades by their first names.' Bar-Lev's campaign proved successful in the upper echelons, but less so at the grass-roots level. The two Labour leaders, Yitzhak Rabin and Shimon Peres, are addressed by party members by their first names, as are their colleagues in the party leadership. But in the party branches people still address each other as 'comrade', and continue to correspond in a manner befitting a self-respecting socialist party.

The red flag is displayed alongside the national flag at official functions of the Labour Party, and on 1 May the Labour Party leaders march in a parade organized by the Histadrut. Many of the party leaders do not feel comfortable celebrating the workers' holiday, are not moved by the red flag, and sing the 'Internationale' without enthusiasm. But, like every other ritual, these have become divorced from their original motives. At the Labour Party Congress in 1991 the 'Internationale' was not sung for the first time and the red flag was well hidden behind the many national flags.

In the Herut movement headed by Menachem Begin, which was a direct continuation of the IZL, many members referred to Begin as 'Commander', the usual greeting is 'Tel-Hai', and the youth movement, Betar, is organized in quasi-military battalions.

The myth of the eradication of personal ambition is one of the most salient components of Israeli political norms. Characteristic of this myth is the idea of a 'mission', particularly prevalent in the Labour movement. Every public functionary is an emissary of the people, namely a person charged with a task he must fulfil in order to live up to the expectations of the public which charged him with his mission. The emissary himself is to all appearances passive; he does not appoint himself; he asks nothing for himself; and there is no talk of a personal career. 'The verdict of the movement' is another concept related to this myth. This denotes the collectivist approach in which, while the individual may prefer a different course, the movement is stronger and decides for him, and he accepts its decision.

In certain circles there is even a ritual for declining an offered position. For example, in the Mapam kibbutzim of the Kibbutz HaArtzi movement, a member is at times asked to assume an important position (emissary abroad, secretary of the kibbutz movement, a Member of Knesset, or a Government minister). He declines on the grounds that his work in the kibbutz is more important. The general assembly of the kibbutz is then convened and forces him to accept the position – in which he is in fact usually very interested.

In the face of widespread political fragmentation, there exists a myth of unity. The term 'statist' serves as the antithesis of 'party'. When people want to present a politician in a positive light and to emphasize that he is not governed by narrow party interests, he is described as having a 'statist' orientation. Non-conformity or a deviation from the consensus was viewed as a very grave phenomenon, both in the pre-state and statehood periods. The IZL and Lehi were always called secessionist movements, and the very fact of their secession was viewed as much more serious than their differing views.

The term *ahdut* 'unity' is one of the most popular in Israel, both in the names adopted by political parties and in multi-party groups (Ahdut HaAvoda meaning labour unity, the United Workers' Party, the BeYahad – together – movement, the National Unity Government in both its incarnations, and more.) But the broad use of this term not infrequently conceals splits and dissension, bearing the name of unity in vain. However, unlike such terms as 'mission' and 'the verdict of the movement' which have been eroded and generally arouse ridicule, unity, like statism, is still current tender.

The ideological language in Israel has changed with the passing years. The term coined by Golda Meir 'socialism in our time', which was used by the left in the 1950s, fell into disuse in the 1960s. The term 'iron wall' was adopted by the Revisionist movement; it meant that only when the Arabs of Israel understood the power of the Jews in Israel would they reconcile themselves to being a minority in the Jewish state. Another ideological social concept which characterized the Revisionists was 'Yes, break it': this emerged after the essay by Ze'ev Jabotinsky which, in 1932, called upon the unorganized workers to break the strike of the organized workers in the Frumin factory in Jerusalem. This later became a disparaging term used by members of the Labour movement against Jabotinsky's disciples, while the right ceased to use the term and even joined the Histadrut in 1965.

According to the Zionist myth prevailing at the beginning of the century, many believed that Jewish immigration to Palestine was in effect the joining of a people without a land to a land without a people, though even then there were some who maintained and wrote otherwise. The unwillingness to recognize the existence of another people in Palestine was based on the understanding that the recognition of a people also meant the recognition of its rights, and hence the negation of the exclusive Jewish claim to the land. Over the years, both major camps moved away from the pretence of exclusivity. The left was prepared to share the land, while the right insisted that the Arabs be satisfied with minority status. In 1978 the existence of a Palestinian people was confirmed, black on white, in the Camp David Accords. Menachem Begin – still apprehensive about the necessary sequel to this statement – clarified in a letter to President Carter that this term would be translated into Hebrew as 'the Arabs of the land of Israel'. Carter was not unduly moved by this addendum, as it was the English text of the agreement that was binding.

The Israeli ideological language was enriched in 1967 by the term 'territories'. This referred to those lands captured during the Six Day War – the Sinai Peninsula, the Gaza Strip, the West Bank of the Jordan River, and the Golan Heights. The adjective attached to this term revealed the political outlook of the speaker: the right called them 'liberated territories', and the extreme left termed them 'occupied territories', while the centre referred to them as 'administered territories'. Those who try to remain neutral and to avoid any ideological overtones refrain from using any adjective, speaking simply of 'the territories'.

In the 1980s the Likud began to term itself 'the national camp', a name which has since become synonymous with the right-wing parties. The left, rather pleased at this choice, sought to establish that it was no less national than the right. However, it failed in the attempt to repudiate this claim, and the right adopted a new tag. The small leftist parties styled themselves as the peace camp – a definition with which the Labour Alignment is afraid to identify itself because it considers it too radical.

Racism is taboo in Israeli ideological language. The horrors of the Holocaust produced a complete consensus against any manifestation of racism, and it is not by chance that right and left united in passing a law in the Knesset barring any party with a racist platform from running for election. Indeed, this law prevented Meir Kahane's list from standing for re-election to the Knesset.

The Holocaust is the ultimate taboo. This is a matter on which everyone is united, and which silences all dissent. For years no German films were screened in Israeli cinemas, no German music was broadcast on the radio, the concert halls boycotted Wagner, and many Israelis boycotted German imports, continuing to do so to this day. An effort is made not to compare any other atrocity to the Holocaust. When the Americans asked that the Israeli government recognize the holocaust of the Armenians, they were told that the Holocaust of European Jewry could not be compared to this massacre, neither in its scope nor in the horrors it entailed. When Palestinian terrorist actions are likened to Nazi deeds, there is always someone who argues that no sporadic act of violence can be likened to the Holocaust. No literature has been written in Israel ridiculing the Nazis – no plays and no films like those produced in the United States and Europe after World War II.

In contrast, the expression 'in order that there should not be another Holocaust' is used as justification for dovish and hawkish ideologies alike. While the former seek to achieve a political solution in order to prevent bloodshed, the latter adopt an unbending stand against Arab demands in order not to invite disaster by yielding to them.

A less acute but prominent taboo is that of Communism, which is beyond the pale in Israeli society. The Communists comprise a small party with an almost entirely Arab membership, considered legitimate for Arabs but illegitimate for Jews. Israelis known to be Communists do not achieve senior positions in public administration, in the army, or in institutions directly or indirectly related to the establishment. They can be found, however, among university faculties, in the arts, and to a lesser extent in the media. The Communists have never been part of a government coalition in Israel, and even leftist circles prefer to distance themselves from them in order not to be stigmatized. The collapse of the USSR will change the Communist Party and the public attitude towards it.

The gathering of the exiles is one of Israel's most important symbols – the task of bringing the Jews to Israel from all over the world, speaking more than seventy different languages, and transforming them into a single nation. The melting pot represents the myth of integration, and maintains that although the Jews come from many different cultures, they are quickly reunited upon their arrival in Israel into one nation. The IDF is also viewed as a melting pot in which all receive equal treatment, regardless of their different origins.

Reality, in this case, is quite different from myth. The process of absorption is accompanied by numerous hardships, and even when the immigrants seem rapidly to be integrated into society and speak Hebrew, many social difficulties remain, some of which come to the fore only much later. There is no doubt that the absorption of the Western/European immigrants into the existing Ashkenazi establishment was more successful than the absorption of immigrants with a Middle Eastern background. Most of the latter arrived without capital, without a language that was common to Israeli society, and without suitable educational qualifications. Behind the facade of military egalitarianism, the Ashkenazim found themselves in the upper command ranks, while many of the Sephardim did not advance beyond the rank of warrant officer. When Ben-Gurion spoke of a dream he had in which a Yemenite served as IDF Chief-of-Staff, this was indeed a remote dream. A Yemenite Chief-of-Staff has yet to be appointed, and indeed many years passed before the appointment in 1983 of a Chief-of-Staff of Iraqi origin (Moshe Levy). Nevertheless, there is no doubt that the army does serve as a meeting-place for people of different social classes who would otherwise not experience such intense contact, and it is also one of the factors promoting marriages between members of different Jewish communities, a practice not common in Israel (about 20 per cent of all marriages).

Population dispersion is another myth related primarily to the immigration from Arab countries. The idea was to direct all the new immigrants to the frontiers of the young state in order to secure the borders through settlement. Many of the transit camps initially set up in the periphery later became development towns. These were originally meant to combine urban settlement with auxiliary family farms, but agriculture was ultimately abandoned. The development towns were originally settled by immigrants from both Western and Middle Eastern countries. The former, however, were gradually attracted to the urban centres, thus creating towns populated almost entirely by Jews of Middle Eastern origin. Many of the second generation of these immigrant families perceived population dispersion as a means to deny their parents the opportunities available in the centre, while the development towns, containing less than a tenth of Israel's population, became known as the 'second Israel', the other

Israel – less well known, appearing less frequently in the media, and developing at a slower pace than the centre. This term referred primarily to the development towns established in the 1950s, and less so to those established in the 1960s, where development was more rapid.

Anyone who examines the demographic map of Israel will easily perceive the failure of the effort at population dispersion. The Galilee in the north and the Negev in the south cry out for inhabitants, while Israel is rapidly approaching a situation in which the majority of its population lives in one large metropolitan area in the centre. Those who remain on the periphery are either people who chose to settle there for ideological reasons, or those who did not have the resources or the ability to leave.

The law enacted to encourage investment capital, which accorded preference to investments in export industries in the peripheral areas, did not bring an abundance of investment to the frontier areas. This was in part because many investors availed themselves of the exemptions granted during the first five-year period, and then moved their factories every five years from one development area to another. Whereas in the past secondary education had been provided free of charge only in the development towns, at the end of the 1970s free education was extended throughout the country, while the average salary in the development towns remained significantly lower than that in the centre of the country.

The high birth-rate among Jewish immigrants from Arab countries was encouraged by the Ashkenazi establishment, who generally had fewer children. As the State of Israel has always been engaged in a demographic effort to increase its population, the authorities wanted the new immigrants, who often arrived with eight, ten or even twelve children, to continue this way of life in Israel. Prime Minister Ben-Gurion declared a prize of 100 lira for every mother of ten. Large families were subsequently called 'families blessed with children', and since 1972 a special national insurance allowance has been accorded to large Jewish families, with eligibility defined by army service of a parent or family member.

It is not without cause that the word 'proletariat' is derived from the Latin word for offspring. A proliferation of children allowed a family to accord less to each child than a family with two or three children could provide. Hence, although the proliferation of children deepened the poverty of these families, who were not well-to-do to begin with, large families remained a desirable image. To assert that a high birth rate reduces the ability of each individual child to cope with his environment is to go beyond the realm of legitimate argument and to enter the realm of taboo.

A prevalent myth in Israeli society is the myth of equality. The relative lack of ceremony, the non-existence of a traditional class structure, the fact that the vast majority of Israelis are newcomers in the country: this all contributed greatly to the sense of equality, until refuted by statistics. Inequality in income in Israel exceeds that in Great Britain and in many other countries where the gap between rich and poor is admitted to be wide.

The equality of women is also a well-established myth in Israel. The pioneers who came to Palestine, believing in the equality of all men, viewed the few women among them as equals, and the women engaged in the same tasks as the men – paving roads, preparing gravel, and farming – sharing the same harsh living conditions and poverty. Nevertheless, Israeli women do not as a rule reach the upper echelons in Israeli administrative, business or public affairs. Women are a small minority in the Knesset; they rarely serve in the cabinet and almost never as mayor; no woman has ever been appointed director-general of a government ministry; few women fill senior positions in government administration; rarely do women attain high military rank except for the OC of the Women's Corps, despite compulsory army service for women; and even in art and literature women do not occupy a central place. There is, however, an awareness of the need to accord women equality, reflected in the equal opportunity legislation passed by the Knesset.

Related to equality is the myth of egalitarian medical services. In fact, more than 90 per cent of Israeli citizens are medically insured through the various health funds, and even people without means receive the necessary minimal medical services. However, it is common practice in the public hospitals to make payments to the individual doctors or to the departments in which they work in order to enjoy a higher standard of service, with a shorter waiting period for treatment. This phenomenon, a kind of 'blackmarket' medicine, has become particularly prevalent in recent years, creating two levels of medical services in Israel – one for people with means, and the other for people of moderate means or less. Although the existence of this phenomenon is universally recognized, the establishment still finds it hard to accept; it prefers to continue to promote egalitarian medicine rather than legitimizing and regularizing the two different levels.

A myth related to the Labour movement's perception of the new Jewish society is the myth of the inverted pyramid. This term was coined by Dov Borochov, a Jewish Marxist, who added to Marx's means of production the importance of production conditions. He believed that only under conditions of independence could the Jews once again become productive. In the diaspora, Borochov maintained, the pyramid had been inverted: then, he stated, instead of a broad base of farmers and workers and a small group who provided services and served as middlemen and merchants, most of the Jews engaged in the latter functions with few farmers or labourers. In Palestine, the pyramid was once again to be inverted. Although the entire Labour movement did not become disciples of Borochov, the idea was adopted by most of its leaders, and an attempt was made artificifically to invert the pyramid: students of yesterday became agricultural workers, swamp drainers and road pavers; education was viewed as bourgeois, and those who held academic degrees concealed the fact; the most prestigious status symbol in the Labour movement was calloused hands. But already in the late 1920s it became clear that pyramids cannot easily be inverted. It later became apparent that, in modern society, Borochov's natural pyramid was no longer relevant, and that what such a society needed more than any other resource was knowledge.

If Dov Borochov, who died in 1917, visited Israel today, he would probably wring his hands at the inverted pyramid which continues to stand on its head in the Jewish state. Israel holds the world record for the number of doctors per thousand people (3.5 per 1000), and the current wave of immigration from the Soviet Union, in which the ratio is ten times as large (almost 35 per 1000), will only serve to break the record again. The number of advocates in Israel is the same, in absolute terms, as the number in Japan (11,000). The public sector is very large (constituting 30 per cent of the labour force), while the number of production workers is relatively small (24 per cent).

Another ideological dream – to establish a workers' society in Palestine – was an attempt to realize Borochovism by creating an economy based entirely on workers, who were to work according to their ability and receive according to their needs. This dream sought a kind of short cut: many of the fathers of the Labour movement believed that in the absence of capital or capitalism in Palestine in the first quarter of the century, it should be possible to skip over the stage of the class struggle and to establish a kind of Communist society in which wages would not serve as an incentive for labour.

Hevrat HaOvdim (the Workers' Society) bore the name of the dream, but immediately relinquished the pretentious claim, becoming an economic sector in Israeli society. Israel itself never became a workers' society.

Full employment has always held special importance in Israel, both because of the need to provide jobs for the soldiers released after three years' compulsory service, and to ensure that the new immigrants would not leave for other countries for lack of suitable employment. Full employment was also presented by the politicians as an important goal in itself because of the inherent value of labour. The mass waves of immigration in the early years of statehood were largely directed to public works, the only purpose of which was to prevent the immigrants from receiving unemployment allowances while remaining idle. Immigrants were thus employed in planting trees and in tasks of less than marginal importance.

The rapid changes of a modern economy curbed unemployment. But it was replaced by hidden unemployment, both in the public sector, which swelled in size, and in the productive sector – particularly in the Histadrut enterprises of Hevrat HaOvdim, in which the dismissal of workers ran counter to ideology. Part of the weakness of the Israeli economy derives from the preference for hidden over blatant unemployment. Hidden unemployment allowed many people who were no longer needed to believe that they were still working, absolving the system from finding alternative employment for them. There is no doubt that this gave rise to distortions, a heavy economic burden and inefficiency. In the mid-1980s, in the wake of the economic recovery program of 1985, many enterprises were forced to face economic truth and to carry out large-scale dismissals. While the dismissals in many productive plants resulted in increased output, the social problem created by the rise in unemployment – partly structural and partly educational – was particularly acute, and remains so in light of the current large wave of immigration from the Soviet Union, which will increase unemployment again, at least temporarily.

Israeli society is becoming increasingly materialistic. The truth is that this process is only natural. The first generation came, at least in part, out of ideological reasons, seeking to realize a dream, to consummate values; the second generation, born in Israel, and viewing its surroundings as natural, makes demands of it and seeks to prosper within it. The anti-materialistic environment of the first decades of the century influenced social norms, and even those with materialistic tendencies preferred to present their motives as national.

As the years passed, materialistic demands achieved greater legitimacy, wealth was less often concealed and indeed began to be
flaunted. Yet Israeli norms in this regard are still far removed from
American norms. Such comments as 'So and so is worth so many
dollars', 'I make so and so many dollars a year', or 'So and so works
for me' are not common in the Hebrew language or in Israeli culture.
One must still apologize in Israel for being well-to-do, for vacationing
abroad, for eating in fancy restaurants, or for driving an expensive
car.

Israel hovers between two symbols which constitute an apparent
contradiction, but which share a common denominator; they express
a special sensitivity to the question of survival. A picture which recurs
in exhibitions, in documentaries and elsewhere is that of the Jewish
boy with frightened eyes in the Warsaw Ghetto, raising his arms in
submission to the Nazi soldiers; a second picture, which appears in
the victory albums of the Six Day War, in documentaries and in
posters, is that of Captain Yossi – who has since become an IDF
brigadier general – standing dressed in his uniform in the waters of
the Suez Canal, raising his rifle aloft in a supreme feeling of implied
happiness: we have been saved from another Holocaust. It is between
these two symbols, – between the Holocaust which befell European
Jewry and the fear of its recurrence – that Israeli society lives.

Ideologies

The new Yishuv in Palestine was established during a period when
ideologies flourished, and ideology indeed played a dominant role in
this community which numbered several tens of thousands. These
ideologies were all-embracing, very demanding of those who believed
in them, and did not leave room for compromise with other ideologies,
whose adherents were viewed at the very least as rivals.

Ideology admits no doubts. Although it applies scientific tools, it
translates hypotheses into premises and conventions. The past is
explained by an overall perspective, and the future is presented as an
inevitable development. Most of the young people who arrived in
Palestine at the beginning of the century left religious homes in
rebellion against their parents' generation. Many agreed with Marx
when he said that religion was the opium of the masses, and they led
secular lives. Socialism, in its various forms, became for them a kind

of new religion, which provided both explanations and predictions. Socialism accorded them a meaningful world which they could understand; helped them to reject 'irrelevant' information; provided excuses for inconvenient situations, past and present; and created a moral system to justify actions.

Zionism itself is an ideology – maintaining that transferring the Jewish people from exile to Palestine would bring about a total change in its way of life, making the Jews productive workers, and transforming them into a nation like all other nations. Like other secular ideologies, Zionism offered the secular Jew of the late nineteenth century an opportunity to live a Jewish life without danger of assimilation and without having to maintain the outward signs of religion. Zionism, as defined by Eliezer Schweid, was and is a programme designed to solve the problems of the Jews and Judaism in the modern age by restoring the Jewish people to their ancient homeland in order to live as an independent nation in a modern national-political framework.

Zionist ideology was based on enhancing the importance of nationality in the life of the individual, assuming its centrality in his life; on the premise that Jewish nationality should be realized in the same place where it originated, namely in the land of Israel, and not in the large Jewish population centres; and on the assumption that this concentration of population would produce a revolutionary change in the life of the Jewish people in employment and social relations. Reviewing the past, Zionist ideology explained the suffering of the Jewish people by their dispersion in many countries, everywhere constituting a small minority. Zionism looked towards the future, which it presented in idyllic colours, totally ignoring the possible development of a conflict between Jews and Arabs in Palestine.

It soon became apparent, however, that Zionist ideology alone was not sufficient to embrace all aspects of life. At the turn of the century, the General Zionists, or the 'plain' Zionists, constituted a large majority. These were people who identified solely with Zionist ideology and did not adopt any social or religious worldview. The socialist parties emerged during the first decade of the century, the religious parties at the beginning of the third decade, and the rightist Revisionist party in the middle of that decade. The controversy among them was total, despite the broad Zionist common denominator. This was a struggle over the course of a society in the making, and each party believed that its victory would determine its character.

The conflict which developed among the various ideologies during the early decades of the century aggravated the dispute within the Zionist movement, with the right presenting the left as Communists, and the left portraying the right as Fascists. While it is true that there were in the two camps those who identified with Communism on the one hand and Fascism on the other, the central streams within each maintained an authenticity which set them apart from these ideologies.

It was hard not to identify with one of the ideologies in the pre-state period in Palestine. While within the Zionist movement one could still be a 'plain Zionist,' in Palestine one had to belong either to the left or the right, or to identify with the ultra-Orthodox camp which refused to reconcile itself to the existence of the Zionist movement, viewing the attempt to anticipate the Messiah and to establish a sovereign Jewish entity governed by secular Jews as a grave mistake. This ultra-Orthodox camp unequivocally preferred foreign rule to Jewish self-rule, and they refused to be part of Knesset Israel – the corporate entity of the Jewish community in Palestine under the British mandate, which maintained an autonomous framework and elected its own democratic institutions.

The Zionist left (and there was always an anti-Zionist left which preferred class affiliation to national Jewish goals) believed that only the workers could establish a Jewish society in Palestine, while the right accused the left of being anti-nationalist. Both left and right had military forces at their disposal (the Haganah and the Palmach on the left, the IZL and Lehi on the right), and both camps, as well as the Zionist-religious camp, had educational, cultural and economic bodies of their own. Ideology was not only a mode of thought, but definitely a way of life, and a shift from one ideology to another was not a political statement, but rather a significant social act viewed by all sides as tantamount to betrayal.

Stein Rokkan explains that the nature of socio-political dispute in every society is determined by the position of the state at the moment when the universal right to vote is granted. The right to vote was granted to the Jews of Palestine in 1920, at the elections to the first Assembly of Deputies, and the political image of the country was shaped in the 1920s. During this decade, the left bloc was formed, the Revisionist movement was established under Ze'ev Jabotinsky, and the religious workers' party was founded. Each advocated a worldview of its own and projected its own image of Jewish society in Palestine. These remain to this day the only major ideologies in Israel.

Unlike other societies where ideologies developed out of a conflict of interests (small versus large landowners; farmers versus city dwellers; workers versus the middle class; periphery versus centre, etc.), the ideological debate in Palestine was characterized by true ideological distinctions. The workers were not workers, but idealists who decided they should become workers; the right was not composed of capitalists, but rather of people who believed that a society engaged in founding a state should not permit strikes and should preferably have a liberal economy. Only the ultra-Orthodox were indeed just that; they viewed these developments as a great mistake, and refused to be part of it.

Against this background of sharp tensions between the two camps, it is somewhat surprising that violence was limited to two political assassinations: Jacob Israel De Haan, an ultra-Orthodox anti-Zionist who was murdered by leftist elements in 1924; and Chaim Arlosoroff, a leader of the left, who was assassinated in 1933. There were other outbursts of violence, which reached a peak in the 1930s in exchanges of blows between members of youth movements from the right and the left, and there were outbursts over strike-breaking efforts by right-wing groups, but on the whole, even in the absence of enforcement agencies, there were norms of discipline which ensured ideological tension within a non-violent framework of debate.

There is a universal tendency to view the behavioural motives of previous generations with nostalgia, and to attribute to them greater innocence and values. In the case of Israel, despite the inevitable exaggerations, there was a certain truth in this, for the simple reason that many of the young people who came to Palestine did so for ideological reasons. Unlike most emigrants from Eastern Europe, these people did not seek to improve their standard of living in the West. They believed in the possibility of creating a new society and of altering the condition of the Jewish people, and viewed themselves as charged with this task. The second generation, born in Palestine, did not face a choice as their parents had. This was a 'normal' generation, educated to 'normalcy'. Its most important achievement was the fact that they lived as ordinary young people, with the problems of ordinary young people. Its second achievement revolved around the fact that they were physically stronger than their parents (or so they believed) and were prepared to bear arms to defend the small Jewish community. It is clear that ideological commitment was less marked in the second generation than in that of their parents.

The attempt by the parents to institutionalize ideology through

youth movements proved only partially successful. The youth movements were designed to provide the answers to all questions, and
every parent could direct his children towards the ideological stream
to which he himself belonged. A child growing up in the city in a
home identified with the Labour movement would have gone to a
'Labour trend' school, would read *Davar for Children* – the Histadrut
youth newspaper – would have belonged to a youth movement such
as HaMahanot HaOlim 'Ascending Hosts', or HaNoar HaOved
'Working Youth', would have joined the Haganah and would become
a member of a kibbutz.

The second generation realized the importance of the chosen ideology, wrote essays and spoke in praise of it, but many of them at one
stage or another abandoned the course set for them by their parents.
With the conclusion of schooling, induction into the army and the
beginning of kibbutz life, social pressure began to exceed parental
influence. As a result, the kibbutz became for many a transit station
rather than a way of life. A very large group of people born in the
country in the 1920s and 1930s note in their biographies a brief
period spent in a kibbutz. Only a minority of the second generation
adopted the kibbutz as their way of life. The 1920s dream of making
the kibbutz the lifestyle of the entire country was replaced by the
kibbutz movement, which throughout the years has comprised about
4 per cent of the population. The collectivist ideology was not
replaced by individualism, but there is no doubt that the readiness of
the founding generation to serve as a kind of 'wilderness generation'
for the sake of a better society did not characterize the later generations, who naturally sought self-fulfilment. However, this was still
a society which viewed the individual in his social context, and which
believed that reforming society would also entail a real reform of the
individual.

There was a sense that ideology had come to an end after the War
of Independence. On the one hand, the ideology of consensus – the
Zionist ideology – seemed to have been realized. On the other hand,
many felt that the young state had not fulfilled their hopes, and that
statehood was no different really from pre-statehood. Young people
who experienced the socialization processes outlined above reacted
with cynicism and even nihilism. Some tried their luck for a few years
in Europe and returned frustrated, a feeling which was also reflected
in Hebrew literature.

During the 1950s and 1960s, there were of course sharp political
controversies, but the issues were not related to the basic differences

between the worldviews of the two major camps. Thus, for example, the acute debate over relations with Germany, or over such issues as religion and state were devoid of any direct ideological basis. Although Golda Meir spoke in the 1950s of 'socialism in our time', this slogan only served to obscure the acceptance of a pluralistic economy – not a class war, nor a classless society, nor even a workers' society. Heated ideological debates were conducted within the Israeli left. Mapam was caught up in a debate between commitment to the composite Marxist-Leninist approach and unhyphenated commitment to both Marxism and Leninism. The debate was later known as the 'hyphen debate' and was presented as an example of a superfluous debate totally cut off from the surrounding reality.

The 1960s were the years of the great political unification. In 1965 Mapam joined with Ahdut HaAvoda after twenty-one years of separation, while on the right the Herut movement united with the Liberal Party. The Israel Labour Party was established in 1968, incorporating Rafi again two and a half years after they had split, and the Labour Alignment in 1969 joining the Labour Party and Mapam. The large political blocs established did not aggravate the basic differences between them. On the contrary, the compromises made within each bloc brought them closer to the centre, and to a certain extent blunted their differences. In the social sphere, the welfare state became the common denominator of left and right, while in the political sphere, there was no central point of dissension prior to the Six Day War.

The National Unity Government established on the eve of the Six Day War in 1967 was undoubtedly the most salient expression of the blunting of differences between the major political blocs in Israel. A government which brought Levi Eshkol together with Menachem Begin was, to a great extent, a government of historic conciliation, established after decades of bitter dissent and personal hostility. One illustrative example is the fact that David Ben-Gurion as prime minister had not only promised to form a government without Herut and without Maki (the Israeli Communist party), but did not even call Menachem Begin by name, but rather referred to him as 'the man seated next to Dr Bader'.

The outcome of the Six Day War was a shock not only to the Arabs, but also to the Israelis – a kind of dream come true – who did not quite know what to do with their new-found wealth. It is not by chance that the failure to conquer the West Bank in the course of the 1948 War of Independence had been called an 'everlasting shame', as it was clear that the armistice lines – the Green Line – would be the border of Israel. In the geography lessons, called 'homeland' studies, I recall a large relief map of Israel on which the border was drawn in green. The generation which entered school after 1967 studied from new maps on which the green line had disappeared; the National Unity Government formally decided to erase it, stating that Israel's temporary border would be the ceasefire line – the Jordan River on the east, the Golan Heights in the north and the Suez Canal to the west.

During my childhood, my parents used to take me during school holidays to Jerusalem. We went up to the roof of a high building near the Old City of Jerusalem and they pointed out the direction of the Western Wall. From that vantage point all we could see was several Jordanian legionnaires, many roofs and laundry hanging on clotheslines, but the Western Wall then seemed to me a very distant goal which could never be attained. Citizens of other countries who visited Jordan would arrive in Israel in the 1950s and 1960s and fill large lecture halls with talks about Petra, the Western Wall, the Mount of Olives, and the tomb of the patriarchs in Hebron. Alongside the great longing for these sites, there was also a general feeling of reconciliation to the realistic impossibility of ever seeing them.

An event occurred after the initial post-war shock which, although not surprising, deserves examination. Most of the political movements in Israel returned to their original positions in the period preceding Jewish sovereignty. There has also been an interesting reversal. Until 1967 the 'land of Israel' was deemed an anachronistic term and nationalist elements tended always to stress that it was the 'State of Israel' (as distinct from the 'land of Israel') which had been relevant only until 1948. However, since 1967 the 'State of Israel' has become a code word for those who attribute greater importance to sovereignty than to territory, while the frequent reference to the 'land of Israel' has become characteristic of those who advocate annexation.

These advocates revealed themselves in an announcement published in the Israeli press on 22 September 1967 entitled 'For the sake of the undivided land of Israel'. It stated:

> The IDF victory in the Six Day War introduced the people and the state into a new and fateful period. The entire land of Israel is now in the hands of the Jewish people, and just as we have no right to surrender the State of Israel, so are we commanded to maintain that which we received from it – the land of Israel. We owe our allegiance to the integrity of our land –

vis-à-vis both our people's past and its future, and no Israeli government has the right to surrender this integrity.

The current borders of our country are a guarantee of security and peace – and also horizons for unprecedented national endeavour, both material and spiritual. Within these borders, freedom and equality, which are the basis of the State of Israel, will be enjoyed by all residents alike.

Immigration and the settlement of the land are the two principles on which our future rests. A large wave of immigration of Jews from all the countries of its dispersion is a basic condition for maintaining the integrity and the national character of the land of Israel. We shall make the goals and the new possibilities of this period a cause of awakening and momentum for the people of Israel and the land of Israel.

The signatories of this document are not Menachem Begin, nor Yitzhak Shamir, nor even Geula Cohen, but veteran and even leading figures of the Labour movement. The others were from the NRP and only a few old-time Revisionists, not the movement's leaders. The major aim of the 'movement for an undivided land of Israel' was to delegitimize the territorial debate itself, thus returning to Menachem Begin's central argument in 1947 – that the Jewish community in the land of Israel has no right to relinquish any part of the land, which belongs to the entire Jewish people.

At first, it seemed that the issue of the integrity of the land would transcend party lines, and that the parties would continue to focus on the old issues – relations with Germany, the role of the Histadrut, etc. Indeed, the six years between the Six Day War and the Yom Kippur War seem to have been characterized by a blunting of the ideological sting. During half of this period there was a National Unity Government, which in itself reduced tensions, and even after the government was dissolved over the refusal of Menachem Begin and his party to accept UN Security Council Resolution 242 (whose main premise was Israel–Arab peace in exchange for an Israeli relinquishment of territory), Golda Meir continued to serve as prime minister, inspiring a firm stand *vis-à-vis* the Arabs and Palestinians, although in principle she supported a solution based on territorial compromise.

As noted, the Israel Labour Party was founded in 1968 when Mapai merged with two parties with more hawkish positions – the leftist Ahdut HaAvoda and the rightist Rafi. One year later saw the establishment of the Labour Alignment between the new Labour Party and Mapam. These mergers accorded the ruling party an absolute majority in the Knesset, which it lost in the 1969 elections (winning only 56 out of the 120 seats). This large party, called a 'supermarket' by some of its members, included people who supported a unilateral withdrawal from the territories (Pinhas Lavon, Yitzhak Ben-Aharon) and a group called 'the undivided land circle'. In the major right-wing party, there were supporters of immediate annexation, such as Begin and his fellow leaders of the Herut movement, and more moderate people who opposed such annexation, such as Liberal leader Elimelech Rimalt, Shlomo Zalman Abramov, and others.

But this situation did not last. Slowly the new-old ideologies began to organize themselves within the existing political structure, without the emergence of new political parties. Those within Labour who advocated an 'undivided land of Israel' either left the party or accepted the majority view; many of them accepted the consensus led by Golda Meir, which advised that so long as there was no peace, Israel would not withdraw from any territory. Many of them felt in their hearts that the chances of peace were so small that there was no need to break up the good old party for the sake of some future illusion.

Within the Herut–Liberal bloc, the militant Herut movement under Begin's charismatic leadership overcame the remnants of Liberal moderation led by pragmatic figures who lacked public appeal. In the 1973 elections, which were to have been held at the end of October that year and were postponed because of the Yom Kippur War, the right-wing party stood for election as a federation of political movements and personalities advocating an undivided land of Israel, under the name 'Likud'. Aside from the Herut movement and the Liberal Party, the Likud also included the Free Centre (a small party which had split from Herut and held a hawkish position on the integrity of the land), the State List composed of hawks under the leadership of Yigal Horowitz (who had split from Rafi and not rejoined the Labour Party), and activists for 'an undivided land of Israel' led by Brig. General (Res.) Avraham Yaffe, former member of HaShomer HaTzair. The Liberal Party was enhanced in these elections by a new personality, Brig. General (Res.) Ariel Sharon, former moshav member and former Labour supporter; his political outlook attracted him to the Likud.

The Yom Kippur War further exacerbated the new situation. The right argued that Israel would only be saved from disaster if the territories remained under Israeli control, and had Israel been attacked in October 1973 from the 1967 borders, it would not have been able to defend itself as it did. Their conclusion was that Israel must continue to hold on to the territories and even to annex them. The left argued that the war had proved the possession of the territories had no value, because the losses suffered by Israel in the Six Day War, when the borders had been much narrower, were much smaller than its losses in the Yom Kippur War when Israel controlled territory three times larger. The shock over the outcome of the Yom Kippur War restored ideological arguments to the arena of Israeli political debate. While for almost a decade the political debate had focused on achievement, management ability, and the personal suitability of the leaders of both parties to run the state, in 1973 – and even shortly before – the ideological debate was rekindled in all its vigour. The left argued that the State of Israel would not be able to survive as a democratic Jewish state if it annexed the territories or continued to control them without annexation. If it annexed the territories and granted all residents full rights, it would be a democratic state with an Arab minority comprising 40 per cent of the population and this minority with its high birth rate, was capable of becoming a majority. If Israel continued to control the territories without annexing them, though, Jewish dominance would be maintained at the expense of it no longer being a democracy; its control of a large group of residents lacking political rights would deny that.

The right, for its part, maintained that the Palestinians in the territories should not enjoy the same rights as the Jews because they had the option to turn to twenty-two Arab states. There was no reason not to annex the territories where they lived, according them broad autonomy but not the right to self-determination, for they chose to continue to live under Israeli rule.

In the new ideological debate there was no room for neutrality. Even the religious parties, whose role in the Knesset had been first and foremost to advance religious matters and to protect the religious interests of their electorate, were forced to make decisions. The NRP, which had in the past been known as a moderate religious party (its leader Moshe Chaim Shapira had, for example, opposed the conquest of East Jerusalem during the Six Day War) decided in favour of maintaining the integrity of the land, largely because of the pressures of the young generation. This generation had been viewed by Israeli society as 'Mapai with a skullcap', namely a pragmatic factor distinguished from their secular friends only by the small knitted skullcap on their heads. They were not identified with heroism, pioneering, or asceticism as were some of their secular friends, nor with deep religious learning, like their ultra-Orthodox counterparts (yeshiva students who pursued their religious studies and were not recruited into the IDF). These frustrated youths were provided now – with the new territories – with an opportunity to prove themselves in a new area – settlement.

The young NRP members returned in their imaginations to the pre-state settlement period. Many of them saw the Israeli government in the image of the mandate government which was to be circumvented, and believed it was permissible to establish settlements against its will. They viewed themselves as pioneers of a new kind, prepared to pay the price of physical discomfort and suffering for the sake of fulfilling the commandment of settling the land. Even before the veteran NRP leadership had finished formulating its position on the occupied territories, they found their sons already living in these settlements, and found it hard to oppose them. This moderate party ultimately inscribed the integrity of the land on its banner, and it agreed to join a Labour-led government only after receiving a promise that new elections would be held before any future decision involving territorial concessions was made. The young NRP members formed the basis of Gush Emunim – the 'Bloc of the Faithful' – which was an ideological movement whose aims were to increase settlement in the territories and to ensure that the land of Israel remained undivided.

Gush Emunim emerged in the course of 1974. At first as part of the NRP and later as an independent body, it was influenced by certain rabbis who viewed the Yom Kippur War as part of a messianic process, part of the suffering of redemption in preparation for the coming of the Messiah. This group, which succeeded in bringing tens of thousands to its demonstrations, enjoyed broad public sympathy; the young men, after army service, bearded and dressed casually – sandals in the summer and sweaters in the winter – became universal favourites. The major success of Gush Emunim lay in its ability to incorporate the Yom Kippur War and its grave results within the framework of an overall worldview which led Israel forward, while the other ideological movements found it hard to explain these events. Gush Emunim was a spirited, fomenting factor, with a constructive programme, which claimed to continue the tradition of settlement at a time when no other movement could offer any cause for enlistment. It aroused envy and admiration even among its greatest opponents, who always emphasized their respect for it. As always, it was impossible to enter into a sharp debate with those who were prepared to suffer. These young men with their young wives, their hair covered with scarves, who were prepared to settle in the heart of Samaria or Judaea – in tents and caravans, without electricity or running water –

presented themselves as the pioneers of the 1970s, and it is hard to argue with pioneers. Their illegal actions; their attempts to establish settlements without the authorization of the military authorities; and even pictures of soldiers forcibly removing young men and women from caravans or tents set up without permission: all these failed to damage the appealing image of Gush Emunim.

Agudat Israel, the ultra-Orthodox party, succeeded in maintaining a low political profile, but its spiritual leaders discussed the issue of the occupied territories, published their positions, and handed down relevant religious rulings. The ultra-Orthodox world was split between the approach of the rabbi of Lubavich, who viewed the return of territories as forbidden by the Bible (he later sharply criticized Menachem Begin for the withdrawal from Sinai in the framework of the Camp David Accords), and the approach of Rabbi Eliezer Schach, also an anti-Zionist, who supported the return of territories for the sake of saving lives, and on the basis of his fundamental view that Jewish sovereignty not based on Jewish religious law was invalid and anticipated the messianic era. The small ultra-Orthodox party Poalei Agudat Israel identified totally with the annexation of the territories, but these two parties were much more involved in religious than political matters, enabling them for many years to support Labour governments, and after the 1977 elections to join the Likud-led coalition. The NRP's joining the Likud coalition was much more natural than its support of Labour, in view of the internal developments within that party.

The position of the left wing took shape quickly: the Communist party, established in 1965 following a split between Jews and Arabs, adopted the Moscow line – namely full Israeli withdrawal from the territories and the establishment of a Palestinian state alongside Israel. The Citizens' Rights Movement, established in the summer of 1973 when Shulamit Aloni learned that her name did not appear on the Labour list which won three Knesset seats, primarily because of the trauma of the Yom Kippur War, declared its unequivocal position to be withdrawal from the territories and recognition of the right of the Palestinians to self-determination.

The visit by President Sadat to Israel in November 1977 and the peace negotiations between Israel and Egypt further shocked the political system. On the right, there was considerable dissatisfaction at Menachem Begin's concessions, and the dispute between the supporters and opponents of the Prime Minister gave rise to the Tehiya movement headed by Geula Cohen. This party, which won five seats, later split, and alongside it there emerged the Tsomet movement headed by former Chief-of-Staff Rafael Eitan. In 1984 Rabbi Meir Kahane was elected to the Knesset at the head of the extremist Kach list, and when his re-election was prevented in 1988 by the new law enacted against racism, the Moledet movement, advocating the 'voluntary' transfer of Arabs from the territories to whatever Arab countries they wish, entered the Knesset.

The Camp David Accords also aroused sharp debate within the Labour Party. When Moshe Dayan said that Sharm a-Sheikh without peace was preferable to peace without Sharm a-Sheikh, he still represented the Labour Party and the party consensus. Several weeks before the Yom Kippur War the Labour Party approved a document inspired by Dayan known as the Galili Document, which promised, among other things, to establish more settlements in the Rafiah salient and to study the possibility of building a deep water port south of Gaza. Such expressions as 'the solution of the Palestinian problem in all its aspects' or 'the legitimate rights of the Palestinian people' had never before been mentioned in any Labour Party document. The Labour hawks encouraged the establishment of new settlements in the Rafiah salient in the course of 1978 – the year of negotiations with Egypt. Settlers in the territories, members of the Labour Party, urged their party leaders to oppose a complete withdrawal from Sinai and accused the Likud of irresponsibility towards the settlements, because it had never been a settlement movement.

At that time I was serving as spokesman of the Labour Party. Rabin and Peres, both in their mid-fifties, were viewed by their seniors as having received the party in good order and of having handed over the government to the Likud. Golda Meir remained to the last a member of the supreme party institutions. Israel Galili, a leader of the hawkish Ahdut HaAvoda faction and Meir's right-hand man in the government, was also a member of these institutions. The arrival of Anwar Sadat in Jerusalem a few months after the Likud's rise to power was undoubtedly a slap in the face for all the leaders of the Labour Party, and they strove to explain this paradox. This was the same Golda Meir who had misjudged Sadat's reply to Gunnar Jarring's proposal in February 1971 and who could, perhaps, have prevented the Yom Kippur War.

The feeling of such people as Meir and Galili was that the state had been placed in irresponsible hands, and that it was their job to prevent the deterioration of the situation. Golda used often to say that Begin deserved an Oscar award, and that he would be ready to do anything to impress the world. She viewed the relinquishment of the Sinai air space as an unpardonable error, and when the phrase 'the solution of the Palestinian problem in all its aspects' was quoted, she stated before the political committee of the Labour Party (which included former Labour ministers and members of the Knesset Foreign Affairs and Security Committee) that this wording was unacceptable, as one of the 'aspects' was a Palestinian state.

Yigal Allon sharply opposed the idea of autonomy in the West Bank and Gaza. Allon, faithful to the Allon Plan of 1967, went from one Labour Party branch to the next in an attempt to convince the members that the autonomy being proposed by the hawkish Begin (in order now not to give up an inch of land) would ultimately lead to the establishment of a Palestinian state. He accompanied his argument with the well-known story that ends with the heroes being expelled from the city and having to eat smelly fish.

On the eve of the historic vote in the Knesset, a stormy debate was held in the Labour Party central committee on the Camp David Accords. Party chairman Shimon Peres asked that the committee support the agreements. The hawks argued – and rightly so – that a total relinquishment of the Sinai peninsula ran counter to the party platform. The decision passed was one which everyone knew from the outset to be impossible – support for the Camp David Accords whilst ensuring the continued existence of the settlements in the Rafiah salient. The Labour MKs ultimately voted according to their conscience, as Labour's central committee's condition was not met. It is not by chance that 81 per cent of the former Mapai members supported the Camp David Accords, as did 66 per cent of former Rafi members, while only 40 per cent of former members of Ahdut HaAvoda voted in favour. In light of this we can perhaps better understand why when Geula Cohen established the Tehiya movement advocating not only the annexation of the territories but also the rejection of the peace treaty with Egypt, several leading Labour hawks – former members of Ahdut HaAvoda and Rafi – joined it.

In 1978, with the negotiations between Israel and Egypt stalled, a group of reserve army officers affiliated with the leftist parties established the Peace Now movement. They held a series of demonstrations, succeeded in arousing public opinion, and attracted the attention of the international media and the support of world public opinion. Peace Now was the peace camp's answer to Gush Emunim. Both comprised young people in their late twenties and early thirties, idealists who, unlike the political parties, did not demand appointments or positions for themselves – on both sides of the political spectrum, idealistic and educated youth from good homes.

The State of Israel had found a paramount issue for real ideological debate, after the earlier ideological issues had lost their importance. During the 1960s and 1970s Labour never dreamt of 'Socialism Now' or of the nationalization of the means of production, while the Likud did not demand a completely free market, and even the matter of relations with Germany was already behind them. The future of the territories has since 1967 become the central, virtually the only issue which divides the Israeli public, and which in the late 1970s shaped the political map in Israel. This is an ideological issue in which each side believes that its solution is the true cure for the ills of Israeli society.

The left believes that relinquishing the territories will restore Israel to the family of nations, release Israel from its tremendous defence expenditures, put an end to the situation in which Israel enjoys cheap Arab labour and thus prevent the exploitation of the Arabs, obliging Israel to carry out modernization and automation. Peace between Israel and the Arabs, according to this approach, will allow Israel to obtain extensive international credit that will enable it to absorb the masses of immigrants arriving from the Soviet Union. The vast resources that will be freed from defence will be directed to education, health and culture, and will allow for more equitable social expenditure.

The right, on the other hand, believes that the left is advocating a short-sighted approach and, if enough time is allowed to elapse for sufficient Jewish immigrants to arrive, then the demographic problem will be reduced, the danger of losing the Jewish majority in Israel will disappear, and the old Zionist dream of Jewish settlement throughout the land will be fulfilled, especially in the areas of strongest Jewish historical ties – Judaea and Samaria. Withdrawal from these areas means withdrawal from the heart of the country and proof of Israeli weakness. Even if a peace treaty is signed in exchange, it will soon be violated because the Palestinians do not want several thousand square kilometres, they want the entire land of Israel.

It could cynically be said that if the problem of the territories did not exist, it would have had to be invented for the sake of Israeli ideological debate. In any event, Israeli society, which was characterized by sharp ideological rifts from the 1930s to the 1950s, and which had begun to formulate a post-ideological consensus in the 1960s, has, since the mid-1970s, returned to sharp, total ideological dissent, and this has produced a new mobilization of personnel to the political system and redivided Israeli society.

By the nature of things, any ideological debate produces its own extremists. The year 1982 was marked by particularly radical views, with the major cause of ferment being the Lebanon war, which many viewed as unnecessary. The transformation of a brief military operation into a prolonged war with hundreds of victims, and especially the massacre of the refugees in the Sabra and Shatilla camps by the Christians, enabled Peace Now to organize their first joint political action with the establishment Labour Party, which had previously always shunned demonstrations. The 400,000 people who participated in the largest demonstration in Israeli history created a new reality, and ultimately forced the government to appoint a commission of inquiry into the events at Sabra and Shatilla. The demonstrators were drawn from the 'haves' – kibbutz members and the well-to-do of the cities – who demonstrated that they, too, could go out on to the streets to achieve their goals. The participation of Shimon Peres and Yitzhak Rabin accorded legitimacy to this type of political activity, which had until then been the domain of extremist social or political protest groups.

Peace Now held a demonstration in Jerusalem shortly afterwards, which ended with the throwing of a grenade and the death of one of the participants. This greatly aggravated left-right relations in Israel, which were then further exacerbated by the surprise exposure of a Jewish underground in 1982. Members of this underground group injured several Palestinian mayors in the territories, killed a number of Palestinians at the Islamic college in Hebron, and planned to blow up the al-Aqsa mosque on the Temple Mount in Jerusalem. The majority of them were young religious Israelis who had served in senior ranks in the army. Most belonged to Gush Emunim and lived in the occupied territories. At a certain stage they concluded that the supposedly nationalist Begin government was in effect powerless, and that they must take matters into their own hands in order to establish order in the territories and to 'correct' the anomalous situation whereby a mosque stands on the site held most sacred by the Jews.

The members of the underground were sentenced to prison for varying terms, from several years to life imprisonment. All Israelis dissociated themselves from the actions of the men, but while the right expressed understanding for their motives, the left was shocked by the very fact that such an organization could arise in Israel. The authorities treated the group with silk gloves. This was a new type of offender – with no criminal past, religiously observant, with family and distinguished military record. The surprise was less at the actions of the underground than at the people who comprised it. These were not new immigrants far removed from the Israeli experience who brought their extremism from abroad, nor obviously disturbed people, but rather young men from the very heart of Israeli society. The right exerted strong pressure on the President to pardon them, and ultimately the entire group was released within less than seven years, with the murderers among them being released at the end of 1990.

Another radical phenomenon on the right was the activity of a group which called itself the Sicarii, after the group by this name which engaged in violence during the Second Temple period in ancient Israel. Those identified with this group threatened leftist elements by phone, sent them letters with bullet casings, and burnt the front doors of the homes of well-known members of the Israeli left.

The radical right in Israel is related to Gush Emunim, to Rabbi Kahane's movement (though he himself was assassinated by an Arab in New York in 1990) and to the Moledet movement established in 1988, which advocates the voluntary transfer of Arabs from Israel. None of these groups advocate violence, but they tend to 'understand' individuals who engage in violent action because of what they perceive as the government's weakness. When the murderers of the Jewish underground were released from prison, representatives of the right-wing organizations waited for them outside the prison walls and danced with them on their shoulders in front of the television cameras. Here was public legitimation of the most serious infringement against the legitimacy of the governing institutions in Israel.

The extreme left in Israel also received reinforcement in 1982, primarily against the background of the war in Lebanon. Their demonstrations were directed both inwards, for domestic consumption by the citizens of Israel, and outwards, to the citizens of the world. More and more signs in English appeared at these demonstrations, obviating the need for translators. Dozens of new groups emerged, whose main message was that the old and legitimate tools were no longer useful, and that new types of activity should be found. They bore characteristic names: Ad Kan ('no further'), Yesh G'vul ('there is a limit'), etc. Only they know how to define precisely the differences between them.

The leftist organizations gathered further momentum with the outbreak of the Palestinian uprising in the territories in December

1987 – the intifada. Faced with the IDF treatment of the Palestinians, and especially of the heroes of the intifada – the stone-throwing children – dozens of reserve soldiers, as well as several in regular army units, refused to serve in the territories. Refusal to serve was not a new phenomenon in the Israeli army; what was new was its scope. During the intifada period the number of habitual offenders reached fifteen and they were repeatedly sentenced to several months in prison. Some of the leftist groups, while not encouraging conscientious objectors, 'understand' them. Even the CRM (Citizens' Rights Movement) held a serious debate on whether or not the time had come to recognize conscientious objection as a legitimate phenomenon. While the debate ended in its rejection, the very fact that it was debated accorded it partial legitimacy and served as a clear signal that if the situation should continue and soldiers were forced to act in the territories against their conscience, a different decision might be adopted.

Dr Ehud Sprinzak, who specialized in the study of delegitimation in the world and in Israel in particular, distinguishes between essential and procedural consensus. He claims that there has never been an essential consensus in Israel, and that the stability of Israeli society stemmed from a procedural consensus. However, such phenomena as Gush Emunim delegitimized even the rules of the game, thus rendering society more fragile. While Sprinzak does indeed point out a phenomenon which it is hard to ignore, I am not convinced that this is a one-way process. Rather, it seems to me a circular pattern; there is a significant ideological consensus in Israel, which comes to the fore whenever the issue of immigration gains prominence. The readiness of an entire society to make economic sacrifices in order to absorb masses of immigrants is quite a rare phenomenon. Even in West Germany it has become apparent that the people are prepared to go a long way in order to prevent a massive influx from the east – and these are their brothers and neighbours, who speak the same language. In Israel, where the immigrants speak different languages, are in many cases more educated than the Israeli norm, and pose a real threat to job opportunities in a country which suffers from unemployment, there is nevertheless a real openness towards immigrants and a tremendous willingness to volunteer to help them. Only on the fringes of society are there a few voices calling for preference for young Israelis in employment and housing.

The evolution in methods of protest does not necessarily involve delegitimation. There have been manifestations of delegitimation in the past – a religious underground in the 1950s, the assassination of Kasztner, and more. On the other hand, mass demonstrations not directed against personal grievances but rather to express public protest, are a relatively new phenomenon. The participants are not necessarily from radical elements, but ordinary citizens, primarily of the middle class. Thus, for example, during the coalition talks with the ultra-Orthodox parties in 1990, a broad public movement emerged, calling for a reform of the Israeli governmental system so that the small parties could not extract far-reaching concessions from the party forming a government. Several very large demonstrations were held, and about half a million people signed a petition for electoral reform which was submitted to the President. This mass movement succeeded in exerting enough pressure on members of Knesset to initiate legislation for the direct election of the prime minister by the electorate (but could not convince the Knesset to enact the law). The use of mass demonstrations and petitions on matters of principle has become more frequent in recent years, proving highly effective both in influencing the decision-makers and in expressing a legitimate form of protest. Manifestations of delegitimation, such as violence on the right or conscientious objection on the left, have in recent years reached a new high, but it would be mistaken to view this as a growing phenomenon.

Another characteristic of Israeli protest is the prominent role played by army reserve officers, who accord a certain legitimacy even to acts of delegitimation. The officers in Israeli society are a focus of broad identification (excluding non-Zionist circles – the ultra-Orthodox Jews and Israeli Arabs). Gush Emunim has therefore highlighted the fact that many of its members are reserve officers; Peace Now, which was inaugurated with the 'officers' letter', did the same. It was a policy continued by the Jewish underground, and even several leaders of the electoral reform movement stressed their military past. The recent public action for an Israeli withdrawal from the Gaza strip began when reserve officers and soldiers serving in Gaza accorded the struggle legitimacy by writing an open letter to the prime minister. It is very hard to present such a group as pacifist or as favouring concessions, when they declare that they will continue to carry out every order, will not violate army discipline, and will not refuse to serve in the occupied territories.

The rapid institutionalization of ideologies in Israel renders any change very difficult. The idea often becomes an institution, and the institution an ideology, and any organizational change is viewed as a value change which must be opposed. The most salient example of such institutionalization and of the difficulty of introducing change is related to Israel's shift from Yishuv to state. The fact that such a central body as the Jewish Agency for Palestine (which was established to represent world Jewry before the British mandate authorities and to involve as well non-Zionists in the building of Jewish society in Palestine) exists to this day, having not been abolished with the establishment of the state, when there would seem to have been no further justification for its existence, raises serious questions.

The symbol of Israeli institutionalization is undoubtedly the Histadrut, the General Federation of Workers – originally Jewish workers – in Israel. For some thirty years it served as a 'state in the making', including a defence force (the Haganah and later the Palmach), a labour exchange, health services, education (the 'Labour stream' and childcare centres), housing, employment (Hevrat HaOvdim), entertainment, culture, and social security. Although a special Histadrut committee which operated from late 1947 to early 1948 decided that with the establishment of the state many functions would be transferred from the Histadrut to the state, most of these decisions were never implemented. To this day, the Histadrut maintains health insurance and services, and there is no national health law. Over the years, the Histadrut transformed its remaining services into an ideology of mutual aid, maintaining that to harm any one of them would lead to the collapse of the entire structure.

Younger bodies have also undergone rapid institutionalization. Gush Emunim, which began as a young anti-establishment protest movement, set up an economic system and settlement movement of its own, as well as a political organization which, by the nature of things, comprises disputes, differences of opinion, institutionalized norms and anti-establishment elements who oppose the movement's establishment. Even a movement such as the Citizens' Rights Movement, which in 1988 won peak political support (five Knesset seats), has become institutionalized over the years, with an oligarchy which is returned to the Knesset every four years, and a younger opposition which protests against the transformation of this protest movement into an establishment party.

The Labour Party cannot escape the establishment image, although since 1977 it has headed the government for only two years, and even then within the framework of the National Unity Government. Its unbroken control of the Histadrut (since 1920), its longtime control of the Zionist movement (1933–1978 and since 1987), and its many years at the head of the state (1948–1977) as a dominant party without which it was impossible to form a coalition, created such a strong establishment image that years after the party had gone into opposition, many citizens continued to blame it for the ills of government.

This party, which constitutes an imperfect merging of several earlier parties, with a delicate balance between doves and hawks and a continuing dispute between Shimon Peres and Yitzhak Rabin who compete for the party leadership every few years, only amends its platform when compelled by outside developments, and does nothing to change its social worldview although most of its leaders are aware of its anachronism and of the need for refurbishment. (Its fifth congress in 1991 was an exception, when changes were achieved because of internal demand.) The Labour Party represents the interests of kibbutzim and moshavim, of employers and employees, of agriculture and industry, of pensioners, of the Histadrut health fund, and more. Representing so many opposites greatly limits its ability to launch a strong effort on any particular issue. Pluralism has become an ideology in the Labour Party, with a considerable measure of justification, for only through such pluralism can large parties exist. However, there is apparently a certain limit beyond which the 'supermarket', as the gamut of views within Labour is called, produces internal paralysis. The most obvious outward expression of the institutionalization of the Labour Party is its ageing. Labour's voters are significantly older than the average age of the Israeli electorate; most of its members are well past their prime; and it has few young elected representatives.

The astonishing success of the Labour Party in the past seems to explain its latterday weakness. Its demonstrated ability to present ideological goals and to realize a large number of them – making the desert bloom, introducing collective agriculture (as against the individualistic outlook of the right), enabling the peripheral communities to flourish, founding a large workers' organization which supplies virtually all their needs, building a highly effective army and maintaining rapid economic growth which exceeded that of most countries at the same time, and with rapid technological progress based in part on an overall vision and well-defined worldview – has convinced the Labour movement that not only the values formulated in the past but also the tools created then must remain unchanged for the sake of continued future success. Part of Labour's success in 1992 should be attributed to changes in its ideological platform.

The Role of Political Parties and their Effect on Israeli Society

The first political parties were established in Palestine at the beginning of the century, long before the founding of the state. Their role extended far beyond ideological expression and the attempt to realize this ideology through parliamentary means, as was the case in other democratic countries. The parties were organizations which accorded their members services generally provided by the state or by private economic enterprises. The parties were social organizations which helped the individual understand his place in his environment. The new immigrant arriving in the country identified himself with a political party. The HaPoel HaTzair party had a hostel in Jaffa to which members were directed, while other lodgings were affiliated with Poalei Zion.

The parties played a central role in immigrant absorption. The formula was very similar to that of the Democratic Party in the United States during the years of mass immigration – services and jobs in exchange for votes. Party membership, especially in the ruling parties – Mapai, the NRP, etc. – was a tool for obtaining the means to earn a living. The ruling parties' control of the institutions that provided housing, employment, and education enabled them easily to win the votes of the immigrants who needed these services, and during the early decades it was very difficult not to belong to a party.

One of the most salient phenomena of the early years of Israeli statehood was the 'party key'. This method served to delegitimize extra-party elements while strengthening the existing political structure. The party key determined who was sent as an emissary of the Zionist Organization to the diaspora; how many immigrants were sent to settlements affiliated with each political movement; how much funding was to be provided by the state to finance Knesset election campaigns. Some of these arrangements – such as party funding – are anchored in legislation, others in official agreements, and still others in tacit understandings between the parties. Allocation by party key is the only method acceptable to the rival parties.

On the surface, this would seem to be a fair arrangement, no one party being accorded an advantage over the others. In fact, it is an agreement between the large parties (the Communist and ultra-Orthodox parties were not included in most of these agreements) which enhances their power and obliges individuals and organizations to identify themselves along party lines. The party key explains why to a large extent Israeli voting patterns did not change significantly with the mass immigration of the late 1940s and early 1950s. Although the new immigrants exceeded the existing population in numbers, the representatives of the establishment with whom these new immigrants had dealings were chosen according to the party key which reflected the earlier division of power. This influenced many of the immigrants who had no previous party affiliation to support the party these selected few represented.

In the Arab sector, where people were barred from the Labour Party until the 1970s, the votes were mostly divided among the left-wing parties. These leftist parties comprised several short-lived lists associated with the Labour Party, established prior to elections, which elected several representatives to the Knesset and then ceased to function until the next election, the United Workers' Party (Mapam), and the Communists. The Labour Party regularly received a majority of the votes, and its supporters won job advancement and coveted licenses. Those who openly supported the Communist Party found it hard to find employment, especially in teaching.

According to the socialist worldview, the left-wing parties were and continue to be mass parties with an apparatus that includes an organization and information department, a municipal department, departments for youth, women and minorities, an international relations department, etc. The apparatus operates both at the national offices and on the periphery, in some 100 party branches throughout the country. In addition to this geographical distribution, the party also maintains a presence in places of employment. The various parties operated 'party cells' in large plants, public institutions and government ministries. Such cells exist to this day, but since the Likud's rise to power in 1977 there has been a significant erosion in the intensity of their activity. During the early decades of statehood these cells flourished, and their elected leaders enjoyed a position of power within the organization. The party cells served as another framework for political debate, and leading party figures occasionally appeared before them; but they were primarily pressure groups for the advancement of employees affiliated with the particular party (most notably the ruling Mapai party).

The party cells in the public institutions, the Histadrut factories and the government ministries created an alternative track for job advancement. It formed one of three parallel options: ability, pressure by the workers' committee which was primarily on the basis of seniority, and pressure by the party cell. An employee of proven ability, who received the support of the workers' committee and the party cell, knew that a desired appointment was in his pocket; but in many cases the committee and cell pressure was exerted on behalf of people who lacked the appropriate abilities.

The party cells in the government ministries enjoyed a unique status. On the one hand, an effort has been made, especially since the 1960s, to build a professional and apolitical civil service; on the other, the party cell has continued to operate and to keep precise membership records – though it was obvious who did not belong. The party cell did not require bureaucratic mediators (personnel director, director-general, etc.) to reach the ear of the minister. Its leaders could always appear before the minister and complain that, either with or without his knowledge, members of rival parties had been given senior positions which 'our people' had for years been waiting for – to the ridicule of all. They have been faithful party members for years, walking their feet off on the eve of elections, and when the time comes to pay, they are forgotten. The cell leaders always claim that failure to advance party members has the effect of alienating potential members, because it demonstrates that there is no advantage in party membership.

The party cell system created an entire group of people who preferred not to display openly their identification with the opposition, and some of them became 'forced converts', namely employees who posed as Mapai members in order to achieve advancement. After the Likud victory in 1977 there were so many people who suddenly remembered that they had been on the *Altalena* (the arms ship brought by the IZL in 1948), that there would have been no room left on it; it became a standing joke. The truth is that a large number of those who declared their allegiance to the Likud at that time had really supported it throughout the years, but preferred to conceal the fact in order not to lose their jobs. The supposed Mapai members were not just opportunists who had taken advantage of a political constellation, but people who lived in the shadow of a dominant party, knowing that failure to identify with it would seriously damage their professional careers for decades to come.

The democratization of the large parties which occurred in the 1980s, whereby candidates to the Knesset were elected by the parties' central committees rather than by appointments committees, accorded the central committee members a new status. They now demanded a price for their support of elected representatives in the form of appointments to various positions, whether directors general of government corporations or tenured employees in enterprises in which the party representatives exerted influence. By the nature of things, central committee members employed in a ministry headed by a representative of their party demanded advancement, hinting that the minister's future was in their hands. This was a new situation, with graver implications than in the past. No longer was this merely a question of party membership; now a minister's political future depended upon members of the civil service working under him. Only in 1990 did the Knesset pass a law barring government employees in the four highest ranks from being members of a party's central committee. If ways are not found to circumvent the law, this problem will be somewhat alleviated, although many lower-ranking employees will continue to wield undue political influence. It would seem that democratization has created an unforeseen problem, the sole solution of which may lie in further widening the circle of those who choose the party candidates, through the adoption of a system of primaries (as has been adopted in the Labour Party). In this way, the electing body will be so broad that any demands for individual reward could be ignored.

While the 1950s were characterized by the clear politicization of the Israeli civil service, the 1960s and 1970s were marked by an opposite trend. However, the 1977 Likud victory set the clocks back, creating renewed politicization, as though to fill a longtime void; this was further aggravated by the process of democratization discussed above. Israel once again suffered from a high level of politicization in the civil service. Positions which in the past had been apolitical in nature, were now assigned by party affiliation. Directors-general of government ministries, who in the late 1970s were usually veteran civil servants, now became blatantly political appointments. The position of cabinet secretary, which had been totally apolitical, became a party appointment when the new prime minister, Menachem Begin, appointed a young journalist very active in the Likud to this post. Five years later the post was again given to a party member, and in 1984, when Shimon Peres was elected prime minister, he too chose a political appointee. As that appointee was myself, I can only say of my predecessors that they filled the post admirably, transforming it into a key position. Yet for decades this had been a post filled by a senior government official.

The board of directors of the Israel Broadcasting Authority, which until 1977 had been a modest body which discussed policy behind closed doors, has since then become a kind of mini-parliament where deliberations and appointments are clearly political. The government corporations, whose directorates are appointed by two government ministers (the minister responsible for the corporation and the finance minister), became an inexhaustible source of political appointments for people who in many cases lacked the necessary qualifications.

We can say that the Likud, after decades outside government, took full advantage of its legal prerogative of making political appointments to state positions in order to fill a longtime void, during which the Likud had not received its share of the public employment pie. In so doing, they set Israeli public administration back many years. Political appointments characterized not only the highest echelons of government administration. Even in the lower ranks jobs were given to party members, many of whom were unsuited to their positions. The State Comptroller has cited this phenomenon, but it continues to recur. In the Foreign Ministry, for example, there were a number of political appointments which had always been filled from within the senior ministry staff – not only ambassadorships, but more junior posts too.

The ultra-Orthodox parties gained prominence in 1984 and demonstrated surprising political strength in 1988, when for the first time in Israel's history they won more than 10 per cent of the Knesset seats. When these parties joined the coalition, they cited three justifications: larger allocations to their sector, especially in the area of education; the appointment of their people to influential positions; and religious legislation. The coalition agreements signed with them made explicit reference to positions below the level of director-general. These were posts which are generally determined by tender, not appointed personally by the minister. In this manner, most of the ministries in the hands of the ultra-Orthodox parties, whether under a minister or deputy minister (some of these parties do not serve as cabinet ministers on ideological grounds, a relic of their historical opposition to the existence of a secular Jewish state and the desire to minimalize friction with it) were filled with people affiliated with them: assistants to the minister and director-general, bureau chiefs and secretaries, as well as relatively high-ranking posts in the bureaucratic hierarchy.

The entry of the ultra-Orthodox Shas party, born only in 1984, into the political system created the need to satisfy a third wave of 'hunger' for budgets and positions, after many years during which the Sephardi ultra-Orthodox community had been alienated from both the Ashkenazi ultra-Orthodox and the secular establishments. Shas, as a party which determined the fate of the government coalition, seized everything it could demand as 'payment'. In this hungry race for appointments and for funds for schools affiliated with the movement, members of Shas crossed normative if not legal barriers, inviting both the sharp criticism of the State Comptroller and intensive police investigation. While this criticism was directed primarily against its financial activities, Shas's staffing of senior ministry positions was no less problematic. These people came almost exclusively from the world of religious study without even minimal formal secular education, and the vast majority of them had not served in the IDF – the entrance certificate to Israeli society.

Sociologically, it can perhaps be argued that the entry of these new groups into government contributed functionally to the socio-political integration of largely alienated population groups into the Israeli establishment and the dominant culture, penetrating to the very heart of the establishment, which was in turn altered by their entry. Although the Likud was also headed by Ashkenazim, the Sephardi community felt that it represented them more than any other party, and viewed its electoral victory in 1977 as a great achievement. For the first time, they felt that people like themselves, who had immigrated in the 1950s, very few of whom had reached key positions within the Labour Party, now found themselves in power, filling government ministries and directorates of government corporations. The Likud victory was a source of pride to them, and they viewed it as a victory over the Ashkenazi establishment which had treated them patronizingly, tried to change them and to adapt them to its culture, and posed impossible conditions for acceptance of certain posts. The Likud, in contrast, was willing to forgo many conditions and to open certain positions to them, even if they lacked formal qualifications.

The Ashkenazi leadership of the Likud was composed largely of the former IZL general staff and their families, who formed a relatively small and homogeneous group. They, too, suspected of secessionist and subversive tendencies, had also largely been kept out of government jobs. Having nurtured strong hostility towards the Mapai leadership under David Ben-Gurion, and having waited thirty years for the closed doors of the government corridors to open before them, they took them by storm.

The integration of the leaders and supporters of Shas was even more revolutionary. Unlike the Likud, whose members had been part of mainstream Israeli life – school, military service, etc. – they lived wholly in the world of the yeshivot (academies for religious study). Most of them were not exposed to the secular media (television, radio, press), lived in communities where they maintained a large measure of autonomy, and felt a deep sense of deprivation. The founding of Shas and the meteoric entry of its leaders into the Knesset and the cabinet brought a large group of ultra-Orthodox Sephardim into friction with the establishment in the highest echelons. The Shas MKs were at first surprising and alien creatures on the Knesset scene. Not all of them viewed themselves as subject to coalition discipline, and several rarely appeared in the Knesset, viewing it as a waste of time better spent in religious study. Later, especially during their second term, they became part of the Knesset, filling important parliamentary positions. Even if Shas eventually becomes a passing episode because of its internal problems and the investigations being conducted against its leaders, it is impossible to ignore its contribution, introducing as it did an important and deprived population group into Israeli life.

The story of Shas has yet to be written, and it is certainly one of the most interesting stories of Israeli politics. Part of the public criticism, as well as the criticism of the State Comptroller against this party, is related to its apparent misuse of its new-found power and of the institution of 'protekzia'. 'Protekzia' is one of the most common and despised words in the Israeli political lexicon, signifying the practice of according preference to people with personal ties to those in positions of power. It is evident in the priority accorded by former immigrants who have already become part of the establishment, over newer immigrants in the areas of housing, employment and welfare.

With the founding of the state, the Israeli establishment – the Jewish Agency, the Zionist Organization and the National Council – was composed largely of Ashkenazi members of the Labour movement, and the new Ashkenazi immigrants relied on the help of their friends and relatives within the establishment. 'Protekzia' was practised not only by the establishment, but also by the veteran population who could accord their kindred temporary shelter. When the War of Independence ended, it was followed by a mass wave of immigration, and the newcomers were at first housed in homes abandoned by the Arabs who had fled the country, and later in temporary transit camps. It was the Ashkenazim among them, however, who found their way sooner to the large cities, where they lived for a time with their relatives already established in the country; it was they who eventually found jobs and housing, while the immigrants from Yemen, Iraq and North Africa remained in the transit camps, dependent on the establishment. They waited their turn to receive jobs in the relief work invented by the government for the new immigrants (such as afforestation projects) and for an apartment in the periphery. While both Ashkenazi and Sephardi immigrants were sent to transit camps in the peripheral areas, it was the Sephardim who remained there until the 1960s when the development towns, grew up, and it is the Sephardim who remain there to this day. The more mobile Ashkenazim moved to the centre of the country, where much more interesting job opportunities were opened to them.

The Sephardim, who came from a different normative framework than that prevailing in Israel, in contrast to the Ashkenazim who were virtually coming home, watched with envy as the latter left the transit camps and settled in the centre. They internalized this sense of oppression during the years of dependence, and externalized it only about twenty years later by supporting and identifying with the opposition party and bringing it to power. The first to express this feeling, as early as the 1950s, was Ephraim Kishon, considered the greatest Israeli humorist, in his play *Salah Shabbati*. The play depicts the tensions and normative gaps between Ashkenazim and Sephardim, describes Ashkenazi patronage, the tremendous dependence of the immigrants from Arab countries on the establishment, and the political payment at the ballot box in exchange for an apartment. But the fact that the play was written by a new immigrant from Hungary, who had quickly found his way to the centre, worked at first for a Hungarian newspaper and was soon adopted by the Hebrew press, perhaps says it all – even Sephardi protest at the time was written by an Ashkenazi.

The change of government in 1977, brought about largely by the Sephardi voters, was a kind of revenge against the Ashkenazi establishment, and accorded the second Sephardi generation a sense of pride in their own power. Now 'protekzia' was practised by all. People who had arrived in the 1950s as children or young adults, and who had remained in the development towns, now occupied central positions in the socio-economic ministries and provided their electorate with the benefits of 'protekzia'. Shas's entry into politics in 1984 (with four Knesset seats) and 50 per cent increase in strength in 1988 was a kind of ultra-Orthodox revolution, bringing new faces to important ministries to provide 'protekzia' for the Sephardi yeshiva students.

The methods of recruitment into the various parties' leaderships differ from one party to the next. In the Labour movement, kibbutz members have enjoyed high prominence, occupying central positions in the Knesset and the cabinet. While the importance of the kibbutzim has declined, both in the Labour Party and in Mapam, their members are still far better represented in these party leaderships than befits their share of the population. The moshavim have also been represented in the Labour Party leadership since the establishment of the state. These two sectors submit their candidates to the party prior to the drawing up of the Knesset list; these are usually people who have developed within their respective movements but have not received broad public exposure. The small appointments committee which functioned until 1988 used to place these candidates on the Knesset list as the representatives of collective agriculture, always viewed as the acme of the Labour movement. Kibbutz members have filled important positions in Israeli government, and the higher one ascends the power pyramid, the greater their share of the power.

In the last Labour government, headed by Yitzhak Rabin (1974–77), Yigal Allon, a kibbutz member, was Deputy Prime Minister and Foreign Minister; Israel Galili, also a kibbutz member, was a very influential minister without portfolio; Aharon Yadlin, Minister of Education and Culture and Shlomo Rosen Minister of Immigration and Absorption, were both kibbutz members; and Aharon Ouzan, member of a moshav, was Minister of Agriculture and Communications. They all represented the Labour Alignment. In addition, there was another moshav member, Michael Hazani, who served in the coalition as the NRP Minister of Welfare. All in all, the cabinet included six kibbutz or moshav members; this represents more than 25 per cent of the cabinet, while the percentage of Israel's population living in these collective settlements never exceeded 7 per cent. It is interesting to note that many other members of that cabinet had at one time been members of a kibbutz or moshav; several were born in moshavim, and others had spent many years in a kibbutz (Shlomo Hillel, Gad Ya'acobi, Avraham Ofer and Shimon Peres).

The Histadrut offers another channel for recruitment into the Labour Party leadership. People who rose within the ranks of the trade unions, and even some who reached the top of the Histadrut pyramid, have found their way into the Knesset, and even the cabinet. The secretary-general of the Histadrut is usually a member of Knesset; in the past this was arranged by the appointments committee, and in 1988 the secretary-general was included among the six MKs who did not stand for election in the party's central committee but were guaranteed a place on the Knesset list.

Party workers operate in a closely related channel – people who climbed within the party apparatus, or occupied positions in the local Histadrut branches or on the municipal level. In the 1950s, a triangle was created in many localities comprising the secretary of the Mapai party branch, the secretary of the local workers' council, and the mayor. One might imagine that the local branch secretary wielded the most power, as it was the local Mapai secretariat which chose the party's candidates for the latter two positions. In many cases, however, each corner of the triangle was a power centre, so that a pattern of rivalry and even hostility developed that was characteristic of a triangular relationship. And Mapai never adopted the Bolshevik model in which the party exerted the most power while less influential people were sent to the legislative and executive institutions. Thus, the most important and locally powerful position was actually that of the mayor, followed by the secretary of the workers' council, and finally the local branch secretary. A fairly typical Mapai party worker's career would be marked by a gradual advancement from one position to the next, after a fairly long tenure in each, with election to the Knesset either the natural continuation of his career or interrupting it at an earlier stage.

The army also provides an important channel for leadership recruitment. In the 1950s generals from Israel's War of Independence adorned the Knesset lists of the Labour movement, and several of them reached the cabinet. Following the Six Day War, senior army officers became even more popular, and several moved directly from the army into the cabinet without going through the party apparatus, and even without having previously served in the Knesset.

The university track is relatively new, because of the traditional reservations about the academic world in the Labour movement. While learning has always been valued, formal higher education has for many years been viewed as 'bourgeois'. Some of the pioneering immigrants who came to the country in the early decades of the century interrupted their university studies to do so; they never completed their degrees, believing that they should engage in more important and real work, such as draining swamps and farming. People who arrived in the country with academic degrees often preferred not to use their titles, and even concealed them.

Until the 1960s, there was a qualified and even negative attitude in the kibbutzim towards academic study. Sometimes the kibbutz would consent to a member's request to study at the university, especially if his request corresponded to the kibbutz's needs, but often people would leave the kibbutz if such requests were denied. During those years, the kibbutzim opposed sitting for matriculation exams or receiving a matriculation certificate, thus denying the young people their chance of going to university. Those who wanted to study were sent to courses conducted in 'seminars' within the framework of the Labour movement (Mapai's Beit Berl, Ahdut HaAvoda's Efal, or Mapam's Givat Haviva), where the course of study varied between several months and two years. A change in the attitude towards higher education occurred in the 1970s. Kibbutzim began to send significant numbers of their members to university, matriculation exams became standard at the end of the twelfth grade, and members were even allowed to study subjects not vital to the kibbutz.

During the early years of the state, several intellectuals adorned the Mapai Knesset list. These were veteran professors, such as Professor Ben-Zion Dinur, who was Minister of Education in the early years of statehood, and Professor Dov Sadan, who later served in the Knesset. Only in the 1980s did politically active senior academic faculty members begin to appear on the Labour Knesset list, chosen by the appointments committee and later, in greater numbers, by the party's central committee.

The political leadership of the Herut movement in the early years of the state was composed of the IZL general staff, virtually intact. Later the leaders of Lehi were added to the Knesset faction. And these former leaders of the underground movements were joined by several veterans of the Revisionist movement.

The Knesset representatives of the second component of the present-day Likud, the General Zionists, were often mayors and heads of the farmers' association. Lawyers have also been prominent on the Likud list (including Begin himself), in part because the movement remained for many years outside the establishment and consequently its leaders did not hold positions in the Histadrut, the Jewish Agency, or even in their own party which was structured as a skeleton party.

At the beginning of the 1970s a new channel for political recruitment was opened in the Likud – the IDF. The first to take this route were Ezer Weizman and Ariel Sharon, as candidates to the Knesset or as mayor, but they were followed by others. Most of these officers joined the Likud at a time when the party was growing in size, beginning to appear as an alternative ruling party of the future. At this stage the party was also reinforced by young Sephardim who had demonstrated leadership in the development towns and had been rejected by the Labour Party establishment. Some were already serving as mayors, and continued in their municipal roles even after election to the Knesset. This group continued to gain strength, providing the second generation of immigrants who had arrived in Israel from the Arab countries in the 1950s with a focus for identification. This generation, having freed themselves of dependence on the Labour Party establishment, expressed their protest at what they viewed as an insufficient effort to integrate their parents and themselves twenty years earlier, by casting their votes for the Likud.

However, the most salient, most interesting, and probably the most influential group within the Likud are the so-called Herut 'princes'. Herut lived for many years as though enclosed in a bubble within Israeli society. In a society which virtually worshipped Ben-Gurion, they viewed the Prime Minister – the father of the nation in the eyes of the veteran Israelis and a kind of messiah in the eyes of many immigrants from Middle Eastern countries – as having erred and misled others. Their esteem was accorded wholly to the late leader Ze'ev Jabotinsky – statesman, poet and writer – in whose works they were well-versed; and to the young populist leader, Menachem Begin, with dark hair and moustache, who threatened, promised and inspired the masses. The 'fighting family', as the IZL had called itself, continued to exist, in the belief that one day this small, right-wing movement would become a real alternative to the undefeated Mapai and parties to its left, which together formed a large majority in the Knesset.

The special lore of the Herut movement (the use of 'Tel Hai' as a form of greeting, such songs as 'Two Banks of the Jordan', the militaristic Betar youth movement, addressing Begin as 'commander', etc); the difficulties encountered by Herut supporters in advancing within the political system because of the suspicions which still adhered to them ('secessionists', an underground movement, delegitimized during the dispute over German reparations, etc.); combined with the fact that for decades no outsiders (retired army officers or others) had joined the party because this meant non-advancement: all this created a feeling of an ever-suffering minority which had to stand united against the whole world, while Ben-Gurion maintained that he would form a coalition with neither Herut nor the Communists.

The Herut Knesset list remained virtually unchanged for many years. It was composed of a group of people who had been in their late thirties with the establishment of the state and who felt themselves to be young even after their best years had passed, and who felt they could function without outside reinforcements. At the same time, Begin saw to it that anyone who showed signs of questioning his leadership or of being prepared to challenge him was removed from the movement.

In the mid-1970s, faced with general disappointment at the performance of the Labour Party in the Yom Kippur War and corruption scandals within the Histadrut, Herut saw an opportunity to grow significantly as a movement. Some members of the 'fighting family' having passed away and the others having or grown older, the Herut leadership turned to its biological sons and charged them with the task of continuity. The 'princes' – all sons of figures who had served Herut at one time or another in the Knesset, all born in the 1940s, all university educated, all members of the liberal professions (mostly lawyers) – maintain a relatively high degree of solidarity which may enable them successfully to challenge the similarly aged group of Sephardi mayors recruited by Herut during the same period.

Recruitment to the political leadership of the National Religious Party, a party which in the 1970s comprised one tenth of the Knesset and which in recent years has been fighting for survival against the growing ultra-Orthodox parties, takes place within the movement's moshavim and kibbutzim and from among party workers, the younger among them being graduates of the religious Bar-Ilan University.

Historically, the NRP is composed of two movements: Mizrahi, founded in 1902, and HaPoel HaMizrahi, founded in 1922. The heads of Mizrahi were middle-class religious Zionists, Orthodox Jews with a modern religious approach and who had tasted a broader general education. While most of the Mizrahi leaders, like many of the other Zionist leaders, remained in Europe during the early years of the century, HaPoel HaMizrahi was founded in Palestine to meet the needs of the young religious pioneers who arrived there with a similar social outlook to that of the Labour movement but coupled with a desire to maintain a religious way of life. They established an extensive institutional network, affiliated in part with the Histadrut: a settlement movement, economic and financial institutions, a system of schools, press, etc. Their political leaders were on the whole those people who helped to build this network and who grew out of it. The Mizrahi leadership, many of whom came to Palestine after the HaPoel HaMizrahi, were older. They included several ordained rabbis, and held a more rightist worldview than the latter. The two movements merged in 1955, Mizrahi largely being incorporated into HaPoel HaMizrahi.

Most of the young members of the united party – the National Religious Party – were Ashkenazim born in the late 1930s who had undergone a similar socialization process, progressing from state-religious schools, the Bnei Akiva youth movement, religious or yeshiva high school to army service and, Bar-Ilan University. They all wore small knitted skullcaps (in contrast to the black skullcaps worn by their fathers), and indeed in the 1960s they became known as 'the generation of the knitted skullcaps'. They established a very powerful political group which challenged the veteran party leadership. In the late 1970s and 1980s, this group tried, albeit unsuccessfully, to introduce into the party leadership several religious Sephardi figures who had experienced a totally different process of socialization. Some leaders of Gush Emunim, formed from within the NRP, who left the party in the late 1970s have returned to the party leadership, which they view as their natural home. However, just as the new Sephardi MKs failed to bring back the Sephardi voters who had left the NRP in favour of the Sephardi religious parties, so the leaders of Gush Emunim did not manage to bring back the Israeli religious voters from the territories, who preferred the radical right-wing parties.

In the ultra-Orthodox parties, the Knesset list is determined by the spiritual leadership of each party. The oldest among them, Agudat Israel, represents the Ashkenazi ultra-Orthodox mosaic, composed of followers of various Hassidic rabbis and *mitnaqdim* which literally means 'opponents', but which represents the rationalist stream, without a central rabbinic figure, which objects to the blind veneration of the Hassidic rabbis by their followers. Some of the MKs were born in pre-state Palestine, and others arrived in the late 1940s after the Holocaust of European Jewry. All were educated in yeshivot, and many, whether yeshiva heads or students, were sent to the Knesset directly from the world of religious study. Virtually none of them had any secular education, though some received a measure of general learning while serving in the Knesset. Most do not serve in the army, and are thus cut off from what is undoubtedly a central Israeli experience. The ultra-Orthodox MKs enjoy a relatively low status within ultra-Orthodox society, because historically their leaders have objected to overly close ties with the government of Israel, because they do not recognize the legitimacy of the secular Jewish state.

During some thirty years of British mandatory rule, until the establishment of the state, ultra-Orthodox Jewry lived as a separate community, were not registered as part of the organized Jewish community, Knesset Israel, and functioned separately *vis-à-vis* the mandate authorities. In 1947, however, on the eve of the establishment of the state, an agreement was signed between Ben-Gurion as chairman of the Jewish Agency Executive and the heads of ultra-Orthodox Jewry. This established two basic principles: the maintenance of the status quo with regard to the Jewish character of Israeli society, and the adoption of the religious laws of matrimony as official Israeli state law. This agreement allowed the ultra-Orthodox voters to participate in Knesset elections, and enabled their representatives to serve as cabinet ministers, until Agudat Israel quit the coalition in 1951 over the issue of the recruitment of women into the IDF. Throughout the years of Mapai–Labour rule, Agudat Israel did not re-join the government, supporting the coalition selectively according to specific issues and on the basis of promises made in order to assure their support. In 1977 the new prime minister Menachem Begin asked Agudat Israel to join his government. The decision of the Council of Torah Sages – the spiritual leadership of the party – was not to join the cabinet; rather, its representatives were to serve only as deputy ministers, in order not to assume ministerial responsibility for the affairs of a secular society, and in order not to be saddled with collective responsibility.

When the Shas faction entered the Knesset in 1984, this practice was departed from as its members joined the cabinet as ministers. This ultra-Orthodox faction, established out of the sense of discrimination against the Sephardim in the ultra-Orthodox yeshivot, was represented in the Knesset in part by people who had risen within the ranks of the NRP, filling political posts on the municipal level or in different frameworks, and who at some stage had become more Orthodox in practice. These were joined by students who had spent their entire lives in yeshivot, who had not served in the army, and who for the first time in their lives were being exposed to public life – and immediately on the highest level. As already mentioned, some of these did not find their place in the Knesset. They rarely attended sessions, did not take an interest in its work, and disappeared after a single term, opening the door to a group of young people in their thirties who had arrived in Israel from the Arab countries as children. Within a short time, this group succeeded in establishing an educational and economic institutional basis for their party, and exploited their power as coalition members. At the time of writing, some of their actions are being investigated by the police.

The spiritual leader of Shas is Rabbi Ovadia Yosef, former Sephardi Chief Rabbi of Israel, who chooses the party's Knesset list and cabinet ministers. In so doing, he has displayed in the second term of this new party a preference for such dynamic young men as Interior Minister Aryeh Deri, who was appointed to the cabinet in 1988 at the age of only twenty-nine – the youngest of them all. In addition to their dynamism, these men demonstrated an ability to obtain the funds needed to lay the basis for a new school system for Sephardi children in the development towns and urban neighbourhoods, and to win a broader base of support for the new movement.

All ultra-Orthodox MKs accept complete subordination to their spiritual leaders, thus limiting their own role to that of agents, who can merely try to influence the rabbis and no more. Occasionally, this means that these MKs participate in a political move, speaking out in its favour, only in the final event to receive instructions that oblige them to adopt the opposite position and to vote accordingly, with no possibility of appeal. It was the young Shas MKs who encouraged the Labour Alignment to resign from the government in March 1990 and to form a Labour-led government, although they themselves were obliged by their spiritual mentors to turn about-face. Thus, they found themselves supporting the Likud government while Labour, which had resigned, remained in opposition. The most obvious expression of the ultra-Orthodox MKs' powerlessness *vis-à-vis* their spiritual leaders can be found in the context of the dissolution of the National Unity Government; the small ultra-Orthodox party Degel HaTorah (which had split in 1988 from Agudat Israel) wanted to bring down the government and its ageing leader, Rabbi Eliezer Schach, refused. Responding in the roll-call vote in the Knesset plenum on the motion of no-confidence in the Shamir government, MK Rabbi Ravitz announced that he opposed the motion 'with great regret'. Apparently expressing his discontent at the order which he was powerless to change, such a statement was unprecedented in the Knesset. In 1992 Shas, led by Deri, joined the Rabin Government while the Ashkenazi ultra-religious MKs refrained from doing so.

The ultra-Orthodox community, which had been small and marginal in the early years of statehood, and which had never elected more than about six MKs, increased its strength in 1984 and surprised everybody with its 1988 political breakthrough when thirteen representatives were sent to the Knesset. The growth of these parties created public interest in their leadership, their representatives in the Knesset and their political leanings. Thus, for example, it was found that the new ultra-Orthodox parties were characterized by a moderate political approach and support for territorial concessions for the sake of peace, though this issue was not top of its list of priorities.

The large increase in the power of the ultra-Orthodox parties was not the result of religious radicalization within Israeli society. Rather, several of these parties received the votes of secular Sephardim because of various rabbinic invocations and promises. The secret of these parties' strength is based in the exemption of yeshiva students from army service. This is one of the most sensitive issues in Israeli society, related to the great weight of the ultra-Orthodox parties.

After the establishment of the state, the heads of the yeshivot came to David Ben-Gurion and asked that the yeshiva students be allowed to defer their army service until the conclusion of their studies. The Prime Minister, also serving as Defence Minister, was impressed by their argument which proposed that following the destruction of the yeshivot in Europe during the Holocaust, the yeshivot would be relegated to history unless regular study was maintained in Israel. Ben-Gurion approved this arrangement for 400 yeshiva students; the general feeling among the public meanwhile was that the ultra-Orthodox Jews, who preserved the special forms of Eastern Europe (the *shtreimel* – a kind of fur hat – black coats, etc.), were a disappearing world of alien people living within the Zionist state, though opposed to Zionism. They availed themselves of few state services because they had their own courts, their own authorities on Jewish dietary laws, their own school system, a communal charity system, etc.; and they conversed among themselves in Yiddish because Hebrew, in their view, was to be used only in the synagogue. I remember being taken by my parents, when we visited Jerusalem, to the ultra-Orthodox neighbourhoods so that they could show me something I would not see when I grew up. The children running through the narrow streets, speaking Yiddish and twirling their side-curls, would no longer, they believed, resemble their fathers. My parents were wrong.

Ben-Gurion's consent to defer army service for several hundred yeshiva students became one of the major reasons behind the surprising growth of the ultra-Orthodox community. In effect, deferment became virtual exemption from service, because the students would inform the IDF of the conclusion of their studies at an age when they were no longer eligible for recruitment, or when they were required to serve for a brief period of three months instead of three years. Over the years the quota of yeshiva students exempted from the army was increased; and later deferment was granted to all yeshiva students. The effect of this decision – adopted in 1980 – was to encourage all children from ultra-Orthodox families to become yeshiva students. Students were accepted to the different yeshivot in accordance with their abilities. However, whereas in the past most young people had sought to earn a livelihood and only a few had devoted their lives to yeshiva study, now a place was guaranteed for everybody in order to enable them to avoid army service. The high birth-rate of the ultra-Orthodox families (a dozen children and more in many families) and the very limited 'drop-out rate' from this community (which entailed immediate recruitment into the army) combine to create a large ultra-Orthodox public in which the number of men of army age, whether regular or reserve duty, today amounts to about 20,000.

The issue of the exemption of yeshiva students is a time bomb. Fewer and fewer secular groups are willing to reconcile themselves to a situation in which a large, growing segment of the population is in effect exempt from military service, while their own sons serve a long three-year stint, followed by many years of reserve duty – and that as the result of a decision taken more than forty years ago in a very different context and scope. The representatives of ultra-Orthodox Jewry in the Knesset, and their electorate, view their primary task to be that of ensuring the continuation of this arrangement and the maintenance of the yeshivot and religious boarding schools bursting with students. The larger the ultra-Orthodox share in the Knesset, the greater the leverage they can wield against the secular parties. The Likud cannot form a government without the ultra-Orthodox parties, nor can Labour. When these two parties together form a National Unity Government, they do not exclude the ultra-Orthodox parties but rather invite them to join the coalition. Neither party advocates legislation which will harm ultra-Orthodox interests, because neither the Labour Alignment nor the Likud is prepared to forgo the chance of forming a future coalition with these parties.

Nevertheless, the conspicuous presence of the ultra-Orthodox parties in the Knesset creates a new self-perpetuating situation. Their political power ensures the steady increase in the number of yeshiva students, which in turn ensures the continued support for the ultra-Orthodox parties by these students and the further strengthening of these parties, thus perpetuating the exemption from military service for this sector of the population. The issue of the yeshiva students' non-enlistment will undoubtedly remain on the agenda of Israeli society, as tension grows between the religious parties, which threaten not to form a government with any party that prejudices the historical rights of the ultra-Orthodox sector, and the secular majority, which is less and less willing to accept a situation in which so many young men are exempt from military service. In any event, it is clear that the ultra-Orthodox parties are the only obstacle to necessary change. If we seek an example of the direct influence exerted by a political party on Israeli society, this is perhaps the most obvious.

The influence exerted by political parties on daily life in Israel, in a variety of fields, is among the highest in a Western democracy. Identification with a party is part of the self-definition of every Israeli. While vote-splitting between municipal, Knesset or Histadrut elections does exist, and is in fact growing, it is not yet a common phenomenon. Party identification is the best explanation for voting behaviour, determined not by the candidate for prime minister, nor by the changing positions of the parties, but rather by long-standing personal habit and identification.

All walks of life are affected by party divisions: the press; the state communications media, headed by a board of directors composed of representatives of the different parties; the economy, which includes a large Histadrut sector with a clear ideological approach; health services, which are provided to a majority of the population by the Histadrut; and more. The election of a new president of the bar association becomes a political race, for example, for when the attorney general, the state comptroller or the chief-of-staff is to be chosen, the first question asked is which party he supports – and the answer is usually readily available. Needless to say, the annual elections to the university student unions are blatantly political too, even when the major election issue may be cafeteria prices. Virtually every election to an important voluntary organization in Israel is related to party rivalries extant on the national level.

It is very hard not to identify with a party in Israel. Social pressure demands such identification. One is expected to attach a political sticker to one's car during the election campaign, in order to distinguish friends from enemies. People tend to mingle socially with people who share their political views, as political differences have throughout the years been so acute that it was difficult to maintain friendships across party lines. Sometimes political disputes create family rifts, even between husband and wife. The most radical expression of this was the 1951 split within the Kibbutz HaMeuhad movement on ideological grounds when, after many years of partnership, people felt that they could no longer live together on the same kibbutz. New kibbutzim were formed alongside the old ones, couples were divorced, and families were split between the kibbutzim.

There have, of course, been changes during the statehood years. Some parties have declined in strength – Ahdut HaAvoda disappeared within Mapai, greatly weakening the old ruling party – and the new ruling party, the Likud, does not maintain the same intensive framework which once characterized Mapai. But even if the parties provide fewer services, and even if their nationwide deployment is not what it once was, they remain a mediating factor in employment and advancement opportunities.

The percentage of party membership in Israel is very high. This partly reflects the arbitrary nature of the figures (the party poll is frequently falsified by the party 'bosses' in order artificially to increase their power within the higher party institutions), and partly results from the fictitious membership of those who believe it worthwhile to appear to belong to a particular party for purposes of personal advancement. Party members in Israel number about one third of the electorate, while the number of activists whom the parties can recruit for an election campaign or in order to promote a specific issue between elections is much smaller. The election results in several localities have shown that the registered members of a certain party exceed four- or five-fold the number of those who actually vote for that party. This is a clear indication of the distortion of the figures – but also of the need felt by many citizens to register as a party member.

The tremendous importance of the parties; their influence on the allocation of resources; the fact that they independently choose all their candidates; and the application of the 'party key' in so many areas of life: all these create a need for state control over internal party activity – financing, internal elections, ownership of assets, etc. There is to date no law in Israel governing the operation of political parties, which enjoy broad freedom of action, with the exception of financing. On the eve of the elections to the Seventh Knesset in 1969, a law was enacted providing for partial state funding of the parties' day-to-day work and their election campaigns. The allocation of funds is relative to party size, and every party is entitled – within certain restrictions – to raise additional funds from other sources, up to a ceiling determined by law.

State funding of parties enables the State Comptroller to examine the parties' accounting books, to examine the size and source of contributions, and to study possible undue influence being exerted on the ruling party by contributors after the elections. As regards this last area, despite recently uncovered aberrations, there are in Israel no signs of corruption or dependence of political parties or figures on economic organizations, as is the case in Japan and even in the United States. Nevertheless, the more democratic election process within the parties does create a need for additional funding, and this may create problematic dependencies.

In any event, state law does not address such questions as how a party should choose its candidate for prime minister, the Knesset or any other positions. The gap between the power exerted by the parties and their unchecked activity clamours for reform, especially in light of the events of recent years – the emergence of such parties as Shas, for instance. Created for a specific purpose, this party's MKs are appointed by an external body (in this case, one man) to whom and to whose interests the party is bound.

7. Who Rules?

The first *aliya*, which arrived in Palestine at the end of the nineteenth century, did not produce its own elite. Its spiritual leaders preferred to remain in Europe, and the young people who did come and who had to cope with existential problems, had little interest in countrywide issues of organization. They belonged to the Hibbat Zion movement which preceded political Zionism, and most were content to concentrate on settling the land and trying to create agriculture in an unfamiliar climate.

Among the members of the first *aliya* were teachers, journalists and writers who could have formed an elite had they functioned as a group. Although their ideology was generally liberal–conservative, they did not hold fervent beliefs and, with the arrival of the second *aliya*, they yielded on the whole to the tremendous power of the collective ideology which characterized the young socialists arrving in the early years of the twentieth century. Collectivism, which required that the individual accept the collective as the primary social unit, was also considered capable of meeting the Zionist challenge which demanded personal sacrifice. Professor Yonatan Shapira has pointed out that while the prestigious teachers' union, which antedated the Histadrut (the General Federation of Labour) refused throughout the 1920s and 1930s to join the Histadrut, with the union's later decline, the teachers came to accept the Labour leadership and even served the political elite.

For many years, Israel's elite was formed exclusively of the leaders of the second *aliya*. This group was formed during the Yishuv period, and continued throughout the first two decades of statehood. A study conducted by Moshe Lissak indicates that the political elite of the Yishuv period was born between 1880 and 1910, and was composed largely of young immigrants from Eastern Europe under the age of twenty-five, who assumed their place in the elite at an early age. Throughout this period, no one born in Palestine joined the elite, though some members of the fourth and fifth *aliyot*, some of them from Central Europe, were accepted. The members of the Labour movement within the elite advanced gradually within the political hierarchy. The civilian elite also comprised many who had previously been active abroad, but these remained part of the political elite for a briefer period than the leaders of the Labour movement.

The economic elite was even younger, with those born in Palestine playing a prominent role. Most of the members of this elite, in all sectors of the economy (private, Histadrut and public) had not been involved in economic activity abroad, nor had they had any professional economic training. The social elite – professors, writers, journalists and artists – were composed largely of East European immigrants, also younger than the political elite. Within this group the length of time spent in the country had virtually no significance.

However, by defining an elite by the official positions held by its members (delegates to political institutions, heads of economic institutions and organizations, academic faculty members, etc.), Lissak's study fails to include a number of people who were undoubtedly a part of the Yishuv elite. There is, however, an important category of people who did not belong to the category of elected heads of institutions and which has been treated unfairly in the historiography of the Yishuv period, namely the industrialists.

Agricultural ideology was accorded preference, influenced by the natural sympathy for the barefooted youths who came to the country imbued with a fervent belief in socialist ideology – reformers and builders of a new society. This worldview transformed all those who characterized diaspora Jewry – tradesmen, craftsmen, manufacturers and financiers – into representatives of the world of the past. But there is no doubt that several of them played a central role in shaping the face of the Yishuv, and no definition of the Israeli elite can be complete without them. Thus, I prefer not to adopt any particular definition of an elite, but rather to use the term in its broad, commonly accepted sense.

The historigraphy of the Yishuv describes the immigrants from Russia and Poland in the early twentieth century within the context of the pogroms perpetrated in Eastern Europe and the strengthening of the Zionist idea. These were young people who left their parents' homes, believed in the need for a social revolution, and who were convinced that the Jews could experience such a revolution only in their own country. They came as youths who chose to forgo personal comfort and were prepared for self-sacrifice for the sake of the people. Those of weaker character among them left Palestine and emigrated to the West, while the stronger remained, struck roots in the country and built a new society.

This is simply not the truth. The young socialists constituted a minority of the second *aliya*, which also comprised a not insignificant bourgeois element. It also included a group of capitalists who lived a completely different life from the ascetic youths who went by foot or donkey from one settlement to the next in search of a day's work from the ill-tempered farmers in order to assuage their hunger, or who lived in a commune, earning a living from agricultural projects of the Zionist Organization. There were also families who came to Palestine at the beginning of the twentieth century with capital and knowhow – people who settled in the big cities, built fine homes, and divided their lives between Palestine and pre-revolutionary Russia, Paris, London or Berlin.

The Wilbuschewitz family was a salient example of this historiographic distortion created, among others, by the fact that the cultural elite, as noted, served the political elite of the Labour movement. The absolute preference for agriculture at the expense of industry and commerce, and the prominence accorded to the self-sacrifice, suffering and malaria involved in the draining of the swamps caused history to overlook people whose influence on the Jewish community in Palestine was greater than that of others whose biographies were recorded in great detail, to the point that they became almost mythical figures.

As one who grew up in this country, Mania Shohat was for me one of the heroes of the Yishuv period. An anarchist with thick glasses who had fought against the Tsarist regime in Russia, this slight young woman immigrated to Palestine and became one of the leaders of the HaShomer movement and of the Poalei Zion party, and was a national symbol. Only many years later, while researching the roots of Israeli industry, did I discover that she was the sister of the Wilbuschewitz brothers who had had great impact on the development of Jewish life in Palestine. None of them was a political figure, and, even if they had been, it is hard to imagine that they would have felt at home in the Labour movement.

The Wilbuschewitz family were the owners of flourmills in Grodno, Poland. They were a wealthy family with a clearly technical bent, who had severed themselves from religious Judaism. The father, who was himself an engineer, sent all his sons to study engineering abroad. The eldest son went to America and died there at an early age. Isaac, who arrived in Palestine together with the Bilu'im in 1882, apparently also died young. His brother, Gedaliah, born in 1865, completed his engineering studies in Berlin and arrived in Palestine in 1892. He was a partner in the first factory in the country – Leon Stein's metalwork factory – where he founded the iron- and bronze-casting section. He was forced to leave the country three years later because his wife was ill; he arrived in Minsk where he became owner of the Technolog machine and metal-casting factory. Only in 1912 did he return to Palestine, where he now specialized primarily in construction engineering, building the Technion and the Reali secondary school in Haifa. During World War I, he served in the Turkish army as chief engineer of its Damascus headquarters, and after the war built the Shemen edible oil factory, the electric company complex in Haifa, and the Nesher cement factory. Together with his brother Nahum, he managed the Shemen factory. He died in Palestine in 1932.

The fourth brother, Moshe Wilbuschewitz, born in 1869, was the inventor of the family, specializing in the food industry. He completed his engineering studies at Zurich University, and was one of the devlopers of margarine and whole-wheat bread. With his thick moustache, long beard and hair, he looks like a real bohemian, very different from his bourgeois and pedantic brothers. He spent most of his life in Europe but in 1919, at the age of fifty, arrived in Palestine and joined his brothers in Haifa. Together with them, he founded and managed the Shemen factory, participated in the building of the Nesher factory and founded Haifa's flourmills. He passed away in 1952.

The fifth brother, Nahum, was the most important industrialist in Palestine. He was born in 1879, studied engineering like his brothers, and worked in his elder brother's Technolog factory in Minsk. In 1902 Nahum went to the United States to receive his brother's inheritance, which he later invested in Palestine. He arrived in Palestine in 1903 to undertake a survey of the country's industrial prospects, a visit which was to take on historic importance. The tour lasted six weeks, during which he was accompanied by his sister Mania who was also visiting the country, a guide and translator, and two Arab servants. This whole group travelled on horseback and slept in tents; they visited Nebi Mussa to examine the bituminous lime, Nablus to study the soap industry, and Damascus to become acquainted with the textile industry. They also travelled in Lebanon, passed through Safed, Acre and Haifa, studied the limestone on the Carmel mountain, and returned to Jaffa.

The survey was to shape the map of industry in Palestine, serving as the basis for the hydraulic electric station in the north, and the cement and edible oil factories in Haifa. Nahum returned to Europe, tried to interest men of means and engineers in his plans, and in 1905 found a site for an oil factory near Lod. Returning to Jaffa only at weekends, he lived alone on the site, hired Arab builders from the area, and studied Arabic in order to be able to converse with them. In 1901 he founded the Atid edible oil factory in Haifa and left for Europe again, this time for further study in Petersburg where, from 1910 to 1914, he served as technical manager of an oil factory. Upon his return to Palestine, he too enlisted in the Turkish army, and served as an engineer in Damascus until the end of the war. In 1924, together with his brother, he founded the Shemen factory, which he managed for many years. He died in Haifa in 1971, at the age of ninety-two.

Yet this important industrialist family entered Israeli historiography only through their younger sister, Mania, born in 1880. Mania was the black sheep of the family. At a very young age, she came to despise the family wealth and devoted herself to anti-Tsarist activity among the workers. In 1899 she was arrested for underground activity and two years later founded the Independent Jewish Labour Party, whose aim was to draw the workers closer to the regime and to improve their conditions through non-revolutionary means. Mania soon found herself in a predicament. The authorities considered her an underground leader, while the workers viewed her as a collaborator with the authorities. She was not a Zionist – at one stage in her life she was even anti-Zionist – but her family was concerned for her safety, and in 1904 she visited Palestine, touring the future industrial sites with her brother Nahum. She later settled in the country, and in 1909 founded the underground defence organization, HaShomer, together with her husband Israel Shohat, several years her junior. During World War 1 the Turks exiled the Shohats to Anatolia. Upon their return, they became active in the leftist wing of the Labour movement, and were among the founders of the Histadrut and the Gedud HaAvoda (Labour Legion). Until her death in 1961, she remained an active member of Mapam.

I felt that the Wilbuschewitz family warranted a departure from the dry data on the elite during the Yishuv period, as there is no more striking example of the double standard by which Israeli historiography judged its heroes. The black sheep became part of the Israeli ethos – the heroic young woman, who rebelled against wealth, was arrested in Russia and exiled by the Turks, led the small Jewish military organization in Palestine and was one of the leaders of the Labour movement – received full historical attention, while her brothers, who were undoubtedly a part of the Yishuv elite, do not figure in the Israeli historical consciousness at all.

Other personalities who were certainly part of the elite include Leon Stein, the pioneer of Jewish industry in Palestine, who in February 1888 founded the first factory in the country with the help of his brother, Dr Mark Stein, one of the first Bilu'im. The metalwork factory produced pumps for the orchards, implements for flourmills, iron gates and ice-making machines. In 1909 there were 150 employees working in the factory – by any reckoning a very large number at that date. However, the Stein factory, like its founder, has merited virtually no historical mention in the past. This was an elite very different from the 'legitimate' elite: Leon was born in Poland and studied in the Ecole Technique Supérieure in Nancy, France. His brother studied medicine in Leipzig, and one year after immigrating to Palestine, was appointed by Baron de Rothschild as doctor of his agricultural settlements. They worked in Palestine, travelled to Europe in order to acquire tools or know-how, and lived a different life from that of the leaders of the second *aliya*.

Eliyahu Meir Berlin, who immigrated to Palestine in 1907, helped Leon Stein to set up his factories, while he himself maintained his business in Russia. Until the revolution, he used to spend nine months of the year in Palestine and three months in Russia.

Shmuel Pavnetzer, who arrived in 1905, was one of the founders of the Atid oil product company in Haifa, and sold the company's shares in Warsaw. Shmuel Itzkovitch, son of an industrialist from Baku who studied engineering in Munich, entered into partnership with this firm in 1908. During World War 1 he went back to the family factory in Baku, and in 1920 returned to Palestine. Michael Pollak, born in 1864, arrived in Palestine in 1922 as a man of means. Born in Russia, he studied mathematics at St Petersburg University, engaged in oil prospecting and shipping, and owned oil shares which he sold for a huge sum to the Shell Company. He founded the Nesher cement factory on the recommendation of Nahum Wilbuschewitz, which he managed for many years.

These capitalists and entrepreneurs who, to a great extent determined the map of the country, did not constitute a well-defined group, did not set the lifestyle of the majority of the people living in the country, and did not try to become part of the country's leadership. The agricultural myth remained dominant, and the leaders of the Yishuv defined themselves as farmers even if they had engaged in farming for only a short period of their lives. The capitalists were viewed as exploiters, and anyone who lived prosperously was bourgeois and belonged to the world of the past. The Yishuv elite viewed collective settlement as the pinnacle of achievement. Although the country's leaders did not live on kibbutzim or moshavim, they admired the asceticism, the rough living, the suffering, the revolt against parents and the old world. The leadership was composed, as noted above, of people from the second *aliya* who created organizational frameworks and functioned as a group, who co-opted other immigrants who arrived decades later. An intellectual elite of scholars, teachers, writers functioned alongside the leadership, supporting the political and economic elite and disseminating its ethos and the norms it created.

The Yishuv entered the period of statehood equipped with institutions, norms, and also an elite. Even the term 'Yishuv' remained in common usage, and, in referring to the public during the first ten to twenty years of the state, the politicians often spoke of 'the people of the Yishuv'. The elite, born at the end of the nineteenth century, former pioneers of East European origin, continued to function as the elite of the new state, even when, in the course of three or four years, the country's population was tripled, new ethnic groups having been added. For many years, with rare exceptions, no new immigrants entered the cabinet, or even the Knesset. Native-born Israelis adorned the First Knesset, but all these young people who appeared in safe slots on the Mapai Knesset list resigned after the elections to resume the tasks to which their elders had destined them.

The political elite remained the most important and the most influential, with the other elites complementing it. The most prominent elite, alongside the political, is the military. The army represents an alternative career for many young people not welcomed with open arms by the political elite. The military track was at the outset completely open; there were no old officers blocking the path of the young. The young commanders of the Palmach and the Haganah, and some of the young officers who had served in either the Jewish

Brigade or another unit of the British army in World War II, became the IDF's new general staff.

During the early years, the scale of military ranks was limited, with new ranks being added gradually. The general staff was composed of thirty-year-olds, with the exception of Chief-of-Staff Ya'akov Dori who was very ill and left the conduct of battle to Major General Yigael Yadin, twelve years his junior, who actually succeeded him in 1949 after just one year. For many years, the position of chief-of-staff was successively filled by members of a single generation. From 1949 until 1983, the chiefs-of-staff were all people born in the latter half of the first or the second decade of the century, and all of them had served in the Palmach, the Haganah or the British army.

Yigael Yadin, born in 1917, one of the senior Haganah commanders and son of the archeologist Eliezer Sukenik (who had been active in Poalei Zion in Poland and a delegate to the Zionist Congress, and who was later responsible for the purchase of some of the Dead Sea Scrolls), filled the post until 1952. He was succeeded by his deputy, Mordechai Makleff, born in 1920, who had served as a major in the British army. A year later he was replaced by Moshe Dayan, son of Shmuel Dayan (an active member of HaPoel HaTzair, a founder of the moshav movement, and a Mapai MK), born in 1915, who had also been a Haganah commander. He served for five years, and was succeeded in 1958 by Haim Laskov, born in 1919, who had served in the British army during World War II and was demobilized with the rank of major. He was replaced in 1961 by former Palmach member Zvi Zur, born in 1925. Two years later Yitzhak Rabin replaced him, born in 1922, son of Rosa Cohen (a leading member of Mapai in the Tel-Aviv worker's council and the party's representative in the city council) and one of the top commanders of the Palmach. He continued in this post until 1968, when it was taken over by his deputy, also of the Palmach, Haim Barlev, born in 1924. Barlev served until 1972, when he was replaced by David Elazar, yet another member of the Palmach, born in 1925. Elazar was forced to resign in 1974 in the wake of the Yom Kippur War. His successor was Mordechai (Motta) Gur, born in 1930, who had served in the Haganah. Gur was replaced in 1978 by Rafael Eitan, born in 1929, a former Palmach member, who served until 1983. Moshe Levi, who succeeded him, was the first non-Ashkenazi chief-of-staff, and the first who did not wear the medal of Israel's War of Independence, as he had been too young to serve in the army at that date.

Many of those who were senior IDF officers at the time of its formation eventually reached the top of the military ladder. These men, all of the same generation, waited their turn, blocking most possibilities for advancement, and enjoying a free rein in the army. The IDF matured with them. The chiefs-of-staff of the 1960s were in their forties, those of the 1970s in their mid-forties, and those of the 1980s in their fifties. The age of the generals increased accordingly. In the 1950s the rank of colonel was added between lieutenant colonel and major general, and in 1967, after the Six Day War, the rank of brigadier was added beneath major general, further slowing the process of advancement. Although the principle of rotation was maintained and the army remained young in comparison to other armies in the world, this was no longer the young army that had characterized the early years of statehood. Not long ago, the oldest active IDF officer, Brigadier David Laskov, died aged over eighty.

The army has always been an important element in the Israeli elite, and, after their retirement from active service, senior officers turned to the management of economic enterprises, to national and local politics, and to a lesser extent to the academic world. The first wave of retiring generals followed immediately upon the conclusion of the War of Independence, in 1949–50. Many returned to their kibbutzim or went to study, but a number of them were soon elected to the Knesset, and several even became cabinet ministers. Yigal Allon, the youngest general in the IDF (thirty years old when the army was established), demobilized in 1949, was elected to the Knesset on the left-wing Ahdut HaAvoda list in 1955, and in 1961 was appointed Minister of Labour. Moshe Carmel, another general, released from the army in 1950, was elected to the Knesset on the same list in 1955 and was immediately appointed Minister of Transport. Aharon Remez, the commander of the air force who retired from the army in 1954, became a Mapai MK in 1955. Lieutenant General Moshe Dayan, released in 1958, entered the Knesset in 1959 on the Mapai list and was appointed Minister of Agriculture.

In the course of the next ten years, there was no significant further entry of IDF officers into politics. Yigael Yadin turned to archaeology, and was considered one of the leading scholars in his field; Mordechai Makleff managed several large government corporations; Haim Laskov was for many years director-general of the ports authority and later served as IDF ombudsman; and Zvi Zur engaged in the management of government and private corporations and served as assistant to the Minister of Defence.

A significant number of career changes for senior IDF officers came after the Six Day War. Yitzhak Rabin, who completed his term as chief-of-staff in 1968, was appointed Israeli ambassador to Washington. He returned home in 1973, entered the Labour Party Knesset list, was appointed Minister of Labour in Golda Meir's cabinet in 1974, several months later to become Prime Minister of Israel. Rabin is to date the only chief-of-staff to have reached this position. Ezer Weizman, the head of the IDF operations branch under Rabin and later Barlev, nephew of Chaim Weizmann and son of a bourgeois family in Haifa, had served in the British RAF in World War II and in the Haganah. In 1969, at the age of forty-five, having concluded that he would not be appointed chief-of-staff, he retired from the army and, accepting the Likud's offer, the next day joined the second National Unity Government as Minister of Transport. In 1977–80 he served as Minister of Defence in the Likud Government; and subsequently in the National Unity Government served as minister without portfolio and as Minister of Science.

Rabin's successor as chief-of-staff, Haim Barlev, barely had time to shed his uniform before, with his retirement in 1972, he was immediately appointed Minister of Trade and Industry for the Labour Party. From 1984 he served for six years as Minister of Police in the National Unity Government. In 1973, the Southern Command OC, Major General Ariel Sharon, resigned from the army when it became apparent that he would not become chief-of-staff, and joined the Liberal Party within the Likud. He ran for the Knesset on the Likud list, participated in the 1973 Yom Kippur War as commander of the corps which established the bridgehead on the west bank of the Suez Canal, and less than two years later became security adviser to Prime Minister Rabin. In 1977, with the Likud victory at the polls, he was appointed Minister of Agriculture, serving in all subsequent cabinets, as Minister of Defence among other posts. David Elazar's successor as chief-of-staff, Motta Gur, joined the Labour Alignment as he retired, appeared on its Knesset list, and served as a minister in the National Unity Government. His successor Rafael Eitan, following his retirement was elected to the Knesset on the Tehiya list, and later as head of the Tsomet movement. In 1990 he was appointed Minister of Agriculture. Rehavam Ze'evi, Central Command OC (1968–73), was elected to the Twelfth Knesset as the head of the Moledet transfer party, and was appointed minister without portfolio in 1991 (both of them resigned in 1992).

During the army's years of glory, generals were often enlisted as candidates for mayor and for senior positions in public administration and national institutions. Generals were frequent guests at social occasions, and some hosted such affairs themselves. The feeling during those years was one of intoxication with power, and absolute confidence in the IDF's ability to meet any military challenge. Every general was considered a superman, and it seemed as though anyone released from the army could fill any civilian position – political, academic, or other.

The veteran senior officers, who had experienced the socialization of the Labour movement (youth movement, Haganah or Palmach, kibbutz or moshav) remained, on the whole, identified with the Labour movement even during their army service, despite Ben-Gurion's insistence on the depoliticization of the army. They were not involved in any political framework at that time. Younger officers, whose political identity could not be determined by the erstwhile litmus test (Haganah and Palmach versus the IZL and Lehi), were not in a position to declare their political leanings. As representatives of the establishment, many undoubtedly identified with the government, with Prime Minister and Defence Minister David Ben-Gurion and the defence ministers who succeeded him; but they entered the army at the age of eighteen (and not in their early twenties like the first IDF officers who had fought in previous battles) and most had not been exposed to political frameworks, so their political support was naturally more superficial. Only when they were demobilized did they have to decide one way or the other if they sought a political career. Many did choose a political career, as it did not require a profession or higher education, and because politics rewarded high IDF ranks.

The Likud, which had to undergo a long process of legitimation before it could be cured of Ben-Gurion's assertion of 'without Herut or Maki', did so in three major stages. Firstly it formed the Herut–Liberal bloc with a well-established party which had already taken part in coalition government. Then it participated for three years in the National Unity Government. And finally it included senior IDF officers on its Knesset list.

No senior officers joined Herut until the 1970s, primarily because there were no central figures in the army who came from the ranks of the IZL and who identified with Menachem Begin's movement. The senior IZL members had turned directly to politics. During the early years of the state, Ben-Gurion had no confidence in the loyalty either of Mapam on the left or Herut on the right, so throughout the 1950s officers identified with these parties had little chance for advancement. Some retired from the army, while others awaited more propitious times.

In 1965 two former major generals appeared on the Labour Alignment Knesset list, and two lieutenant generals (Dayan and Zur) on the Rafi list headed by Ben-Gurion. In 1969 the Labour Alignment list included one lieutenant general and two major generals, all of whom had retired from the army in the 1950s, while Gahal still contained not a single former army man.

Ezer Weizman's decision to join the National Unity Government in 1969 was extremely important for the Likud. (According to Israeli law, a cooling-off period of several months is required between release from the IDF or from a government administrative position and election to the Knesset, but because a cabinet minister need not be a member of Knesset, Weizman could retire from the IDF one day and become a minister the next.) However, shortly after the dissolution of the National Unity Government, a rift developed between Begin and Weizman, and Weizman was not included on the Likud Knesset list in 1973, making Ariel Sharon that year the first former army general to stand for election on the Likud list. The 1973 Labour Alignment list included two former lieutenant generals (Dayan and Rabin) and three former major generals (Allon, Carmel and Yariv). Rabin and Yariv were products of the 'years of glory' (1967–73). Minister of Trade and Industry Haim Barlev was not a Labour candidate to the Knesset, but continued in his ministerial role after the elections as well.

In 1977 the Likud list included Major General (Res.) Ezer Weizman and Lieutenant General (Res.) Mordechai Zippori, while Major General (Res.) Ariel Sharon, elected on a separate list, joined the Likud immediately afterwards. The defeated Labour Alignment elected three former lieutenant generals (Dayan, Rabin and Barlev) and one former major general. The newly formed party – the Democratic Movement for Change (DMC) – had a notable military contingent: headed by Lieutenant General (Res.) Yadin, its fifteen MKs included two former major generals (Amit and Zorea) and a former colonel (Assaf Yaguri) who had won considerable fame in the Yom Kippur War as the most senior officer to have fallen into Egyptian captivity, and who had severely criticized the IDF's conduct of the war.

Begin, surprised like many others by his electoral victory, and still viewed by many as lacking legitimacy, immediately surrounded himself with former generals. He invited Moshe Dayan, a member of the Labour faction, to join the cabinet as Foreign Minister, although he did not require his vote to obtain a coalition majority. To Ezer Weizman he offered the defence portfolio. Ariel Sharon's small party was merged with the Likud, and Sharon became Minister of Agriculture; and when the DMC joined the government, Yadin became Deputy Prime Minister, and Meir Amit Minister of Transport. These former generals, most of whom had come from the very heart of the Labour movement (some had been born in a moshav or kibbutz, or held important positions within the Histadrut) accorded Begin and his government the legitimacy they lacked.

The life story of ex-IDF brigadiers and major generals follows a recurring pattern. A typical example is that of Shlomo Lahat, mayor of Tel-Aviv. Lahat – known to all as 'Chich' – was born in 1927, immigrated as a child from Berlin, served in his youth in the Haganah, filled a series of positions in the IDF culminating, at the height of his military career, as head of the manpower branch in the general staff with the rank of major general. He retired from the army during the the six years of glory. Prior to the 1973 elections he came to Finance Minister Pinhas Sapir, the 'kingmaker' in the Labour Party, and offered himself as candidate for mayor of Tel-Aviv. The mayor at the time was Yehoshua Rabinowitz, a sixty-three-year-old veteran party member, a diligent, honest and painfully reserved man. Sapir, unwilling to offend his old friend, suggested that Lahat accept the second slot on the Labour list in the municipal elections. Lahat refused, and went to the Likud. The Likud placed Lahat at the head of its municipal list, and since then has won every election in the city.

Such tales generally include an appeal to Labour, although Lahat, like many others, was not deeply identified with Labour. For him, the mayorship of Tel-Aviv was much more important than in which party he ran for for this position. Lahat is still on independent person, whose political views are far from those of his chosen party; he supports negotiations with the PLO, is prepared to relinquish the occupied territories and to allow the establishment of a Palestinian state. When asked how his position squares with his membership in the Likud, he counters by suggesting that in his opinion only the Likud will be able to implement his views.

The great importance of political parties in Israel, and the fact that it is virtually impossible to obtain a political post without going through a party, requires the officers to identify with some party regardless of their ideological background. Today many Likud candidates for mayor are former brigadiers and major generals who were previously inclined towards Labour, several of whom enjoy the public support of the 'old boys network'. Thus, for example, when Brigadier (Res.) Rami Dotan ran as the Likud candidate for mayor of Haifa in 1990, Major General (Res.) Yanush Ben-Gal who, after his retirement from the army, joined the Labour Alignment and worked in the Labour campaign headquarters, appeared on his behalf.

A characteristic trait in the political behaviour of many of the 'generals in politics' is objectivity. They feel much less obliged than the veteran party members to toe the party line. They frequently say what they think; do not hesitate to criticize their party and its leaders, emphasizing that the party is a tool and not an end in itself; and find it relatively easy to move from one party to another. Indeed Ezer Weizman, who was a leader of the Likud, resigned and later formed his own party, Yahad, which subsequently joined the Labour Party. Ariel Sharon, who was born in the moshav Kfar Malal and served in the Haganah, prides himself on having managed in his time to have been a member of Mapai, to have joined the Liberal Party in 1973, founded his own party in 1977 at the head of which he ran for the Knesset, and then to have joined the Likud and become a member of Herut. Brigadier Binyamin Ben-Eliezer, who served as head of the civil administration in the occupied territories, became secretary-general of the Sephardi religious Tami movement after leaving the army, later joined the Yahad movement headed by Ezer Weizman, and with him joined the Labour Party.

The cabinet behaviour of the 'generals in politics' is also unique. They are a much more consolidated group than other politicians, with a sense of being 'brothers in arms' – shared memories, similar connotations and even a special language. Inter-party rivalries often appear to them anachronistic, when urgent challenges must be faced. Among themselves, ideological rivalry is replaced by long-standing personal rivalry, based on events in their shared military past.

Three former chiefs-of-staff (Rabin, Barlev and Gur) and two major generals (Weizman and Sharon) served in the National Unity Government of 1984; four represented Labour, and one the Likud. Four of the five were members of the political-security inner cabinet which was composed of ten ministers. Despite the complex relation-ships among them, they functioned as a group, especially when confronted by people from the army and the defence establishment. They often seemed to feel closer to the young officers fifteen or twenty years their junior than to the veteran politicians around the table. The use of military abbreviations and military terms; the professional questions they posed; calling army officers by their nicknames; the pride of former commanders in having known the young officers ('I gave him his wings', or 'I was his commander in the officers' course'): all these combined to create the impression that the ministers wished to prove to the young generals that they were still in the know, that they were still part of the military reality and that the dozens of years they had spent in the army were the most important and the best of their lives.

The disappointments and the losses suffered by the IDF in the Yom Kippur War and the Agranat Commission appointed in its wake, leading to the resignation of the Defence Minister and the dismissal of the Chief-of-Staff and a large number of senior officers, damaged the IDF's image. While the 1976 Entebbe operation somewhat repaired this image, it was again impaired by the Lebanon War. Perceived in hindsight as unnecessary, the war indirectly involved Israel in the massacre of Palestinians by Christians in the Sabra and Shatilla camps, which became the subject of investigation by the Kahan Commission. As a result of the report submitted by the commission, the Defence Minister was obliged to step down, the Chief-of-Staff only narrowly escaped being dismissed – being allowed instead to complete the brief remainder of his term – and several very high-ranking officers were forced to retire from the army.

The fact that a considerable number of former generals failed in their civilian positions, on both the political and the administrative and economic levels, also cooled the automatic enthusiasm for anyone holding the rank of general. Generals who retire from the IDF today are obliged to make do with less important positions than their predecessors, and there is a growing number of brigadiers and major generals who fail to find suitable civilian employment.

Nevertheless, the senior IDF commanders still enjoy great prestige, and a high military rank is still an important asset. The military elite does not constitute a separate group but is rather a complementary elite, in effect a kind of 'prep school' for the political and economic elite. Officers who retire at the age of forty or forty-five view themselves as candidates to launch a second career, and they begin this career at the top, not from the bottom. The continuing centrality of the army in Israeli society ensures that, despite its diminished glory, the IDF will continue to be an inexhaustible source for the recruitment of leaders in different walks of life.

Israel's economic elite is composed of people with private capital, as well as professional management in the private, government, Histadrut and kibbutz sectors and in large public concerns. In this it differs from the economic elite in the Yishuv period, when those with private wealth were divorced from the other elites, even when they filled public positions. Arie Shenkar, who served as president of the manufacturers' association for thirty years, adhered to an apolitical ideology until his death in 1959. One year earlier, when he reached the age of eighty, Prime Minister David Ben-Gurion wrote to him: 'I do not know whether we were always in agreement on all issues, or for whom you voted in the municipal or Knesset elections, but I know that you were a loyal builder-son of our homeland.' The apolitical position adopted by Shenkar and the manufacturers in a country where the political parties played such a central role was one of the factors in the weakness of the industrial sector *vis-à-vis* the agricultural interests.

The party members who managed the economic institutions of the Jewish Agency and the Histadrut during the Yishuv period were on the whole not trained for this task, although many proved successful. For them, the senior positions they filled in the Histadrut companies and enterprises – the public banks, the Jewish National Fund and elsewhere – constituted a kind of public service which was, in effect, a part of their political career. In contrast, those who filled the important positions in the economic companies connected with the British mandate government were largely professionals (economists and engineers), who were a part of the economic system and who viewed it as their career. Close ties did not develop between the few capitalists – the financial aristocracy of the Yishuv – and those political figures who managed a large segment of the economy, or the professionals who headed the Electric Company or the Potash Company. They shared neither a joint framework of activity, nor a similar worldview, nor did they have common interests.

The situation today is very different. There are families in the various economic sectors who have acquired wealth in recent years or who brought their wealth with them to Israel. Such important families include the Recanati family in banking, the Sakharov family in insurance, the Federman family in the hotel business, the Mayer family in construction, the Moshevitz and Proper families in industry, and more. However, unlike their fathers, the young generation who are today running the family businesses, underwent a socialization process similar to that of the economists unrelated to the financial aristocracy; they went to the same schools and the same youth movements, served together in the same army, and studied in the same departments in university (law, economics or business administration).

It is not by chance that the manufacturers' association was broadened in the 1970s to include also the salaried managers. The distinction between ownership and management that characterizes the modern Western states created a class of technocrats who move in three circles: university, government and the market (both public and private). The most senior economics professor in the Hebrew University is Professor Dan Patenkin, born in Chicago in 1922, who immigrated to Israel with the establishment of the state as an associate professor. He has published many scholarly papers, and raised a generation of economists known as the 'Patenkin boys', who have already produced their own generations of economists in Israel's other universities.

Many young people who complete their degrees in economics seek employment in the Finance Ministry. Although government wages, especially at the lower ranks, are relatively low, the experience thus acquired is unique. The young economists are given tremendous authority. Those working in the income tax department, the accountant-general's department, and the budgets department work on the one hand with the business sector of the Israeli economy, and the government ministries on the other. They determine the margin of profit, tax exemptions, and the scope of government aid for the various business sectors, and draw up detailed budgets for the government ministries. These young men and women in their late twenties and early thirties, who are more expert in juggling numbers than those in charge of them, often arouse the anger of businessmen and ministers alike. The 'budget boys', as the employees of the budgets department are called, often cause resentment among the decision-makers. Since he who determines the budget in effect also sets the priorities, the ministers frequently maintain that is the budget department which makes their decisions for them.

Several years on, now in their late thirties, armed with a bachelors degree and sometimes a masters degree as well, together with vigorous experience in the Finance Ministry, these young people enter either the private or Histadrut market, or become deputy directors-general in government corporations, and begin to move in the three typical circles. Some of them develop an incidental academic career, giving one or two university lectures, while others place greater emphasis on the university.

The previous Governor of the Bank of Israel, Professor Michael

Bruno, studied economics at the Hebrew University of Jerusalem and abroad. For eight years he served in various senior positions in the Bank of Israel, and afterwards pursued his academic career at the Hebrew University as a prominent professor of economics. In 1985 he was informally involved in the preparation of the economic programme which put an end to Israel's inflationary spiral. One year later he was appointed by the National Unity Government to the high post of Governor of the Bank of Israel. At the end of his term, in 1991, he decided to return to the University.

Eitan Berglas, a well-known economics professor at Tel-Aviv University, agreed in the late 1970s to serve as head of the budgets department at the Finance Ministry, but afterwards he returned to the academic world. In the late 1980s he was appointed chairman of the board of directors of Bank Hapoalim (he died in 1992). Professor Eitan Shishinski, one of the leading economists of the Hebrew University, was elected chairman of the Histadrut's Hevrat Ovdim in 1990; and a young professor of economics from Tel-Aviv, Efraim Zadka, accepted the position of chairman of the Histadrut's construction company, Solel Boneh. Amiram Sivan, formerly directorgeneral of the National Insurance Institute and later director-general of the Finance Ministry, took on the management of Bank Hapoalim. Eli Hurwitz, one of the owners of a large drug company called Teva, and former president of the manufacturers' association, became chairman of the board of directors of Bank Leumi. He is a good example of the change which has occurred in the image of Israeli industrialists in recent years. Hurwitz was a member of the Labour Party youth movement and of Kibbutz Tel-Katzir; he married the daughter of a manufacturing family, and became one of the most successful industrialists in Israel. Hurwitz is also one of the leading figures in Israeli society, his opinions are listened to, and he belongs to the group of 'natural candidates' for such economic positions as Finance Minister. His affinity with the Labour movement facilitated a closer relationship between the manufacturers who had traditionally been identified with the conservative right, and the Histadrut and the Labour Alignment movement. It is therefore not surprising that in 1984, with the establishment of the socio-economic council with representatives of the government, employers and Histadrut, it was he who expedited its day-to-day work and helped to bring about its most important achievement – the economic programme which in July 1985 saved the Israeli economy.

His predecessor, Avraham (Buma) Shavit, son of the owners of a large oven factory, also had greater affinity with the left than the right. In his youth he was a member of HaTenuah HaMeuhedet (the Labour-affiliated school youth movement) and later a member of the Palmach, and he was active in Rafi (the Israel Labour List) headed by Ben-Gurion. Although he did not play an official role in the economic programme of 1985, he was its regular spokesman on television, and contributed greatly to its success.

The fact that the heads of the manufacturers are part of Israeli life, and that they may belong even to left-wing parties can be attributed primarily to Israel's system of uniform education. The sons of wealthy families study side by side with those from poorer homes in the same schools, and belong to the same youth movements. One often finds oneself in a particular youth movement not out of ideological preference, but because its local branch is close to one's home, but the result may be a long-standing effect on political behaviour.

The economic elite is composed of the second generation of manufacturers, bankers and hotel proprietors, salaried directors-general, and a large group of lawyers and accountants who represent the economic organizations. The salaries of the directors-general and of senior managers in the large economic enterprises are very high, certainly by Israeli standards, and their lifestyle is similar to that of the moneyed class: they own private homes in prestigious neighbourhoods or expensive condominiums in Tel-Aviv, a holiday home (usually in Eilat or Caesarea), fancy cars; they have personal chauffeurs, live-in domestic help, fashionable clothing, play tennis and golf at the weekends, travel abroad frequently etc.

In a society whose ethos is still pioneering, simplicity and asceticism, based on an equal distribution of the burden, and which, on the other hand, is very small, with the consequent feeling that 'everyone knows everyone else', there is a dual attitude towards wealth: on the one hand jealousy and the desire to emulate it, and on the other contempt and even anger. In recent years wealth has been transformed from a private into a public matter, with a growing tendency to adopt the American practice of publishing the salaries of the senior salaried employees who earn between $250,000 and $360,000 per annum. Although MKs periodically propose setting a 'maximum salary', such motions never reach the final stages of legislation, both because there is no obstacle to paying high salaries in a free market, and also because it is clear that any attempt to limit salaries would simply lead to additional payments 'under the table', thus circumventing the law.

The members of the top percentile in the Israeli economy are themselves often uncomfortable about the lifestyle they lead, but as the years pass wealth becomes both more legitimate and more conspicuous. Because of their high lifestyle, there is virtually no shift from the economic elite to other elites, and even when such a shift does occur, it is generally short-lived. Thus, for example, it is commonly accepted that the senior positions in the Finance Ministry are filled by economists from outside the government who have previously served in the government. In recent years, the position of director-general of the Finance Ministry has been filled, in turn, by Dr Emanuel Sharon, Ya'acov Lifshitz and Shalom Singer, amongst others. Each of them was obliged to forgo about 80 per cent of his previous salary when he accepted a civil service position. The accountant-general and the head of the budgets department are also positions generally filled by people who have already made their way in the business world.

Shifts from the economic elite to the political elite are even rarer and less successful. In 1977 several figures from the economic elite – Meir Amit, then director-general of Koor, the huge Histadrut enterprise; Stef Wertheimer, one of the most important private manufacturers in Israel; and Shlomo Eliahu, owner of a large insurance company – were elected to the Knesset on the DMC list. Amit was appointed to a ministerial post, but resigned shortly afterwards. The other two were very frustrated as MKs left no mark on parliamentary life, and did not return for a second term.

In 1981 the leader of the opposition, Shimon Peres, decided to designate candidates for positions in a possible Labour-led government to be established after elections later that year. He asked Professor Haim Ben-Shahar, then president of Tel-Aviv University, to agree to be the Labour candidate for finance minister, and Naftali Blumenthal, director-general of Koor, for deputy finance minister as a Member of Knesset. The Labour Alignment did not win the election, and Ben-Shahar continued his academic pursuits, later entering the business world as Armand Hammer's representative in Israel. He has continued to advise the heads of Labour on economic matters, both during the preparation of the 1985 economic programme and when Shimon Peres himself served as Finance Minister in 1988–90. Never again did he stand as a candidate for any political position or for the Knesset, and instead abandoned political activity. Although Naftali Blumenthal was in fact elected to the Knesset, as a representative of the opposition party he naturally received no executive position and, like many fellow members of the economic elite, felt frustrated in the Knesset, and did not seek re-election in 1984. There is today no one from the economic elite serving in the Knesset, possibly the result of the unsuccessful attempts by economists to enter politics in the past.

The economists' 'years of glory' were the 1960s and early 1970s – years marked by economic prosperity, high rates of economic growth, the establishment of new enterprises, and the emphasis on modern technologies. The success stories of young Israeli entrepreneurs frequently engaged the media, and through them the public. The growth policy of Pinhas Sapir on the one hand, and the rapid growth of the defence industries after 1967 on the other were the 'pep pills' which fuelled the Israeli economy. The heroes of the day were such private manufacturers as Mark Moshevitz, Beno Gitter, the Mayer brothers, etc.; members of the Histadrut economy – Zvi Rechter, Asher Yadlin, Meir Amit, etc,; and the government – Pinhas Sapir, Moshe Zanbar, Michael Zur, Moshe Kashti, and others.

During the 1970s several scandals were uncovered, tarnishing the image of the economic elite, some of whose giants were revealed as criminals. The collapse of the Israel–British Bank in the summer of 1974 opened a Pandora's box of white-collar offences. The director-general of the bank, Yehoshua Ben-Zion, was tried for the disappearance of a huge sum from the bank's coffers and was sentenced to fourteen years' imprisonment. Michael Zur, director-general of the large Hevra LeIsrael enterprise, was sentenced in 1975 to fifteen years' imprisonment for having stolen millions from the company. Zur, who was born in Germany in 1928 to a religious family, immigrated to Palestine as a child, received a religious education, and was active in the Mizrahi youth movement. He entered the Ministry of Trade and Industry in 1950 when its director-general Herman Hollander (also from Mizrahi and German born) invited him to work with him. He remained in government service even after Hollander left his post, and developed excellent relations with Pinhas Sapir. When Sapir was appointed Minister of Trade and Industry, he appointed Zur as the ministry's director-general. Zur was known for his original thinking, for his sharp tongue in occasional fierce arguments, and for the absolute loyalty of his assistants. Although considered a technocrat and not a politician, Zur was a candidate for Minister of Trade and Industry, and was viewed as an economic wizard and a powerful man.

With his retirement from the civil service in 1966, he was appointed chairman of the board of directors of the Haifa oil refineries. He was also a member of the board of other important government and private corporations. In 1969 he was appointed director-general of the Hevra LeIsrael, initiated by Pinhas Sapir in 1968 with the aim of creating a company that would raise 100 million dollars for investment in basic industry, and established following a gathering of Jewish millionaires. While the company failed to raise the money, it enjoyed sweeping tax exemptions granted by special legislation. The arrest and trial of Zur were an earthquake which shook the Israeli economy.

It was not to be the last, however. A legal investigation initiated against Zvi Rechter on criminal suspicion of dubious deals ended with Rechter's resignation as director-general of Solel Boneh and the closing of the file against him. Rechter had also been a leading figure in the Israeli economy. Born in Vienna in 1921, he immigrated to Palestine in 1940 and joined a kibbutz, remaining a kibbutz member for almost 30 years. As such, he was appointed to a number of economic positions, and was finally made director-general of Solel Boneh, the largest construction company in Israel.

The Yadlin affair was undoubtedly the most serious economic scandal in Israel's history, and that which caused the most serious damage to the heads of the economic elite. Born in Jerusalem in 1923, Yadlin was secretary of the Labour youth movement, a kibbutz member for many years, and an integral part of the group known as 'Mapai youth'. He later went abroad and studied in the United States, where he received his bachelors and masters degrees before returning to Israel, where he filled various positions in the Histadrut, and in 1966 was appointed secretary of Hevrat Ovdim. Yadlin brought a new spirit to this organization; he insisted on higher salaries for managers, fought against the proliferation of strikes, demanded that a worker's wages be commensurate with his output, and demanded that Hevrat Ovdim operate solely on the basis of profitability rather than taking on ungainful national tasks. Yadlin accumulated tremendous power, controlled many constellations, made significant changes in appointments, and six years later, in 1972, took over the management of the Histadrut's health fund, Kupat Holim. In this position, on the eve of his appointment as Governor of the Bank of Israel, he was apprehended for carrying out illegal deals as director-general of Kupat Holim; he was tried, pleaded guilty, and was sentenced to five years' imprisonment.

In the late 1970s and early 1980s the bankers were widely respected. Bank shares rose steadily during these years, and many Israelis purchased these shares on the banks' encouragement, for the banks guaranteed their yield. Advertisements announced that 'The banks are the oxygen of the state.' One claimed to be 'the bank that marches with the times'; another that the bank is 'also a friend', and many new bank branches were opened throughout the country, each more luxurious than the next.

The most highly respected bankers were Ernst Jaffet, chairman of the board of Bank Leumi; Ya'akov Levinson, chairman of the board of Bank Hapoalim; Eli Cohen, director-general of the Discount Bank; and Bino Zadik, director-general of the First International Bank. The collapse of the bank shares in 1983, obliging the government to purchase the shares at a cost of nine billion dollars, together with the commission of inquiry subsequently appointed, which led to the resignation of most of the directors-general and chairmen of the board of the different banks, profoundly damaged the myth of the banks with their supposedly unfailing backing.

The acme of the Israeli economy, the financial wizards, disappeared from the scene. Ya'akov Levinson, the man who wielded the greatest power in the Histadrut economy, and who had groomed himself for the position of finance minister and perhaps even prime minister for the Labour Party, committed suicide. Michael Albin, one of the prodigies of the Israeli economy, one of the heads of magnate Eisenberg's empire also took his life by jumping from the window of the lock-up where he was being held for questioning. Ernst Jaffet, considered the most important banker in Israel, left for the United States and has not returned to Israel since he was forced to resign from the chairmanship of Bank Leumi. About a dozen bankers who had high-handedly managed Israel's banking system, and who had maintained extensive ties throughout the financial world, are today obliged to accept such positions on the margins of the economy as representatives of investors from abroad. There is no doubt that the shock waves produced within Hevrat Ovdim by the Yadlin affair in the 1970s, combined with the collapse of the bank shares in the 1980s, altered the face of Israel's economic elite.

The cultural elite is drawn from the fields of electronic and written media, literature, the arts, academia and sports. The number of Israeli newspapers, some of which are politically affiliated, is large relative to the size of its population. The average Israeli, who closely follows the news, is an avid newspaper reader, and many read more than one daily paper. The editors of the important newspapers (*HaAretz*, considered to be of the highest quality; *Yediot Ahronot*, with the largest distribution; and *Ma'ariv*, formerly the most widely read and today second in distribution) are on personal terms with the heads of state, as are the veteran publicists. Journalists take meetings with senior Israeli politicians in their stride, and they feel free to telephone a minister or even the prime minister and, without apologies, addressing him by his first name, ask him any question. They exert considerable influence on the decision-makers, which continues to increase with the broadening of the base of those who elect the party candidates for the Knesset. The politician's most important form of communication with his electorate is not via letters sent at the conclusion of the Knesset session, but rather through what is written about him in the press, and it is very hard for a politician to act in a manner which will not be condemned by the media.

In the last twenty years, television has played an increasingly important role in the life of the state, and although a second television station is currently in its infancy and many Israelis are already hooked up to local cable television, the state television station – run by a board of directors appointed by the Minister of Education according to a party key – still enjoys tremendous influence. The television broadcasters to a large extent determine the fate of ideas and their proponents. They belong to the elite, are highly popular, and are much more well known than many of the personalities they interview or on whom they report. Radio, which is on the air for many more hours of the day, has a status of its own, and its leading personalities are also part of the Israeli elite.

There is an almost symbiotic relationship between the communications media and politics. The journalists draw the politicians' attention to certain situations; the politicians place the issue on the cabinet or Knesset agenda, and in return receive media coverage. Israeli journalists are news-makers no less than the ministers on whom they report. The most salient example of this was Dan Margalit, a correspondent for *HaAretz*, who, while in the United States, discovered that the then Prime Minister, Yitzhak Rabin, continued to maintain a dollar bank account having completed his term as Israeli ambassador to Washington, in contravention of the law. It was Margalit, in effect, who brought about the resignation of the Prime Minister.

Journalists usually advance within their own hierarchy, although there has been some mobility between journalism and politics. The late editor of *HaAretz* Gershom Schocken was an MK for the small liberal party (the Progressives); the late editor of *Yediot Ahronot* Herzl Rosenblum represented the Revisionist party on the Provisional State Council which preceded the Knesset; while Herzl Berger, a leading journalist for *Davar*, the Histadrut daily, was for many years an MK for Mapai. Not a few MKs have engaged in journalism in the course of their lives, but, in recent decades, there has not been a single journalist of national renown who has gone over to politics. It would seem that many journalists satisfy their own political ambitions through political writing, or through explicit political identification.

The most prominent Israeli writers are those with clear ideological and even political identities. For decades during the pre-state period, most literature was politically committed. Many of the literary organs were associated with the Labour movement, and the various publishing houses were affiliated with the various leftist political movements: Am Oved with Mapai, Sifriat Poalim with Mapam, and HaKibbutz HaMeuhad with Ahdut HaAvoda. The right also had publishing houses, though much smaller ones. The fact that each party had a daily newspaper, and that each paper had a literary supplement which published works or excerpts from the writings of selected writers, led even those writers without strong political opinions to choose among them.

The literature written by the early immigrants dealt largely with realistic accounts of the pioneering experience, contributing directly to the building of the myth of asceticism on the one hand and to the rejection of the diaspora on the other. It portrayed an image of the diaspora as the source of all evil, while most of the immigrants to Palestine were people with an ideological worldview who were prepared to pay a high personal price for the sake of those who would follow. Many of the writers viewed themselves as making a modest contribution to the Zionist-socialist effort through such 'positive' writing.

The 1948 War of Independence produced its own generation of writers. Such authors as Moshe Shamir, Yizhar Smilansky, Dan Ben-Amotz, all born at the end of the second or at the beginning of the third decade of the twentieth century, published war stories which described the dilemma of the young soldier, called upon to play his part in the national challenge and thus required to kill his enemies. In the late 1950s political identification was obscured as the nihilist current prevailed; disappointment at the achievements of the state were expressed and questions asked about whether this was indeed the state to which the fighting generation had aspired.

The 1960s and 1970s were years of depoliticization in all areas, including literature. Many party newspapers were closed for lack of readers, and new publishing houses without an ideological orientation were founded, while those with party affiliation ceased to issue tendentious material, choosing rather to publish what they considered good literature. While in the past most leading writers were organizationally affiliated with the Labour movement (as former Palmach members, kibbutz members, journalists who had written for the Labour movement newspapers, Histadrut employees, etc.), most of the prominent writers towards the end of the century are identified with the Zionist left, primarily because of their position on the Israeli-Palestinian conflict. Some are identified with the Labour Party, while others prefer to be associated with a smaller party with a more sharply defined message, such as the Citizens' Rights Movement headed by Shulamit Aloni.

A few writers from the dominant generation born in the 1930s and 1940s earn their livelihood by literature, through a contract with a publishing house. Others teach literature at university or edit a literary or other column, while still others are regular journalists or broadcasters. Even if most writers and poets are not actively involved in political issues, the minority – who are also among the best of them – are prominent and sophisticated, and are listened to. The most conspicuous among them are Amos Oz, Avraham B. Yehoshua, Yizhar Smilansky and Haim Guri. Their names often appear on petitions on political issues, and their opinions influence wide circles within and even beyond the Israeli left. Their efforts to persuade the large parties to establish a National Unity Government in 1984 made an important contribution to this result. Their voice is considered the voice of morality, and many come to them to win support for a political move. When in 1990 Shimon Peres and Yitzhak Rabin again vied for the leadership of the Labour Party, Yizhar Smilansky took the podium on behalf of Peres.

Few writers have achieved political appointments. Uri Zvi Greenberg, one of Israel's greatest poets and one of the only ones to be identified with the right, was an MK for Herut in the early years of statehood. Smilansky was on the Mapai list for the First Knesset, but resigned before the Knesset convened, although he returned to the parliament for a brief period in 1965 on the Rafi list. Moshe Shamir, long-time member of Mapam, entered the Knesset only after he had switched camps, appearing on the Likud list on behalf of the 'Labour Movement for an Undivided Land of Israel'. He later left the Likud – together with Geula Cohen – over his opposition to the Camp David Accords; he went on to form the Tehiya movement.

The various elites have 'eternal candidates' for political activity on the highest level. One such candidate was the late Yigael Yadin who, for a quarter of a century, was considered by many to be a suitable candidate for a political post. He himself preferred to keep away from politics, relenting eventually in 1977 only to fail to realize the hopes placed in him. The eternal candidate in the economic sphere is the above-mentioned Eli Hurwitz, former president of the manufacturers' association; in the field of literature it is Amos Oz, whose name is mentioned not only as a natural candidate for minister of education, but even as the leader of the Labour Party.

'People of the Book' remains a relevant appellation to Israel even in an age when the electronic media are claiming ever-growing importance. The publication of a new book by Oz, Yehoshua, David Grossman, Yitzhak Ben-Ner, Shulamit Lapid and others is seen as a real event in Israeli society. Everybody, it seems, reads them and argues about them, and many telephone the writers to compliment or criticize them. The great popularity enjoyed by the writers together with the fact that they expose themselves to the public accords them special importance; it allows them to express controversial views, even on political figures and issues (such as supporting self-determination for the Palestinian people), which would be unpardonable coming from anyone else. Between the 1940s and 1960s such a status was accorded only to Natan Alterman, the poet and playwright who was an intimate of the establishment and of Ben-Gurion himself, though he could also admonish him. (In his last years – he died in 1970 – he supported the movement for the undivided land of Israel and even backed Gahal in the Knesset elections.)

Theatre actors in Israel are not directly involved in politics and do not fill political positions, but they are active on ideological issues, especially on questions related to the Israeli–Palestinian conflict, and most are identified with the dovish camp. During election campaigns some identify with particular parties and appear on their campaign broadcasts, but their identification is usually limited to participation in demonstrations and support for petitions. The number of artists who sign petitions (against expulsions, administrative detention, and continued Israeli control in the territories, for the advancement of the political process, etc.) is large and conspicuous.

In the past, actors were also organizationally affiliated, though less so than journalists and writers. The Ohel Theatre, founded in 1925, belonged to the Histadrut. It was from the Histadrut that it received financial support, and its governing institutions were appointed by the Histadrut with the actors working on a cooperative basis. During the years of de-politicization, the Ohel Theatre was closed (1969), thus putting an end to the only political theatre in Israel.

The Habima Theatre, founded in Russia at the beginning of the century, Israel's oldest company and considered the national theatre, was a repertory company whose members functioned as a cooperative. While not considered a political theatre, its close affinity with the establishment, its cooperative framework, and the fact that many of its actors lived in housing projects built by the Histadrut in the 1930s for workers, all made Habima the theatre of the political elite. To go to Habima was not mere entertainment, but a question of devoting an evening to culture. I remember in my youth weighty discussions on whether such a serious company could present 'vulgar' plays: while Habima argued that without such plays it would go bankrupt, the critics claimed that such plays would put an end to its position as the Israeli national theatre.

Despite its general identification with the establishment, though, Habima's veteran actors did not engage in intensive political activity. It was rather the younger actors of the Cameri Theatre, founded with the establishment of the state in protest against the closed and established nature of the national theatre, and other non-affiliated actors who allowed themselves to be much more prominently and publicly active. One of the explanations for this may be the Likud's rise to power in the 1977 elections which brought leftists out to demonstrate and protest. Another explanation may be the cultural change which occurred in Israel, in which political issues were transformed into broad public issues which could not be dealt with solely in smoke-filled rooms. In any event, the actors constitute an elite of their own which, though it does not mix with other elites, is involved in and related to the political elite, and certainly to the literary and journalistic elites. Its voice is frequently heard, usually on behalf of the dovish camp.

Singers are even more conspicuous in raising their political voice, using their natural instrument. They often express their opinions in songs, which promptly become the focus of political controversy. They sing at demonstrations or gatherings of a political nature, sign petitions, and identify with political parties. Such popular performers as Shlomo Artzi, Yehudit Ravitz, Nurit Galron and others make it a point to include songs of an ideological nature, whether implicit or explicit, in each new album. Most singers who express political opinions voice leftist-dovish views, although there are also singers identified with the right (such as Zvi Pik), who accord their views great prominence.

Israeli sportsmen are generally identified with political movements through the sports clubs to which they belong, although with the passing of the years the various clubs' links with political ideology have become increasingly tenuous. The Betar sports club belongs to the Herut movement, Hapoel to the Histadrut with a clear Labour influence, and Maccaabi to the General Zionists (later the Liberal Party). Among sports fans, political identification is more pronounced. Betar fans are generally supporters of the Likud, while Hapoel fans lean towards Labour.

Sportsmen do not often express opinions on political issues, but some of them have a large following, to the point that political parties have on occasion tried to enhance their Knesset lists with the names of well-known players. Thus, for example, the Labour Alignment included Moshe Sinai, captain of Hapoel Tel-Aviv's soccer team, on its 1988 Knesset list – in one of the unrealistic slots reserved for celebrities. It is hard to know whether this symbolic gesture won Labour additional votes. In any event, Sinai himself removed his name from the list when he learned that Knesset candidates cannot appear on television during the month before elections, irrespective of whether the candidate is in a realistic slot or not; this would have meant that his team's games could not have been televised throughout that entire month.

A group very closely related to the political elite is the academic elite. Prior to the establishment of the state there was a breach between the two: the political elite scorned the university professors as part of its revolt against the European bourgeoisie, while the professors, most of whom had come from Central Europe with a different educational background, regarded with scorn the immigrants from Eastern Europe who disparaged formal study. Part of the academic elite formed Brit Shalom ('The Peace Association') under the leadership of Professor Judah L. Magnes. This small movement, which did not try to garner political power, was considered the most dovish Zionist group before the establishment of the state, proposing as it did equality between Jews and Arabs in the governing institutions (regardless of the number of Jews or Arabs in the country), and demanding that the Arabs be taken into consideration when determining the scope of Jewish immigration. This position distanced the prominent professors who joined the movement from the decision-makers in the Yishuv's governing institutions.

The 'boycott' of the academic cadre ended after the establishment of the state. Given the fact that most of the members of the political elite, certainly those born in the 1930s and 1940s, held academic degrees, the rapprochement between the two was only natural. University department heads, faculty deans, rectors and presidents had often been and are still fellow students, teachers or former pupils of members of the political elite. Two faculties proved to be particularly successful cultivators of politicians – law and social sciences.

While people with distinguished academic careers have found their way to the Knesset ever since it was established, this trend is particularly characteristic of recent years. The flexible nature of the academic world facilitates leaves of absence and some take advantage of this option, while others continue to give a weekly lecture in order not to sever themselves from the university.

The integration of senior members of the academic world into the political elite generally proves successful. There is a certain similarity between their behaviour and that of the 'generals': they share an objective approach free of party obligations, as most of them, unlike the professional politicians, have somewhere to return to. What is more, most of them have not undergone the long process of party socialization which teaches party discipline – 'freedom of discussion and unity of action'. The general respect accorded to a professor is much higher than that accorded a politician, and parties pride themselves on the senior faculty members who join their ranks. In many cases a party will ask a prominent university professor to serve in the Knesset on its behalf. There are those who accept willingly, while others are wary of politics, preferring a different kind of involvement (as ambassadors in important posts, directors-general of government ministries, or in a position such as that of attorney general). Professors are more prominent in the small parties on both the right and the left than in the large parties, and more in the Labour Alignment than in the Likud. There are five professors in the 12th Knesset, three representing Labour, one Moledet, one the Tehiya movement, and one Shinui.

The elite of Israeli society, which includes the top of the political, military, economic, cultural and academic pyramid, comprises about 400–500 people. Its members frequently meet both informally and at official receptions for important visitors from abroad, and almost all of them can be seen annually on the Fourth of July in the American Ambassador to Israel's large garden.

This is a relatively homogeneous elite, with a much higher percentage of Ashkenazim than in the population at large. Most of them reside in the major cities and are linked by a close network of relationships based on a similar socialization process. Sephardim are very rarely found in the academic and economic elites, and constitute a small minority in the military elite. The entry of this sector into politics is more significant, although even here the top of the pyramid remains in Ashkenazi hands. It is interesting to note that the Likud, most of whose supporters are Sephardim, is headed by an Ashkenazi leadership, while the essentially representational positions (e.g. deputy prime minister) are accorded to Sephardim.

The Sephardim are particularly prominent in the area of sports where they constitute a clear majority, especially on the soccer field. They are also prominent among popular singers, where their number is steadily growing. Moreover, while in the past these singers would often perform Western songs in preference to the Oriental music viewed by the elite as primitive, in recent years a new ethnic pride has emerged: young Sephardim perform more Oriental music as Ashkenazi ears become accustomed to it, and even some Ashkenazi singers have also begun to specialize in this music.

Inter-elite mobility is not common. While movement is more common from the army to the political elite, both on national and local levels, and from the academic world to politics, the other elites retain their position in their own areas of specialization and exert political influence only from afar. Despite its homogeneity, the Israeli elite is open-doored. There is no need to attend a particular school in order to gain entry, nor to be born into a distinguished family. This is a society which admires excellence and which rewards it. One need not be wealthy in order to enter politics, and one need not be the son of a professor in order to achieve a senior academic position, although it never hurts ...

Israeli society is still young, and this is the main reason for its relative openness. But youth is a temporary state. In the economic field, there are today family enterprises run by the second or third generation (Recanati, Proper, Levy of Nilit, Taiber, and others); there are large law firms run by the second generation; and there is a clear accumulation of wealth in Israel's affluent families. Among artists there is a proliferation of second-generation performers, while in politics a growing number of sons are following in the footsteps of their fathers – 10 of the current 120 members are second-generation MKs, the Likud holding a relative majority of them.

The openness of the Israeli elite may be temporary. Israel is beginning to adopt some of the characteristics of a maturing society, and family dynasties may begin to limit this openness. On the other hand, the welcome influx of hundreds of thousands of Soviet Jews may help to perpetuate the openness, especially given the high percentage of scientists, doctors and engineers among them, who will undoubtedly enhance the quality of Israeli society.

Of course, not all the influential people in Israel can be seen on the US Ambassador's lawn on the Fourth of July. One influential group who are not invited, and who would not dream of attending even if they were, are the ultra-Orthodox rabbis who govern the lives of the ultra-Orthodox MKs. These parties have achieved peak power in the present Knesset, and many – politicians, journalists and scholars – are displaying a new interest in this strange and alien world, which has the power to determine what kind of government will be formed and who will head it. This may well be an exaggerated interest and their power may be a temporary one, but, as the leaders of tens of thousands of Israeli citizens, they cannot be ignored.

At the top of the pyramid of Israel's ultra-Orthodox population, which numbers about 200,000 people, are some ten influential rabbis, who have the power to determine for whom their followers will vote. They can demand that their supporters vote for new parties, abandoning the traditional parties, and even that they refrain from voting altogether. For their supporters, voting for the secular-Zionist state institutions is relatively unimportant, and they would not dream of disobeying the instructions of their rabbis. None of these rabbis view the secular state as a positive phenomenon. Some are anti-Zionists, while others have accepted its existence with reservations – refusing to allow their representatives in the Knesset to serve as cabinet ministers but only as deputy ministers, and refusing direct government support. About 10,000 ultra-Orthodox Jews comprising an extremist group still refuse to accept the existence of the state, do not carry identity cards, do not vote in Knesset elections, and conduct an on-going dialogue with the United Nations which they view as responsible for their existence.

Ultra-Orthodox Jewry has been divided between Hasidim and 'Lithuanians' since the eighteenth century. Hasidism, since the time of its founder Israel Ba'al Shem Tov, has viewed prayer and devotion as the essence of Judaism. The Lithuanians, or Mitnaggedim ('opponents'), by contrast, view religious study as the essence. The Hasidim are more emotional in their approach and have developed a system of almost regal rabbinic courts headed by a Hasidic rabbi, or 'rebbe', addressed as *'admor'* ('our master, teacher and rabbi'), with the omnipotent rabbi wielding absolute control. The Lithuanians are more intellectual, lacking the element of veneration of their rabbis. They constituted the majority of ultra-Orthodox Jewry before World War II, and still constitute the majority of this sector in Israel today.

There had been a community of ultra-Orthodox Jews living in the holy cities of Palestine for centuries, and on the eve of the establishment of the state the two large ultra-Orthodox centres were located in the Me'a She'arim quarter in Jerusalem and in the city of Bnei-Brak near Tel-Aviv. After World War II, the remnants of European ultra-Orthodox Jewry made their way to the United States and to Israel. Hasidic rabbis or members of their families arrived and began to re-establish their courts. In Israel, most of them settled in Jerusalem and Bnei-Brak, but some made their homes in Tel-Aviv, Netanya, Rehovot, and elsewhere.

The Hasidic rabbis who arrived as refugees from Russia, Poland and Hungary were mostly broken men, many of whom had lost all or part of their families and most of their following in the Holocaust. They began to gather new followers and to rebuild from scratch the world which had been destroyed. As discussed above, the exemption of the Yeshiva students from military service was the main secret of their success. They founded *yeshivot* and various institutions of religious learning, synagogues, a network of religious services, a welfare organization, old-age homes, medical services including even hospitals, cooperative food stores, cemeteries, an internal judicial system, ritual baths, *kashrut* (Jewish dietary law) certification, low-cost housing for young couples, match-making services, and their own newspapers. While some of the Hasidic rabbinic courts have remained small and devoid of influence, others (such as the Gur and Vizhnitz courts) number thousands of followers, each constituting a quasi-autonomous state with a clear hierarchy. The authority the rabbi wields is not a function of age, and even an heir of twenty immediately becomes the leader of his community. The rabbi issues rulings which are proclaimed in the synagogues of his followers and published. (For example, in response to queries about whether men should shave their beards in order to be able to use gas masks during the Gulf war, the Hasidic rabbis instructed their followers not to shave, even when faced with the threat that Iraqi missiles with chemical warheads could strike Israel.) The Hasidim consult their rabbi on many aspects of life, but primarily on questions of marriage, medical operations and business deals. No one argues with the rabbi, who is assumed to know what is best for them.

The Lubbavitcher Rebbe, Menachem Mendel Schneersohn, who resides in Brooklyn, New York, is now about ninety years old. His followers, both in the United States and in Israel, accord him messianic attributes which he himself makes no effort to refute. Rabbis are noted for their 'missionary' approach; they devote considerable effort to persuading secular Jews to become religiously observant, encouraging them to perform religious commandments and trying to convince them to change their ways. In recent years the Lubbavitch has held audiences with large groups; he shakes the hand of everyone who attends, rich or poor, and gives each a single dollar bill. No one seems to know whence this singular idea came, nor what the elderly and heirless rabbi seeks to express by this, but his followers all place their trust in their rabbi and believe that it undoubtedly has some important purpose.

The Council of Torah Sages, the governing body of Agudat Israel since its founding in 1912, comprises about a dozen rabbis, Hasidic and Lithuanian, and for many years it constituted the elite of ultra-Orthodox Judaism in Israel. The Council's presidium is composed of four rabbis who head the major Hasidic courts, and they are absolutely obeyed. The rabbis do not retire from the Council, but are appointed for life. Several of the Hasidic rabbis are over ninety and suffer from a variety of ailments associated with old age. Yet they remain unchallenged, and teachings are issued regularly in their names as proof of their mental faculties, while control of their courts actually resides in the hands of the eldest or other son.

The Hasidic rabbis behave like kings and live like kings. Most live in private homes in the heart of the city (Jerusalem, Bnei-Brak or Tel-Aviv). Some of these houses resemble small 'palaces' of several storeys. The rabbi sits in his home in a high-backed armchair, generally made of heavy wood, ornately carved, and topped by a crown. His house is indeed his castle. Anyone who wishes to see him must call on him. Some rabbis virtually never leave their homes. The Lubbavitcher Rebbe in Brooklyn, for example, only goes out to pay his respects to his late father-in-law at the cemetery. The Hasidic rabbis in Israel leave their homes to worship at their synagogue unless they live above it, to attend large religious gatherings, and to participate in the rare meetings of the Council of Torah Sages (two or three times a year). All are known by the names of the East European towns where their dynasty reigned until the Holocaust (the *admor* of Modzhitz, of Sadagora, of Vizhnitz, of Belz, etc.). This is a clear ideological statement about the way they view their life in Israel as having been necessitated by tragic circumstances and on their self-perception as carrying on diaspora life in Israel.

All Hasidim dress throughout the year as though in the midst of an East European winter. This special dress – dark suit, black coat and black wide-brimmed or fur hat – along with beard and sidelocks, is a major tool in preventing desertion from the Hasidic camp or any kind of assimilation into the modern religious or secular world. The Hasidic rabbi wears a dark silk robe and fur hat (*shtreimel*), and outside his home carries a stick topped with a silver or gold knob. Throughout the day, which he spends at home, he sits at a table and receives callers who wait in an adjoining room. Placed before the rabbi is generally the volume of the Talmud that he is currently studying and a plate of fruit from which he offers refreshment to his callers. An attendant, known as the *shamash*, serves him, ushers people in and out of the room, records what he says, peels his fruit for him, pours his drinks, or summons people at the rabbi's bidding. The *shamash* almost always remains standing, being seated at the table only on rare occasions. Other members of the court – those in charge of finances, and heads of educational and welfare institutions – also generally stand in the presence of the seated rabbi, expressing admiration for his words; he rarely invites them to be seated.

Many of the Hasidic rabbis maintain expensive cars and a regular chauffeur, and spend several weeks each year in homes outside the city or abroad. They are especially fond of spending a holiday in Switzerland with chosen family members. They neither give interviews to the media nor, in fact, have any interest in the media; they do not stand for election, their followers are not exposed to the media, and the wider readership it involves is of little interest to them. While Hasidim may occasionally glance at a secular newspaper or even at television while in the home of friends, the *admorim* never watch television, never listen to the radio, and read only the ultra-Orthodox press. The information which reaches them from the outside world is highly eclectic. Most of them are deeply hostile to the non-Jewish world, which they also fear. Their greatest animosity is directed towards the Arabs. However, this is not necessarily combined with hawkish demands for the annexation of the territories conquered by Israel in 1967, as they do not attach great importance to sovereignty of a state which presumes to anticipate the coming of the Messiah and which is not based on Jewish religious law. Moreover, they attach the highest importance to the principle of the sanctity of human life and are therefore prepared to make major concessions in order to avoid bloodshed.

The world of the *admorim* and their flock is very different, though, from that of their Israeli milieu. Theirs is an island where views and norms are an inverted mirror of the society around them. Thus, for example, rabbis who were prepared to relinquish land in order not to arouse the anger of the gentiles and to prevent bloodshed, encouraged Rehavam Ze'evi's joining the government in February 1991, viewing his call for the transfer of Arabs from Israel as a legitimate demand. Like other religious movements throughout the world, the ultra-Orthodox leadership believes that the secular world will ultimately recognize the error of its ways and return to religion, in a deterministic process which most believe requires no special intervention on their part. They view secular life as pleasure-seeking, devoid of any value, a kind of persistent hedonism which will ultimately be scorned even by those who now lead it. They treat the secular leadership with a combination of forgiveness (as Jews who have sinned but have not lost their right to be Jews or to return to God) and of respect, because of their control over the distribution of funds. But whereas in the diaspora they used to pray for the well-being of the leaders of the country in which they lived, in Israel they do not, rejecting all symbols of Israeli independence – the national flag, memorial day to the fallen IDF soldiers, and independence day. While the rest of the nation celebrates its independence, they continue ostentatiously to demonstrate their own independence – and carry on with their normal daily lives.

Almost all the current *admorim* were born in Eastern Europe and arrived in Israel in the 1940s with their parents. They speak Hebrew but prefer to converse in Yiddish; the meetings of the Council of Torah Sages which they attend together with several Lithuanian rabbis are generally conducted in Yiddish. This is one of the reasons – or excuses – why not a single Sephardi rabbi participates in these meetings. The Council is one of the only forums in Israel which can maintain secrecy, although even from here there are occasional leaks. Apart from the Council members, only its secretary is present at meetings, and it is he who issues its decisions. Since 1988, this forum – the official elite of ultra-Orthodox Jewry in Israel, most of whose members are totally divorced from Israeli life – has become one of the most influential bodies in Israel. It was this forum which in 1988 instructed Agudat Israel's representatives in the Knesset to support the Likud-led government although they had previously expressed a preference for Labour; and it was the same forum which one year later instructed them to resign from the National Unity Government after Prime Minister Shamir failed to keep his promises to them. It was this forum also which, in March 1990, ordered the Agudat Israel MKs to vote to bring down the government and one month later to form a government with Labour and which, when two of its MKs disobeyed this instruction and thus foiled the attempt to form a Labour government, instructed them to join the Likud government some six months later.

But the most important figure among ultra-Orthodox Jewry, the above-mentioned Rabbi Eliezer Menachem Schach, has not been a member of this forum since his resignation in 1983, and he has since established a separate but no less important elite. Schach, born in 1898, is the leader of the non-Hasidic ultra-Orthodox majority in Israel. The most important *yeshivot* view him as the supreme authority, and indeed, at the time of writing, he continues to head the Ponevezh (Panevezys) *yeshiva* in Bnei-Brak where he lectures once a week and near which he lives in a modest apartment. Looking at his behaviour, he is very different from the 'regal' Hasidic rabbis, but examining the deep respect he enjoys within the ultra-Orthodox world and the absolute acceptance of his authority on every subject, they are indistinguishable. Schach, who immigrated with his family during World War II, taught at many *yeshivot* and is considered a learned and important rabbi. However, the major source of his authority lies in the fact that most of his contemporaries died decades ago, leaving him virtually the sole bearer both of vast experience and memories of the days of glory of ultra-Orthodox Jewry prior to the Holocaust. This is enhanced by the fact that many of the heads of the *yeshivot* in Israel today were his students.

Schach is a sick man, hard of hearing and with poor eyesight, and his toothless mouth speaks indistinctly both in the Yiddish he prefers and in Hebrew. He is blunt, extremely anti-Zionist, stringent on religious matters and almost totally divorced from the world around him; he maintains contact with it mostly through the man who serves as both his chauffeur and his personal attendant. His family has rejected his approach and identifies with the Zionist religious branch in Israel; his grandsons even served in the army, which is for him almost sacrilegious. He has no heir, neither within his family nor without, and Lithuanian ultra-Orthodoxy will find him hard to replace. Rabbi Schach has for many years waged war against the Lubbavitcher Rebbe because of his messianism and because of the importance he attaches to missionary activity among secular Jews. In the wake of the Six Day War, the Lubbavitcher Rebbe expressed strong opposition to any territorial concession and sharply attacked the peace treaty with Egypt, while Rabbi Schach supported both, presenting the other as an invalid Zionist approach. This is a war between a 'hawk' who has never left Brooklyn and a 'dove' who views the existence of the state in which he lives as a terrible mistake.

After Rabbi Schach had resigned from the Council of Torah Sages over the issue of Agudat Israel's representation in the Knesset, he decided to establish a separate ultra-Orthodox political framework. Exploiting the long-standing resentment of the ultra-Orthodox Sephardim at the discrimination against their institutions by the Ashkenazi ultra-Orthodox establishment, he joined with Rabbi Ovadia Yosef, the most important Sephardi rabbi in Israel, to form the party of 'Torah-Observing Sephardim' – Shas. Its Knesset candidates were chosen cursorily, at the last moment. They were people who were unknown to Israel society, who had never been interviewed by the media, and who did not appear on any list of 'who's who'. Indeed, even many ultra-Orthodox Jews had never heard of them. Rabbi Ovadia Yosef placed himself at the head of a new forum of Torah Sages, together with three heads of Sephardi *yeshivot*, but spiritual authority remained primarily in the hands of the elderly Rabbi Schach who is not a member of this forum. The Torah Sages cannot be considered part of the ultra-Orthodox elite as their influence is limited to a small group, and even among them is not total. It is valid to say that while the secular Ashkenazi elite is open to its environment and tries to include non-Ashkenazim, the ultra-Orthodox elite is a closed group which scorns the Sephardim, accepts very few of them into the important *yeshivot* and does not include them in its influential institutions.

The efforts of Rabbi Schach were surprisingly successful. He instructed his followers, both Ashkenazi and Sephardi, to vote for the new party which, though only several months old, won four seats in the 1984 elections, while the veteran Agudat Israel lost 50 per cent of its strength, sending only two representatives to the Knesset. The election results greatly sharpened the conflict within the ultra-Orthodox leadership. These differences had nothing in common with the debates waged within Israeli society during those years – the serious economic crisis, whether to withdraw from Lebanon even without a peace settlement, and the dilemma regarding Israeli participation in an international conference. The war within the ultra-

Orthodox world was a triangular war of prestige waged between the Council of Torah Sages which governed Agudat Israel, Rabbi Schach who sought revenge against them, and the Lubbavitcher Rebbe looking on from New York and seeking revenge against Rabbi Schach who opposed him and his methods.

Just as the discrimination felt by the ultra-Orthodox Sephardim served as a tool in the hands of Rabbi Schach against Agudat Israel, so did this veteran and disappointed party become a tool in the hands of the Lubbavitcher Rebbe. The Rebbe, who maintains almost military discipline among his followers, had never identified with any political party in Israel. Rather, he had been careful to maintain relations with all of them, particularly those in power, in order to ensure the free access of his followers to schools and even army bases to preach his teachings. On the eve of the 1988 elections, Rabbi Schneersohn put all his weight behind Agudat Israel, and his followers were dispatched to proclaim that a vote cast for Agudat Israel was a vote for the Rebbe.

The ninety-year-old Schach did not sit idle. On the eve of the elections he founded a new party of Lithuanian ultra-Orthodox Ashkenazim called Degel HaTorah, which was answerable to a new 'council of Torah sages' headed by Rabbi Schach himself. Schach selected the party's Knesset candidates and accorded it his public support, though not withdrawing his support from Shas.

The contest between the followers of the Lubbavitcher Rebbe and of Rabbi Schach reached its climax in the autumn of 1988, overstepping the well-defined boundaries of ultra-Orthodox Jewry in Israel. Shas appealed to the Sephardim, exploiting their sense of discrimination and even offering free day care for many children in development towns and urban neighbourhoods in a newly established independent school system. Rabbi Ovadia Yosef flew by helicopter from one election rally to another, speaking of the lost Sephardi honour, of the Sephardi mothers, of the broken families, of the great tradition of which they had been robbed. He promised to restore the former Sephardi glory through the head of the Shas list, Rabbi Yitzhak Peretz. The Lubbavitcher Rebbe's followers travelled throughout the country, but focused primarily on the lower classes, distributing photographs of the Rebbe wrapped in a prayer shawl and promising his blessing for longevity, fertility or life in the next world in exchange for a promised vote for Agudat Israel. After all, as important as elections may be, is it not more important for a man to ensure his admission into heaven or simply to live longer than to give his vote to a party which he would not have considered supporting anyway? The leaders of Shas were duly alarmed by these promises, which constituted a clear precedent in Israeli political history, and they prepared a special television campaign broadcast in which several leading rabbis, including members of the Council of Torah Sages, after praying, informed the public that they were released from their vows to vote for Agudat Israel, even if they had promised to vote for the Lubbavitcher Rebbe.

A stranger finding himself by chance in Israel at the time would have rubbed his eyes in disbelief at this broadcast, but even native Israelis found it hard to follow this sharp dispute relevant to so few. Some laughed in ridicule, while others feared a wave of ultra-Orthodoxy, speaking of the dark Middle Ages or of Khomeinism. Postcard-sized photographs of Rabbi Ovadia Yosef on the one hand and of the Lubbavitcher Rebbe on the other were found in the most unlikely places – on the dashboard of taxis whose drivers did not even wear skullcaps, in hairdressers' shops, in grocery stores, and even on the desks of government employees.

The election results were no less startling. Agudat Israel, with the generous help of the Lubbavitcher Rebbe, for the first time in its history won five Knesset seats. Shas won six, while Degel HaTorah, which had been formed at the last moment and had not even presented its candidates or its platform to the public, won two seats. The Council of Torah Sages now controlled five MKs, and Rabbi Schach eight. The importance of the power they thus wielded can hardly be exaggerated in view of the situation prevailing since 1977, in which the religious parties hold the key to the formation of the coalition government.

The ultra-Orthodox elite was interested in obtaining additional funds for its educational and religious institutions as well as the enactment of religious legislation (the invalidation of conversion by Reform rabbis, stricter observance of the Sabbath, the prevention of abortions, a ban on the sale of pork, censorship of permissive advertising, etc.). But its excessive demands – prompted by its surprising power (particularly the demand not to recognize Reform conversion which caused shockwaves among American Jewry) and its internal disunity – led once again to the formation of a National Unity Government in 1988. The Lubbavitcher Rebbe, who rightly felt himself a major 'stockholder' in Agudat Israel, insisted on the amendment of the Law of Return (which defines 'who is a Jew?') so that only Orthodox conversion would be recognized as valid for registration as a Jew in Israel. While the Labour Alignment rejected this demand, the Likud agreed, and Agudat Israel gave its support to the Likud. Rabbi Schach had never expressed interest in such an amendment, and Shas wavered between Labour and the Likud, ultimately backing the Likud – primarily because its electorate identified more closely with the positions of that party. Degel HaTorah, which with its moderate political positions was inclined to support Labour (this is a party which advocates territorial concessions and does not reject negotiations with the PLO and the establishment of a Palestinian state), found itself isolated in the ultra-Orthodox camp, decided not to support either party and did not join the National Unity Government.

The tables were later turned. Because of the Shamir government's failure to fulfil the promises made on religious issues, the Council of Torah Sages decided to withdraw from the coalition, bring down the government and join a Labour-led government. Shas absented itself from the no-confidence vote, thus helping to bring down the government, while the small Degel HaTorah faction, which was not even a coalition member, supported the government which had blocked the Baker peace initiative. Rabbi Schach ultimately succeeded in forcing the hand not only of Degel HaTorah, which was under his direct control, but also of Shas. After a short-lived attempt to rebel against his authority, the representatives of Shas quickly understood that the Sephardi *yeshiva* students in the Lithuanian academies viewed their rabbi's decisions as unimpeachable. The MKs, who had been inclined to rely on their mentor Rabbi Ovadia Yosef, realized who the real 'boss' was, and understood that the so-called 'world of the Torah' was in fact headed by the Ashkenazi Rabbi Schach.

These two rabbis, both over ninety, also determined the fate of the coalition formed after the 1990 government crisis – Rabbi Schach by forcing Shas and Degel HaTorah to back the Likud, and the Lubbavitcher Rebbe by preventing his two followers among Agudat Israel's MKs from supporting Labour. The National Unity Government was replaced by a Likud government supported by the right and all the religious parties. In 1992, however, the order of Rabbi Schach was ignored by his non-Ashkenazi disciples.

It is hard to say whether the power exerted by such figures will remain as a lasting phenomenon in Israeli society. It is the product of two parallel developments which are not necessarily interrelated. One is the growth in the ultra-Orthodox population in Israel (primarily the result of the exemption of their sons from military service, on which I have already expressed my opinion). The second is the exploitation of religious feeling among the lower classes in Israel, most of whom are not actually religious, and certainly not ultra-Orthodox in practice, to support religious leaders who can make promises to which no political leader would ever commit himself.

The fall of the government in 1990 and the events which followed created hard feelings within Israeli society against the ultra-Orthodox community. This was a period when society at large was allowed more than a glimpse into the ultra-Orthodox world. The media wrote widely about them and several books were published on the subject, but this new familiarity did not endear them to the public. The most surrealistic event in this context was undoubtedly Rabbi Schach's appearance at the Degel HaTorah rally held at the Yad Eliahu basketball stadium on 16 March 1990. No newspaper, television or radio station would have taken the trouble to send a representative to cover such an event were the fate of the future government not dependent on the religious parties. Indeed, the stadium was filled to capacity; not only were there some 15,000 *yeshiva* students who had purchased tickets for the rally, but also a very large number of journalists, both domestic and foreign, who awaited the aged rabbi's instructions to the MKs he controlled as to which candidate for Prime Minister – Shimon Peres or Yitzhak Shamir – they should recommend to the President.

Israeli television broadcast the event live on its only channel, and in every Israeli home people watched this strange spectacle. Following a brief introduction, during which Rabbi Schach was seen dozing on the podium, he stood up and for about half an hour, alternating between Hebrew and Yiddish, he mumbled about the importance of upholding the Jewish tradition and the gravity of abandoning it, bringing himself to tears about the widespread lack of observance of the religious commandments. Only few understood him, as his rare television appearances had in the past always been taped in advance, and his remarks, whether spoken in Yiddish or Hebrew, translated into Hebrew. It later became apparent that he had devoted a large part of his discourse to a time-worn harangue against the kibbutzim, because he remains convinced that people there eat rabbit, an animal forbidden by Jewish dietary laws. Schach made no reference at all to the issue on which everybody awaited his decision, and the various commentators immediately began to interpret his criticism of the kibbutzim (which are part of the Labour movement) as a preference for the Likud. And so indeed it was.

The mass public movement for electoral and government reform which arose at the time, amassing 600,000 signatures on a petition submitted to the President, seemed to have gained sufficient power to force the politicians to adopt some such reform, even against their will. But the religious parties which joined the Shamir government made any reform conditional on their agreement, thus limiting the chances for any change in the form of government and nullifying any chance for electoral reform. What this means, in effect, is that it will be technically impossible to prevent a recurrence of a situation in which small parties determine the fate of Israel.

The scope of the ultra-Orthodox phenomenon in Israel and the extent of the influence exerted by its elite produce a serious problem of accountability in a democratic society. These are parties with no real 'address', whose presence in recent years at the centre of Israeli government (at the time of writing they hold the positions of Minister of the Interior, Minister of Immigration Absorption, Minister of Communications, Deputy Minister responsible for the Ministry of Labour and Welfare, chairman of the important Knesset Finance Committee, and several other deputy minister positions) calls for fundamental answers which were not necessary when the ultra-Orthodox representatives were few and situated on the fringes of the political system.

The funding of the political elite has also been raised in relation to the increased importance of this group which, only fifteen or twenty years ago, was considered a disappearing phenomenon, a kind of tourist attraction. The fundraising of the ultra-Orthodox community which does not participate in elections, maintains total separation from the Israeli establishment, and which to this day maintains a kind of 'vigilance' on the Council of Torah Sages, is entirely carried out abroad, enjoying no support from the Israeli government. The heads of the community periodically hold 'dinners' (a term they have adopted in both Hebrew and Yiddish) for supporters of the Satmar Hasidim in the United States; the primary message at such an event is the continued struggle against the Zionist government which is supposedly trying to force its ultra-Orthodox residents to violate both the Sabbath and Jewish dietary laws.

The Hasidic courts in Israel receive funds through various means: the taxation of their followers in Israel; contributions from Hasidic abroad (an inexhaustible source for 'laundering' money); and government support – accorded to educational institutions according to the number of students and to other institutions, without fixed criteria –

in response to pressures from within the ultra-Orthodox world. These so-called 'exclusive funds' originated when the ultra-Orthodox parties first joined the Likud-led government, inaugurating the 'tradition' of investing an Agudat Israel MK with the key post of chairman of the Knesset Finance Committee. He would ensure that the state budget was not approved until various ultra-Orthodox institutions – especially those with which he was affiliated – received direct funding. A well-ordered state cannot justify financial support to a particular synagogue or *yeshiva* while ignoring others. Indeed, the State Comptroller has come out strongly against this phenomenon and it has likewise been disallowed by the High Court of Justice. The funds are therefore allocated by special legislation. In the absence of a constitution, there is nothing to prevent the passing of a law which is by definition discriminatory, and these funds are allocated annually in ever-increasing sums (reaching a total of 110 million dollars in the 1990 budget).

As Deputy Finance Minister, I tried in vain to abolish this unhealthy practice and to distribute the same sum of money to the various religious institutions on the basis of clearly defined criteria. I encountered a sharp disagreement here between the spiritual leadership of the ultra-Orthodox world and its representatives in the Knesset. While the rabbis prefer the funds to be granted to the *yeshivot* in order to provide the students with better conditions (living and study conditions in most *yeshivot* are indeed quite harsh), the MKs prefer personally to distribute the funds designated for an institution within their own court or community. They thus demonstrate their indispensability to institutions in difficult straits, virtually the sole justification for their existence. The moment such funds were allocated according to set criteria, as Ministry of Education funds are allocated to all other schools in Israel, the MKs would lose their position of power. The rabbis tried to circumvent their representatives and set up a framework that would ensure a fairer distribution of funds among the various institutions, but the MKs thwarted this effort, making it clear to anyone who tried to persuade them that, in day-to-day Knesset affairs, it was their vote that counted.

The Hasidic courts receive additional direct income from individuals who come to ask the rabbi's opinion. Those wishing to consult with the rabbi hand a note to the *shamash* posing the question to which they desire the rabbi's response together with a sum of money. Gift baskets sent by the Hasidim to their rabbi on holidays – usually containing bank notes – are another source of income. Hasidim in

Europe and the United States finance many of the *admor*'s activities: air tickets, holidays abroad, and sometimes even the purchase of his first or second home.

The Hasidic rabbi generally refrains from engaging in financial matters, and even if his court suffers financial difficulties, he personally wants for nothing. His immediate circle provides all his needs, and he is totally divorced from daily life. The environment of the Lithuanian rabbis is very different. They are much more closely involved in their community, and the funding for their activities comes primarily from tuition fees and state funding of their schools. Their needs, however, are growing, as the Ministry of Education covers only part of the cost of these special schools. (Alongside the state religious schools attended by the national religious sector and the 'independent' schools affiliated with Agudat Israel, which have a different curriculum from that followed in the regular schools, though still subject to Ministry supervision, is another 'recognized but unofficial' school system with a totally independent curriculum in which the language of instruction is often Yiddish.) Since government supervision is out of the question, funding is partial and, as the number of students grows, so does the deficit and the need for state funds. The MKs are, in effect, sent by the rabbis to the Knesset to obtain funds to cover the deficit. Thus, so long as *yeshiva* students are exempt from military service, the ultra-Orthodox community in Israel continues to grow; and the more it grows, the greater the needs which are not met by the state budget, and therefore the greater the need for MKs who will uphold the exemption and exert pressure for special funding to cover the deficit.

Another elite group which is not necessarily invited to the American ambassador's garden party are the veteran members of the civilian defence establishment. This is a unique group, far from the limelight, who are known primarily to the military and political elite and whose influence is unrelated to any formal hierarchical position. Some still hold positions in the defence establishment, while others retired from these positions many years ago. Today in their sixties and seventies, most of these people filled important defence positions prior to the establishment of the state, and can be seen on such occasions as parties for the outgoing head of the Mossad. Many who were cultivated by Ben-Gurion and his circle voted for his Rafi list although they were not politically active, and continue to express admiration for the 'old man'. Retirement has no meaning for most of them; they continue to work, whether full- or part-time, within the defence organizations which were their life's work and with which they identify totally.

Some belonged to the Defence Ministry, others to the General Security Services, and still others to the Mossad, the various military industries, the aircraft industry, or other sensitive security organizations. Almost all have access to the Prime Minister and the Defence Minister. Their calls are returned without delay; indeed, they are consulted on sensitive and problematic issues; and are appointed to various committees which are not always made public. Some of them are more influential than many government ministers. They obtain information through formal channels, and especially through the 'old boys network', and thus they are always among the first to receive security-related information.

Haim Yisraeli is one such figure, assistant to the Defence Minister since the time of David Ben-Gurion. Only in the late 1980s was he given the title of deputy director-general of the ministry. As he served under all Israel's Defence Ministers, none dared to replace him, and there is universal agreement that he is indispensable. For decades he has sat in his small room just a few metres from the Defence Minister's bureau, automatically attending to a large number of issues. There is no one who knows the defence system better than he, and few wield as much power – derived from his knowledge, experience and modesty. He is a man of few words, always concise and to the point. He always looks as though the entire burden of state security rests on his shoulders. An appeal from him receives an immediate response, and it is rarely negative.

To this special elite also belong such figures as Shaike Dan, who parachuted behind enemy lines in Europe during World War II and who has for the past generation devoted himself to the task of bringing East European Jews to Israel; Al Schwimmer, former director-general of the Israel Aircraft Industries, who arrived in the country during the War of Independence as a volunteer from abroad and who is still learning Hebrew; and Isser Harel, who for many years headed Israel's secret service. They are joined by another thirty or forty people who continue to guard old secrets and who are proud to belong to this intimate 'aristocracy' on whom those who need to, know they can rely.

8. Political Lobbies

During the Yishuv period, there were no institutionalized political lobbies. Organizations of workers from various sectors functioned alongside merchants' and manufacturers' organizations, making demands of one another and presenting demands to the British mandate authorities – but always in the name of the national interest rather than a particular sector. The farmers spoke of the return of the Jews to normalization as a nation through agriculture, and equally important – of ensuring control over the land purchased by the Jewish people by tilling the soil; while the manufacturers spoke of the need for economic development which could not be accomplished solely with the tools of the previous century.

A pressure group is, by nature, an egotistical, self-interested group which makes demands for its own benefit and not for society at large. However, the norm of the Yishuv elite was collectivism. Individual groups were therefore compelled to put forward a common argument, denying that they were a pressure group which sought to advance particular interests or to defend a specific group.

The proportional electoral system introduced in the Yishuv period, which was maintained after the establishment of the state, combined with the low threshold for election to the Knesset (one per cent of the total vote and $1\frac{1}{2}$ per cent since 1991) created a great temptation for special interest groups to present a list of their own. Groups with very specific concerns which did not meet the generally accepted definition of a political party (such as the ultra-Orthodox sector, which sought to safeguard their particular interests without affecting other population groups, various ethnic communities, pensioners, etc.) preferred to run for the Knesset, hoping to hold the swing vote and thus to obtain funds and concessions as actors on the stage rather than as people waiting in the wings. Several parties have an institutionalized lobby formed by 'reserving' slots for MKs representing specific interests. Thus, for example, Mapai, as the ruling party, for decades reserved slots on its Knesset list for representatives of the kibbutzim and moshavim, as well as the public transport cooperatives and the small tradesmen. Once assigned to a cabinet position or to an important Knesset committee, it was obvious for whom these representatives worked, and no one saw the efforts of the public transport delegate to increase transportation subsidies as the work of a pressure group.

With the passing of the years, the work of lobby groups became more legitimate. A society which encouraged the Jewish lobby in the American government system could hardly continue to scorn the existence of such groups within itself. The large pressure groups still tend to claim to represent the general good, seeking to benefit from the general improvement and not at the expense of others. However, the readiness of a growing number of groups within Israeli society to call themselves 'pressure groups' testifies to the change which has occurred in the society's attitude towards such groups and its readiness to listen to them. There is a recognition of the need for their existence in order to accord expression to many social issues which are not raised by the parties represented in the Knesset. As elsewhere in this volume, I prefer not to enter into a protracted discussion of the various definitions of pressure groups, but will refer to two primary types: interest groups representing specific segments of the population, and interest groups fighting for an issue relevant to the nature of Israeli society.

The most established and veteran pressure group in Israel is the Histadrut, though it took quite a few years for it to realize and accept this fact. The Histadrut was founded in order to create a new, just society in Palestine, not to represent the employees against the employers. Only in 1936 was a national trade union framework established. Until then, the trade union was viewed as a very secondary function to the primary task of building an economy, creating jobs, and formulating and implementing the cooperative ideology. Even when the national trade union federation was established and the trade unions began to play a central role, the principle of universality continued to prevail, as it does to this day. A person first joins the Histadrut, and only then does he join the individual trade union; in contrast to the general practice elsewhere in the world, where a person joins a trade union and, as a union member, also belongs to the nationwide organization. The Histadrut establishment views both the principle of universality and the maintenance of a large Histadrut economy – making the Histadrut also a major employer – as a shield against being transformed into a loose federation of trade unions vying for better conditions, at the expense of the good of society, rather than as an organization with a clear social message.

The Histadrut is considered the representative workers' organization (it in fact represents over 85 per cent of Israel's employees), and its major effort is directed towards maintaining real wages through negotiations with employers' organizations and the government, usually held before April each year. These talks set a framework, and each trade union or workers' committee can then reach a specific agreement. The absence of any linkage between wages and productivity is one of the ills of Israeli society. Wages increase faster than productivity, but neither reaches the average level of the European Community. In 1985, as part of Israel's economic recovery programme, there was a drastic drop in real wages for several months, though this was later corrected. Here the Histadrut demonstrated its ability to convince the various trade unions to forgo immediate demands in return for long-term benefit.

The Histadrut also fights for universality in social services and national insurance payments, and opposes aid given solely to the lower income groups in order to avoid the stigma of poverty. It has historically been opposed to superfluous legislation on labour relations, preferring that this remain a matter for negotiation between Histadrut and employers. It is opposed to the introduction of compulsory arbitration in certain services, and has succeeded in preventing this despite its advocacy by the Likud government. It opposed bringing foreign workers to Israel and, together with the manufacturers, has been fighting since the Yishuv period to protect local manufacture against imports, in order to ensure employment for Israeli workers. It therefore supports high tariffs on foreign products and even administrative restrictions on imports.

Its representatives also exert pressure to obtain support for the Histadrut's economic enterprises. The recent financial crisis of Hevrat Ovdim has increased the Histadrut's dependence on the government and its willingness to provide the financial aid needed to save its enterprises. The government, for its part, is prepared to extend such aid, both because the Histadrut enterprises employ tens of thousands of workers, and because it can in this way obtain concessions from the Histadrut in an area where it exerts considerable pressure – the trade unions. The Histadrut's economic enterprises (Hevrat Ovdim, the health fund and the workers' pension funds) have over the years been transformed from an economic and political asset into a very heavy burden on the shoulders of the Histadrut, held hostage by the government. Although the Histadrut leadership is unwilling to admit it, it is prepared in its the present difficult straits to surrender a major share of its wage demands in order to save its economic enterprises.

'Growth and employment' are the twin slogans of the manufacturers' association. When we examine these words and who stands behind them, we find something much more practical, namely an unwavering demand for currency devaluation in order to ensure the profitability of exports and the maintaining of tariffs 'in order to prevent the flooding of the market with cheap products from countries which pay slave wages' – but in fact in order to allow factories which sell at inflated prices to continue to operate, despite the lack of economic justification. They demand further encouragement for capital investment in industry (primarily through government sureties) as well as private and corporate tax reductions.

There has been an historical conflict of interests between the manufacturers and the chambers of commerce, although the people involved in them belong to the same social and economic group, and some have switched over the years from one side to the other. The government has always handled industry and trade within the same ministry, despite the rivalry between the two organizations. Importers object to frequent currency devaluations which increase the price of imports, and call for the cancellation of customs duties in order to bring down prices, and they are champions of a free market.

For many years, the manufacturers were viewed as a constructive and legitimate element in the Israeli economy, while merchants were viewed by the establishment as shopkeepers seeking to protect their own interests and contributing nothing to Israel's society or economy. The younger generation, who today head the chambers of commerce, have succeeded in according the merchants' associations legitimacy on the basis of their shared socialization with other elite groups. They have adopted manners similar to those of the manufacturers (studying the history of Israeli commerce and holding festive gatherings marking commercial efforts in Israel), and transformed their special interest (exposing the economy to competitive imports) into a free market ideology, discussed at study sessions by economists from Israel and abroad.

The banking association lost some of its prestige in the 1983 bank shares crisis, but the banks were and remain an important economic factor which play a central role in any economic programme. They serve as a channel for loans to those entitled to government subsidies (such as new immigrants and young couples), and the interest rates they fix have a direct impact on inflation. They can offer special plans for sectors which the government favours (a special fund for immigrant entrepreneurs, for example); they conclude agreements with the government on debt repayment schedules in various sectors (kibbutzim, moshavim, local authorities); and through them the government grants loans to enterprises in temporary difficulties. They often fight for higher bank charges, higher permissible profits (such as fines for early loan repayment), the rate of compound interest, etc. This is a pressure group which has the ear of the cabinet and the Knesset, despite being critized for excessive profits, grandiose bank buildings, and the exorbitant salaries of many bank heads.

The agricultural pressure group is considered one of the most powerful in Israeli society. It comprises the various kibbutz and moshav movements (including many kibbutzim based largely on industry) as well as private agriculture, represented by the farmers' union (with a right-wing leadership which has enjoyed particular importance since the Likud's rise to power in 1977). The Minister of Agriculture has always been drawn from one of these groups, and views himself as the farmers' representative. All three are well represented in the Knesset, and a considerable number of these MKs view themselves as responsible solely for agricultural matters.

One of the most important agricultural issues is the subsidized price of water. The farmers in fact set the price of water via a subcommittee of the Knesset Finance Committee. Israel's waterworks (the water commissioner, water planning, and the national water carrier, Mekorot) are under the jurisdiction of the Ministry of Agriculture. In 1991, faced with a severe water shortage, the State Comptroller published information on their failure properly to prepare for the shortage, in part by setting unrealistically low prices for water for agricultural use.

The farmers also fight for subsidies for other means of production, for a pre-set price for part of their produce, and for extensive government compensation in the event of drought, excessive heat or frost – which occur almost yearly. They oppose the sale of agricultural produce from Gaza and the West Bank, which is much cheaper than their own, and the export of agricultural produce from these territories through independent channels. (All Israeli produce is exported through a national company which is responsible for standards and for transport to markets abroad.) In recent years, the major effort of this pressure group has been directed towards improving the debt repayment arrangements for farmers in the various sectors, totalling several billion dollars, which resulted from the severe crisis in Israeli agriculture. Both the government and the banks are reluctant to meet the farmers' demands to erase a large portion of these debts and to extend the repayment schedule for the remainder. However, given the prominence of agriculture as an important value in the Zionist ethos and the social importance of the various forms of agricultural settlement, they will in the end probably yield to pressure.

The two public transport cooperatives – Egged (throughout the country) and Dan (serving the Tel-Aviv metropolitan area) – are virtually the last vestiges of the dream of service cooperatives. They employ thousands of members and employees, and hold a monopoly encompassing almost all of Israel. The fact that they serve the army in times of emergency, are required to provide bus services to dangerous areas (such as settlements in the occupied territories during the intifada) and at dangerous hours (night services during the Scud missile attacks against Israel) make them part of the 'routine emergency' fabric of Israeli life, rather than a purely economic concern.

Public transport prices are set by the government, and the difference between income from ticket sales and operating costs is subsidized by the government. The cooperatives, of course, present their expenses and their outlays for equipment in such a way as to obtain larger subsidies, as well as demanding government assistance to cover extensive past losses. Another important issue for the cooperatives is to ensure their monopoly on public transport. Small bus companies in various parts of the country can offer their services to the Ministry of Transport at a much lower cost than Egged or Dan, because of much lower wages and management costs. Over the years, the Ministry of Transport has tried to reduce the monopoly of these two companies and to introduce competition on certain routes, but to no avail. The cooperatives appear before the relevant ministries (specifically Finance and Transport) with a battery of lawyers and economists; they explain the importance of the monopoly even if it is expensive, confirming that only a monopoly can ensure service to inconvenient places, at dangerous hours and with problematic passengers – such as the workers from the occupied territories – without cutting and running in a moment of danger or when the route is unprofitable. The fact remains that no Israeli government has succeeded in altering the situation or in limiting the transport monopoly.

A demand on which the cooperatives have been lobbying for years is a tax exemption on members' share profits. A member purchases a share in the cooperative, the value of which he receives upon retirement – linked to the consumer price index plus interest. The cooperatives claim that this does not constitute speculative profit but rather an investment by the member, which should therefore not be subject to tax. The tendency within the Finance Ministry in recent years has been to reduce marginal taxes and to broaden the tax base, so that all sources of income will be taxed. Although this approach is today accepted by most of the political spectrum, on the eve of the 1988 Knesset elections, two MKs – representing Likud and Labour – joined in presenting a bill granting tax exemption to cooperative members' shares. This came after explicit letters – signed by the heads of both parties on the eve of the 1984 elections – had been submitted to the respective parties' Knesset factions, promising to pass such a law in the Knesset. The bill was pushed through all four readings before the elections, and the exemption went into effect. The cooperatives 'repaid' the parties: some buses displayed Labour campaign stickers, and others Likud stickers.

A highly institutionalized pressure group is the local government association; it is composed of all heads of local authorities, who elect its governing institutions through party coalitions. Since the establishment of the state, there has been tension between central and local government over the division of budgets and powers. The British mandatory Municipal Corporations Ordinance, on which these relations are based, accords a clearly inferior position to local government. A district officer of the Ministry of Interior approves municipal decisions; the government decides by how much local authorities may raise municipal rates; the level of government assistance to local authorities is subject to the fairly broad discretion of the Ministry of Interior; and the government ministries responsible for social services (education, labour and welfare), which fund a fixed share of local services generally do not allocate sufficient sums to finance these services. Mayors spend more time in the government ministry corridors in Jerusalem than in their own offices. Some take advantage of individual political and personal ties with the decision-makers in the national government, but they also find it convenient to appear as a group which can exert pressure by shutting down the municipal system throughout the country – a threat they frequently use.

Between the personal level, on which political ties are exploited by mayors in explicit demands on the national leadership ('I won't be re-elected unless I get the budget I need,' for example) and the collective level, there is also sectorial activity within the local government association. Sectorial interests are expressed by the development towns and Arab municipalities, as well as by *ad hoc* organizations of local authorities in various parts of the country, the northern border area, for instance, which for many years was subject to Katyusha rocket attacks from Lebanon.

The development towns are particularly dependent on the central government because income from municipal taxes is relatively low, especially from the industrial and commercial sectors. In most development towns located on the periphery and populated by non-Ashkenazi Jews (the Ashkenazi Jews who were absorbed there having found the ways and means to leave the development towns and to move to the centre), a major effort is being devoted to halting the flight of residents to the centre of the country and attracting young people from the centre by offering tax benefits; the lower the local tax rates, the greater their apparent attraction to new residents. However, this also means lower municipal income and a greater dependence on the central government. The development towns are also constantly aware of the need to protect the partial income tax exemptions accorded for many years to their residents, which the central government has for some time been trying to eliminate. The heads of the development towns view this as a serious threat to the towns' future, and have succeeded from year to year, through pressure on the Knesset Finance Committee, in fending it off.

The situation of the Arab local authorities is appalling. Their budget per person is about one-third of that in the Jewish municipalities; income from local taxes is very low, and government assistance is limited. This is reflected in the outward appearance of these villages, which lack the necessary infrastructure and are overcrowded: there are lavish villas which the residents build by themselves or with the help of relatives, but there is no city plan, and sewage runs through the antiquated, winding streets. The heads of the Arab localities have organized themselves as the Committee of Heads of Arab Authorities, with their major demand being parity between Arab and Jewish municipalities. This committee, which has become the most important representative of Israeli Arabs, raises many political issues and voices its views on the Palestinian question.

While the government is prepared to discuss local affairs with the committee, generally admitting the inequitable treatment of the Arab sector and making proposals to bridge the gap over the course of several years, it is not prepared to recognize it as the representative body of Israeli Arabs. While the former Labour Alignment cabinet ministers displayed a fairly open attitude, recognizing that the Arabs had no other representative framework, the Likud ministers have tried, so far without success, to boycott the committee on political issues. The fact is that the Israeli Arabs view the committee as their true representative, and view its head, Mayor Ibrahim Nimr Hussein of Shefaram, as the most important Arab figure in Israel, despite the fact that he has no party affiliation and is less well known in Israeli society than several other prominent Arabs.

A concept which has become increasingly important in recent years is that of the 'neighbourhood'. This term is used to refer particularly to the disadvantaged urban neighbourhoods which have attracted considerable attention, especially since the Black Panther demonstrations of the 1970s. Their residents came to these neighbourhoods either when they first arrived in Israel or after a period in a transit camp, others coming later from the development towns to seek work in the big city and settling nearby. With a mostly Sephardi population, these neighbourhoods have a relatively high crime rate, especially drug-related crime. While in the past the code name for the lower income groups composed largely of Sephardim was 'development towns', in recent years the development towns and disadvantaged neighbourhoods have been spoken of in tandem. On the eve of the 1988 elections, pressure was brought to bear within the Labour Party to reserve a slot for a representative of these neighbourhoods, and today a resident of a southern Tel-Aviv neighbourhood serves in the Knesset. He frequently raises problems specific to this sector (the demolition of houses built without a permit, for instance, or the provision of various services, such as bomb shelters which were found to be lacking during the Gulf War, treatment for drug addicts, etc.).

The contrast between the success of the local authorities since the end of 1989 in absorbing the mass wave of immigration from the Soviet Union and the problems displayed on the national level, together with that thrown up during the Gulf War when the mayors of those cities hit by the Scud missiles coped admirably while the government's handling of the matters showed a marked lack of coordination, has created broad legitimacy within public opinion for the demand both to reduce the dependence of local government on the central government and to grant additional powers to local government at the expense of the government ministries. However, it is unlikely that this will happen. The Zanbar Commission report, which recommended a series of decentralizing measures and the transfer of power to the municipalities, was approved by the cabinet in 1985 but has never been implemented. The ministers will continue to pay lip-service to decentralization while preferring that the periphery remain dependent on them on both major and minor issues, while local government will continue to function as a pressure group, demanding the defrayal of their unending deficits as well as broader powers.

The consumers' organizations in Israel are weaker than many of their counterparts in the West, although Israel is a consumer society which to a great extent emulates American society. One such organization functions within the Histadrut (the consumer authority) and the other is partly funded by the Ministry of Trade and Industry (the consumer council). The Histadrut finds itself in a constant dilemma, not only as an employer which represents the workers, but also as an advocate of full employment and the protection of local products which is responsible for protecting the interests of the consumers. Its opposition to the exposure of Israeli industry to imports and its advocacy of a high tariff policy significantly increase the cost to the consumer; this is a direct infringement of the consumers' freedom of choice, often obliging them to purchase an inferior product at higher cost. The high price of local products, of course, has a direct impact on the rate of inflation, and this constitutes an unofficial tax on the lower income groups. As one consumers' organization is related to the Histadrut with its historical preference for protecting the worker rather than the consumer, while the other is related to the Ministry of Trade and Industry which historically protects the manufacturer rather than the importer, they generally confine themselves to providing consumer information. They express criticism, draw public attention to the injustices of large companies, and make constructive proposals for legislation and regulations to ensure price listing, the itemization of ingredients and compliance with the criteria set by the standards institute. Neither, however, has sponsored such an activity as a prolonged consumer strike or any more unconventional measures in order to force the government or the manufacturers to change their ways. Consumer awareness in Israel is not highly developed, creating a vicious circle. The consumers' organizations do not arouse public protest or educate the public to demand their due, and the consumers do not expect the organizations to represent them or to become more militant.

The various immigrant organizations (*landsmanschaften*) constitute a pressure group of a special nature. They assist immigrants from wherever they come from during the initial stages of their absorption; as well as general orientation, they help them learn Hebrew. Afterwards they provide them with a social framework, and at a later stage stress and cultivate the cultural traditions of their respective home countries. In the recent immigration of Ethiopian Jews (since 1984) and Soviet Jews (since 1989), the respective immigrant organizations have played, and continue to play, an important and prominent role. The organization of Ethiopian immigrants has fought mainly for the recognition of this community as Jews who need not undergo ritual conversion, on the grounds that (despite their special customs) they are *bona fide* Jews who should not be treated differently from other Jewish communities. This effort won broad public sympathy and proved successful.

Soviet Jewish immigrants have been fighting for years to increase the public demand to open the gates of the Soviet Union to Jewish emigration. The Israeli government, on the other hand, maintained that quiet diplomacy, especially through the United States, was more effective than an open struggle, with demonstrations and mass gatherings. This debate was never resolved: the government pursued its diplomatic efforts, while the immigrant organizations held demonstrations. At the end of 1989 the gates of the Soviet Union were opened to the Jews. At the same time, there was a significant reduction in the number of US visas granted to Soviet Jews, producing a wave of immigration to Israel which exceeded 400,000 at the end of 1992. The immigrant organizations abandoned the old debate, replacing it with demands submitted in the name of the new immigrants for better absorption conditions: adequate provision for the shipment of personal belongings, insistence on larger grants to immigrants during their first year in Israel, larger mortgages, a reduction in the number of guarantors required to apply for a mortgage, etc. The young immigrant leaders have proved quite effective in reaching the media, partly because a number of them were people who had spent many years in Soviet prisons for Zionist activity. They meet frequently with cabinet and Knesset members, and enjoy observer status on several committees which make decisions relevant to Soviet immigrants.

Organizations of immigrants from countries from which few new immigrants are now coming are today involved in a variety of issues.

They provide scholarships to the children of immigrants, help finance communal buildings and libraries, encourage the writing of books which honour their community's past, etc. The greatest success of the immigrants from North Africa has been the broad acceptance of the Mimouna – a holiday celebrated only by North African Jews upon the conclusion of the Passover holiday, when people visit each others' homes and are offered specially prepared foods. When they first arrived in Israel, the immigrants refrained from celebrating the holiday, which was unknown in the newly established state. Only several decades later, through a concerted effort of the Moroccan Jewish leadership, was the holiday restored to the calendar. It is now mentioned in the school curriculum as an officially recognized holiday, and is one of several elective holidays an employee can choose during the year. In recent years it has been celebrated as an evening on which the Israeli elite is invited to the homes of Moroccan Jews throughout the country, followed the next day by a mass picnic in Jerusalem's Sacher Park. Among those who make the rounds of the open homes of Moroccan Jews each year are the Prime Minister and other cabinet ministers, the head of the opposition, and many MKs. They are photographed for the media dressed in a red tarbush and white robe in the Moroccan tradition, and they praise the warm hospitality of the community and its leaders. On the following day the heads of state address the tens of thousands of celebrants, and anyone not invited to this event feels slighted.

The Saharana – the special holiday of Jews from Kurdistan – is celebrated in a similar manner, and yet another such holiday is celebrated by the Jews of Iran. These celebrations are clear proof of the success of the various immigrant leaderships in maintaining the organizational frameworks even after they have fulfilled their major purpose. These are holidays with no national or religious content, and have sometimes even included activities which run counter to the Jewish religious tradition (such as belly-dancing), arousing the anger of the rabbis. Nevertheless, the Israeli elite does not dare to criticize them for fear of the negative political consequences. They play their part in these celebrations year after year, telling themselves that the price is worthwhile.

Insurance companies constitute another significant pressure group, involved as they are in an effort to prevent the entry into Israel of foreign insurance companies which would charge lower fees. This position runs counter to Israel's desire to become part of the unification of Europe in 1992; it will not be able to close its doors to

Europe and to compete by itself against the entire continent. Another goal of the insurance companies which has been only partially successful is to ensure a high interest rate for the state bonds which they purchase with the money of their clients. The insurance agents' union has also fought to close the profession to those who do not meet certain criteria.

The bar association is the only professional association in which membership is obligatory. It is involved in public action on such issues as administrative detention, opposes the opening of private law schools as this would increase the number of lawyers in Israel, and there are already as many as there are in Japan – 11,000. Yet the profession and the bar association continue to enjoy high prestige, and a good Jewish mother still dreams that her son will become a lawyer.

The accountants' association exerts pressure primarily on the tax departments of the Finance Ministry. The accountants are interested in increasing public dependence on themselves. Thus, for example, while the tax officials are opposed to compulsory tax reports in order not to clog the system with reports of small taxpayers and thus limiting their ability effectively to monitor the large companies, the accountants favour compulsory reports for all. The accountants are also concerned with closing the profession to outsiders and are opposed to the phenomenon of 'tax consultants', claiming exclusive authority in the preparation of tax reports.

The contractors' association – for several years represented in the Knesset's right wing – are most concerned with improving their position on the government housing projects in which they are involved; they want to increase the percentage of guaranteed pre-sold apartments. The contractors demand cheaper raw materials and lower taxes. In addition, they seek to be allowed to bring in more foreign labour and to prevent the licensing of competitive foreign contractors in Israel.

Two pressure groups which have been politically active for many years are the homeowners on the one hand and the protected tenants on the other. The homeowners, whose political ties are primarily with the Liberals within the Likud, claim that maintaining low rental rates prevents them from earning on their investment; the tenants argue that raising rents would be a severe blow to their already low standard of living. The tenants usually emerge from these confrontations with the upper hand.

A pressure group which has gained strength in recent years' on the other hand, is that of the pensioners, their ranks having been augmented by figures who used in the past to head large trade unions. A very young society in the 1950s and 1960s, today 10 per cent of the population of Israel is over the age of sixty-five, and this figure will probably increase slightly with the arrival of the Soviet immigrants, about 15 per cent of whom fall into this age group. This is a large group with specific demands of its own in various fields, but their major, direct issue focuses on the size of their pension allowance. The pensioners demand that the old-age pension paid by the national insurance institute to all retired workers in Israel continue to be linked to the average wage and not to the cost-of-living index. They oppose the taxation of these payments, even when a pensioner also receives a high pension from his former place of employment. The pensioners vigilantly guard the pension funds, demanding government support – in the form of particularly high interest rates for government bonds sold to the pension funds – and the addition of certain salary package components on top of the basic salary in the computation of pension (such as extra pay for car maintenance and overtime).

Many pensioners are in financial straits, having received only a small share of their income while they were employed. However, most of those who represent them today enjoy a relatively high standard of living and are part of the Israeli elite. On the eve of the 1984 elections a pensioners' list was formed which unsuccessfully ran for the Knesset. In 1988 a different pensioners' list headed by former Foreign Ministry employees and a former member of the Labour Party central committee, almost won a Knesset seat, mostly at the expense of the Labour Alignment. It may well be that had Labour not lost this important mandate, it would have achieved parity with the Likud, thus improving its bargaining position. In any event, it is clear that the growing organized power of the pensioners is a factor which the political system must take into consideration. The fact that Shimon Peres, when serving as Finance Minister, was forced to abandon his plan to tax the allowances of pensioners with relatively high incomes is clear proof of their power.

The disabled people's organizations have also gained strength in recent years. This is a particularly large group; as elsewhere in the world, it is composed of people handicapped from birth or injured in road or work accidents, plus those disabled in the Nazi Holocaust and casualties of Israel's wars. The IDF disabled receive the highest benefits, and those handicapped from birth the lowest. While there are disputes among them over demands for equal treatment, they pool their efforts to lobby for conditions that will allow them all greater mobility (pavement ramps, for example, to enable those confined to wheelchairs to cross the street without assistance), for the abolition of taxes on auxiliary aids for the disabled, for rehabilitation, and for higher allowances. The disabled enjoy the 'power of weakness', as defined by Anna Fauker. It is very hard for elected representatives to ignore demonstrations by the blind, amputees and others, who barricade themselves into an office – possibly even a government office – vowing not to leave until their demands are met. The police are not called in to remove them from the premises, and the authorities are forced to abandon their usual practice and to negotiate with a group engaged in illegal protest.

The most powerful general interest groups are the political organizations: Peace Now, which exerts pressure to advance the peace process; and Gush Emunim, which promotes the annexation of the territories (both of which have been discussed above). There are other groups which, though related to them, function independently. For example, Betselem has been gathering information on events in the occupied territories since the beginning of the intifada. It distributes its reports among the Israeli decision-makers and tries to help in individual cases – persons arrested without trial or innocent people abused by the authorities. On the other side of the political map, the organization of Jewish regional councils in the occupied territories is becoming a factor to be reckoned with. It works not only for the expansion of Jewish settlements in the territories and the referral of new immigrants to these settlements, but also for the arming of the settlers, the liberalization of open-fire regulations against Arabs, and the reduction of sentences for Jews convicted of causing injury to Arabs. Despite their declared opposition to the Jewish underground, members of this group campaigned for the early release of its leaders from prison, with marked success. They were also involved in the attempt to prevent soldiers accused of illegal conduct against Palestinians during the initial period of the intifada from being charged on the grounds that orders given at the time were ambiguous.

An interest group emerged in the late 1980s comprising a handful of law professors from Tel-Aviv University. Joined by several other leading figures, they demanded a constitution for Israel, and the group has since demonstrated an ability to exert considerable pressure. They even prepared a draft of such a constitution which included a proposal for the direct election of the Prime Minister by the Israeli voters, the reform of the Knesset electoral process, and a civil rights law. Such efforts usually produce no more than a newspaper article or two, and a nod from the politicians at the legalistic professors' innocence; not this time. The group succeeded in obtaining significant funding from American Jews who had never been happy with the Israeli coalition system of government and who had for many years believed that electoral reform would magically improve Israel's domestic situation. They embarked on a massive publicity campaign, including full-page advertisements in the press, study days, and huge demonstrations; it was carried along by a tremendous wave of scorn that was directed at the politicians, a wave which swelled during the months between the fall of the national unity government and the formation of the Likud government.

The pro-constitution group, which focused its efforts on the direct election of the Prime Minister, recruited the help of broad sectors of the public who telephoned politicians to ask for their support. Ultimately, four MKs – two from the coalition and two from the opposition – presented a draft bill for the direct election of the Prime Minister, which passed the first reading with wide support. In this second reading Labour supported the bill, Likud was against it, and eventually the bill was passed and the direct election of a Prime Minister will take place in 1996.

The social workers' union has been a prominent interest group in recent years which, although a trade union, has chosen to champion an idea. Israeli social workers have for many years viewed themselves as virtually the sole spokesmen of those in distress. Indeed, the emergence of the Black Panthers in the 1970s is attributed in part to the social workers. They present the gravity of such problems as drugs and prostitution among the lower classes to the media and the decision-makers; they draw attention to pockets of severe poverty, to the plight of the elderly, to battered women and to child abuse. Increased awareness of these problems, prompting the opening of shelters for battered women, the elevation of child abuse to a major public issue, and the establishment of an authority to deal with drug problems: all these are attributed in large measure to the efforts of the social workers' union.

The Israeli civil rights association is an interest group which from time to time expresses an opinion on such issues as euthanasia, but its influence is limited. Environmental groups also carry little weight, as demonstrated by the Reading 4 power station case in the 1960s (discussed above). These are two areas in which interest groups in the Western world are much more prominent than they are in Israel.

The centrality of the government in Israel makes it the major focus for pressure, the main lobbying effort being directed towards cabinet ministers, directors-general and senior officials of the government ministries. In the Knesset, the primary target of pressure is the Finance Committee which, because it must approve every budgetary allocation, is seen to have been accorded real power. Other MKs are subjected to pressure when a specific sector is trying to promote its interests through a bill or when a public interest group is supporting a major issue like the direct election of the Prime Minister.

Many economic matters – most notably the efforts by monopolies to maintain their monopolies, the manufacturers' opposition to exposing Israeli industry to imports, etc. – are discussed between the relevant lobby and members of the coalition or the Knesset. Issues related to the nature of Israeli society and government are generally channelled through the media, especially the electronic media; because as yet selection is relatively limited, this brings the question into almost every Israeli home via the televised evening news. This is usually enough to ensure a follow-up in the written press and to launch a public debate if the issue is perceived as sufficiently important.

The permanent Knesset lobbies include both external and internal groups. The external lobbies are the Histadrut, the manufacturers and the immigrant organizations. These have permanent representatives in the Knesset, who participate in meetings of the Knesset committees on an almost regular basis. They meet with influential MKs and present their organizations' positions on current issues. The internal lobbies, which have become especially prominent in recent years, are comprised of groups of MKs from different factions who designate themselves as a lobby for a particular cause. They hold regular meetings and adopt decisions on relevant issues. Thus, for example, the 'social lobby', composed of MKs from the right and left, opposes any legislation which they perceive will adversely affect the lower income classes. The 'agricultural lobby' – the oldest of them all – concerns itself with guaranteeing the farmers' subsidies for the means of production and agricultural produce, as well as arranging terms for the repayment of debts in the agricultural sector. In contrast to these two, the lobby of the 'land of Israel faithful' comprises members of the Likud and factions to the right, and rouses itself to action primarily when it feels that the government is seriously considering a proposal for the political solution of the Arab–Israeli conflict. In the past, there has also been a dovish lobby composed of MKs from Labour and parties to the left, which encouraged the government to adopt a peace initiative. The problem with the internal lobbies is that the MKs tend to function within them as members of a pressure group and not necessarily as elected public representatives who must constantly weigh the benefits to the public of a particular decision against the price which the public, in whole or in part, will have to pay if it is adopted. Membership of a lobby is often more important to an MK than abiding by party discipline, and he is often torn between his dual loyalties.

The major tool of the political interest groups is mass demonstration. These always receive press coverage, serve as proof of strength, and necessitate some response. Several organizations have distributed the private telephone numbers of ministers and MKs to their supporters, asking them to 'bombard' the politicians with phone calls advocating a particular position. A much less annoying method involves supplying supporters with prepared postcards to sign and mail to the decision-makers. Mass demonstrations are held in the Malkhei Israel Square in Tel-Aviv which can accommodate hundreds of thousands. To choose this location for a demonstration is a risk, because if the number of participants is not sufficiently large, this is readily apparent in such a large site. On the other hand, a successful demonstration here is clear proof of a group's ability to muster wide support. Smaller demonstrations in Tel-Aviv are held in the Museum plaza.

In Jerusalem, almost every Sunday, demonstrators can be found opposite the government offices where the weekly cabinet meeting is in session, and sometimes they remain there for many days. In 1989, for example, a number of local authority heads who were unable to pay their employees' salaries, set up tents in a demonstration which lasted a number of days. They were even joined one night by the Minister of Interior. Opposite the Prime Minister's residence one can almost always find representatives from the right or the left holding prolonged protest vigils. Other demonstrations are held at a central intersection nearby, the most famous of these being that of the Women in Black; they have appeared there every Friday afternoon for the past several years, calling on Israel to withdraw from the territories.

Economic pressure by the 'have nots' (those subsisting on some kind of pension or allowance, the homeless, etc.) is expressed through demonstrations, individual harassment, or illegal action against which the authorities dare not take action. One such example was the above-mentioned takeover of an office in the Finance Ministry by the disabled. Another case in 1990 involved tents being set up in public parks throughout the country by homeless families, in protest against the rise in rent. Some mayors tried to impose the law and called in the police, but it soon became apparent that this was not practical. Not only did the majority not remove these tent-dwellers, they even provided them with electricity, water and sanitary facilities. And ultimately, housing was found for most of these families.

The pressure of the 'haves' is less public in character. Relations between public and private economic organizations and senior government officials is highly complex; here the carrot is used much more than the stick. The gap between the two sides is very wide. On one side stands the senior government official, with broad discretionary powers, and the power to bring a suit against a taxpayer who has committed an offence, or just a fine if he see fit; he can decide that the expected yield from a certain investment does not justify government subsidy, or he can help obtain significant government funding for a concern which will go under without the necessary sum. With a net monthly salary at the top of the pyramid of less than $2,000, he cannot maintain even a moderate standard of living, particularly if his wife does not work. On the other side are the economic concerns, with the best accountants and lawyers at their disposal, who come begging to the government officials. While such a glaring disparity might well give rise to corruption, such cases are rare in Israel; indeed, I believe it would not be overly naive to say that the acceptance of bribes is not symptomatic of the Israeli public administration.

The most lucrative allurement that the economic concerns can offer such an official is the offer of future employment. Of course, even without an explicit offer, the interest shown by them in an official can foster expectations which will affect his behaviour. I encountered several such cases during my term as Deputy Finance Minister, and all were legitimate, as the natural sequel to the career of a senior government official in the economic field is the private market and the various economic organizations. The director-general of the Ministry of Trade and Industry became director-general of the manufacturers' organization; the income tax commissioner joined one of the largest accounting firms in the country; the deputy superintendent of wages in the Finance Ministry, who participated in very tough negotiations with the Histadrut health fund over the irregular wage benefits it granted its employees, accepted a job with that very health fund. The deputy head of the Finance Ministry budgets department was appointed economic adviser to the Egged public transport cooperative, which every year haggles with the budgets department over tens of millions of dollars, if not more; the budgets department official in charge of education was appointed economic adviser to Beit Berl, one of the large educational institutions in Israel, which also conducts an on-going 'dialogue' with the budgets department.

The representative of an economic organization will often invite a senior official to lunch, and even those officials who deliberately decline such invitations will not turn down an opportunity to tour a major economic concern or factory, or to attend a prestigious function sponsored by these organizations. These functions accord the officials and their wives social status, thus rewarding them well without being in bad taste. These pressure groups thus open the doors to the decision-makers for themselves, for it is hard to turn down requests once a personal relationship has been created, however superficial.

The 'old boy network' is very characteristic of relations between the economic sector and public administration. Firms involved in the weapons industry (such as the Israel Aircraft Industries, the various military industries, Sultam, and others) often appoint former army officers to leading or senior positions, usually those previously responsible, whether directly or indirectly, for IDF arms acquisitions. The fact that the IAI is headed by a former air force commander, who knows the force's top brass personally (many of them having received their wings from him), certainly does not hurt its efforts to compete with foreign companies for tenders to produce various types of aircraft. These former officers focus their efforts on the army officers currently in charge of weapons procurement, many of whom were formerly under their command and with whom they have often maintained close ties of friendship. The recommendation of a former commanding officer who is wholeheartedly convinced that the product he is promoting is eminently suitable for the IDF and more reliable than its competitors (and this coming from a commander who still holds a high reserve rank and may have to rely on the equipment he is now recommending), is a very special endorsement.

A similar situation prevails in the civilian sector. When top people in the income tax, accountant-general and budgets departments in the Finance Ministry, as well as former senior employees of the ministries of Trade and Industry, Agriculture or Defence, appear in the corridors of the ministries with which they were formerly associated, they radiate credibility. In many cases, civil servants and former civil servants belong to the same social sets. They get together at weekends and frequently consult with one another, and these officials' doors are always open to their friends – who now represent diverse economic interests.

The situation in the political world is not very different. Businessmen prefer to present their demands to the highest echelons. In many cases they believe that while the senior government officials operate within rigid and conservative frames of reference, the politicians at the head of the ministry can apply greater discretion in the public interest. (For example, a holiday centre in northern Israel which had few customers during the years of Katyusha attacks in the Galilee may, having exhausted all its resources, request aid to cover its debts, claiming special consideration for having continued to operate on the 'front line' even during the hardest years.) But when businessmen phone the bureau of the minister or his deputy, they are usually referred to the appropriate official in the ministry. They find it hard to reach the politicians themselves unless they are prepared to sit patiently in the corridor waiting either for them to leave their rooms or to approach them at the end of a public appearance. The alternative is to use a go-between whom the politicians cannot turn away. Quite often, an MK would request a meeting with me to which he would bring along a businessmen with a 'special' problem; he would ask whether I had any objection to hearing him out, at which point the MK himself would leave the room. Sometimes old friends from university or the army would phone my office for an appointment, knowing that they would not be asked why; it was only when they arrived that I would find that they were accompanied by some businessman whom I could no longer turn away.

In conclusion, pressure and interest groups in Israeli society have in recent years won a measure of legitimacy which they did not enjoy either during the pre-state period or in the early years of statehood. Pressure groups operate in a similar manner to those in the United States, although the types of pressure group differ. As to their effectiveness: given the small size of Israeli society, with its small elite and uniform socialization, creating the general feeling that 'everyone knows everyone else', it is probably actually the old boy network that exerts more influence than any of the pressure groups.

9. Epilogue

Something happened to us on our path to the fulfilment of Herzl's vision. No reality ever resembles the vision out of which it was born, but this reality seems especially different. The Dreyfus case, which shocked Herzl, became mere child's play in comparison to the Holocaust of European Jewry which hastened the establishment of the State of Israel; while the Arab problem, which he treated romantically, has become the central problem in the lives of the Jews living in the country for almost the past hundred years. It is this problem which weighs heavily upon us; it is this which diverts our resources from the really important things needed to ensure our physical survival; it is this which divides us in our search for a solution.

In hindsight, enhanced by the writing of this book, it seems to me that the years between 1957 and 1967 were our finest years. They included very difficult times – with the Kasztner and Lavon affairs, and a year of severe economic recession – and they were marked by sporadic incidents along the Syrian border and some along the Jordanian border as well. There were ethnically sparked riots in Wadi Salib, and the question of 'Who is a Jew?' became a major debate within Israeli society. On the whole, however, these years demonstrated what Israel is capable of achieving in a period of relative tranquillity.

Israel experienced many difficulties in its early years, having to cope with both security and immigrant absorption problems on an unprecedented scale. They were characterized by a certain sense of transience, especially in the area of national security, in which Israel was still not sure of what it was capable. The trivial matters which surfaced after the heroic days of the establishment of the state and the War of Independence produced a measure of frustration among the young generation, some of whom left Israel to seek their fortunes elsewhere. The economic hardships, the austerity policy, and the rationing of consumer goods created a sense of poverty in a society which had flourished economically during World War II and in which the level of education, prior to the establishment of the state, had been among the highest in the world, if not the highest.

The Sinai Campaign provided Israel with proof of its own strength; within about 100 hours the entire Sinai peninsula was in Israeli hands, creating a sense of permanency and stability as regards Israel's future, both inwardly and outwardly. The withdrawal from Sinai and Gaza several months later left a bitter taste, but did not have a traumatic effect. Israel in 1957 was a self-confident country which, by raising outside capital and through industrialization, was proving successful in raising its people's standard of living. It served as an example to the Third World states liberated from colonialism, to which it provided considerable agricultural and economic aid, whilst completing the process of internal integration and developing its scientific infra-structure.

These were years in which Israel accomplished the impossible. With a population originating largely in the Third World, it steered a course towards the Western states and quickly reached the level of southern Europe, with an astounding annual growth rate of 10 per cent. These were years in which Israel freed itself from many of the norms that had taken root in the pre-state period – the depolitization of such institutions as the broadcasting authority and the employment service, the building of a professional public administration and army – all this within the narrow borders of Israel. The dream of conquering the West Bank or Gaza was harboured only on the irrelevant fringes of the Israeli political system.

The occupation of the West Bank and Gaza proved to be, more than anything else, the opening of a Pandora's box. Israel found itself responsible for those very people who had fled the Jewish state or who had been expelled from it nineteen years earlier; once again it had to confront a problem which had troubled the pre-state Jewish community for decades – the numerical ratio between Jews and Arabs in the land of Israel. The new Israeli rule, the constant friction with Israeli authorities, the employment of Palestinians in unskilled jobs in the Israeli economy: all these created deep hostility towards the Israelis among the Palestinians, feeding the nationalist flame, and led to renewed manifestations of Palestinian terrorism. Since then this has been the major issue on our agenda, thrusting almost all other issues aside. Thus, Israel's sensational victory of 1967 became a curse.

The Gulf War may alter the situation. If among its by-products Israel achieves a settlement with the Palestinians and the Arab states, if in the wake of the Scud missiles fired at Israeli population centres, a political process leading to peace emerges, Israel will enter a new era unlike anything it has ever known.

Will Israel succeed in returning to Herzl's vision? Will the partial removal of the defence burden not simply remove the excuse and expose our nakedness? Will Israel be able to become the spiritual centre of which Asher Ginsberg (another Zionist-thinker who called himself Ahad Ha-Am, meaning 'one of the people') spoke? I believe that we have a chance. I believe that this country – with more doctors per 1,000 people than anywhere else in the world, with the same number of lawyers as Japan, with many universities and scientific institutions – can become a world centre of research and development within the space of a few years.

Israel will rapidly become accustomed to the change in its condition. The long army service, the annual reserve duty, the sanctity of everything related to security, the allocation of huge sums to defence: all this will change substantially, if not completely, in peacetime. Israel's security problems and heavy defence burden have served not only to excuse certain actions, but also in a positive sense. The army became the 'melting pot' of Israeli life; it is a framework in which all are equal, in which people can advance relatively quickly, in which young people from the country's centre meet with those from the periphery in an encounter that would not take place unless forced upon them. It is an inexhaustible source of friendships between people from very different backgrounds, and even for intermarriage between the different Jewish communities. The army is also a breeding place for political leaders. It serves as an extended maturity rite for Israeli youth, and is a source of pride for all those who serve in it.

However, the security problem has also been used as an excuse which facilitates state control, sometimes by circumventing democratic and legal procedures. The official state of emergency prevailing in Israel since the establishment of the state enables every minister to declare emergency regulations for a three-month period in any area, without the approval of the Knesset. The state of emergency also accords legitimacy to the use of administrative detention – by which a person can be detained for six months without the submission of an official indictment. The state of emergency accords the defence forces informal power which has no place in a democratic state. And although Israel is a democracy in every sense, and despite the fact that throughout these years of emergency Israel has never for a single day ceased to be a democracy, this fact still casts a heavy shadow.

During the Gulf War, a new phrase was coined in Israel – the 'emergency routine'. It referred to that strange state of readiness which we experienced for six weeks, during which the gas masks never left our sides, and a sealed room was maintained in every home where we locked ourselves at the sound of an alarm. The 'emergency routine' is a vulgar oxymoron, but it epitomizes for me life in Israel during the past decades, before and after the establishment of the state. We have become accustomed to the 'emergency routine' as a hunchback becomes accustomed to his hump. People are born into it, and proceed from it into the next world. People like myself, born together with the state, have never known a routine other than the emergency routine. When we travel abroad and see a local newspaper with a sports headline, we are sure that we are looking at the back page and instinctively turn the paper over, because in Israel no sports event can ever compete with the news of a soldier wounded by a stone thrown in the occupied territories, or in a border clash with a group of terrorists, etc.

The challenges that will face Israel when peace is achieved will be very difficult. The problem will not be a mere longing for the hump (a feeling of emptiness and nostalgia for 'the good old days', when everyone had a role to play and there was a purpose in life), but first and foremost the need to redirect all existing resources, new ones inclusive, in order to absorb the large wave of immigration from the former Soviet Union, whilst at the same time introducing significant changes in Israeli society. These changes are necessary if Israel is to be transformed into an attractive incentive for world Jewry, rather than being a 'second choice' for Jews in distress to whom the gates of the United States are virtually closed.

We shall have to deal with the wide gaps that have been created in a society still clinging to the myth of equality, with no statistical justification. This will be accomplished not necessarily by increasing allowances to low income groups, but primarily by making broad social services and education available to all. This is the key for creating equal opportunity, while the heavy demands made by security have led in the past decade to a continuing erosion of school hours, the time has come to reverse this trend, to introduce a long school day, perhaps also to start schooling at an earlier age, and to provide special help for those who lag behind.

Government involvement in the economy must be limited to policy-making within the framework of appropriate legislation. There must be a 'health basket' and a national health law; there must be an 'education basket', a 'pension basket' and a 'housing basket'. But the 150 government-owned companies are an anachronism, and they must be disposed of as quickly as possible by transforming them into stock companies which issue shares to the public. The same applies to the Histadrut-owned companies. Central management of the economy has proven inefficient, while failing to fulfil the major purpose of union-owned companies – the abolishment of workers' alienation. The workers have remained alienated from management, even if the management is salaried. The companies would do better to issue shares on the stock exchange, according employees preference in purchase. Thus, a more modern and more efficient economy would be built.

Electoral reform is inevitable. Such reform, which Labour has supported for almost forty years and to which the Likud has historically been opposed, is essential if we do not want small parties representing a marginal minority in Israeli society to dictate our way of life. Nor, in order to prevent this, should we be forced to trample democracy by once again forming a National Unity Government, which attempts to pull the cart in opposite directions with no real parliamentary opposition. Ben-Gurion dreamt of adopting the British system; later the Knesset seemed ready to adopt the German system. One way or another, we must reduce the tremendous bargaining power of the small parties which are, in effect, no more than pressure groups. For some of these, it makes no difference whether the state is led by the Likud or Labour, so long as their interests are safeguarded.

One more challenge remains, not unrelated to the latter: to enable the secular majority in Israel to live as they wish, abolishing the religious marital laws which place every Israeli citizen at the mercy of the religious authorities in matters of marriage and divorce. This is a challenge which may prove more difficult than the others. However, like them, this is not the position of a minority which dreams of becoming the majority, but the majority will, blocked at every step by an interested minority which prevents them from conducting their lives as they see fit.

These challenges, and many others, cannot and will not be realized in a single day, nor in a decade; but it is these that will change the face of Israeli society when the major item on the agenda – security – is no longer the top priority.

This unprecedented attempt to transplant a nation whose members have lived for thousands of years in dozens of countries to a new home, prompted by persecution on the one hand and the nationalist ideology of the late nineteenth century on the other, is in itself a success story. The rapid economic growth and the establishment of a stable and developed Western democracy in the heart of the Middle East is Israel's second success story.

Nature provides few surprises in Israel: only a madman would carry an umbrella in July, and the sun is always much more generous in its gifts than the clouds. The State of Israel is much less predictable and monotonous; it will for many years remain a young state, ever ready to experiment with fascinating new challenges and new social patterns.

Bibliography

English

Deutsch Karl W., *The Analysis of International Relations*. Englewood Cliffs, N.J., Prentice Hall, 1968.
Holsti K.J., *International Politics*. Englewood Cliffs, N.J., Prentice Hall, 1967.
Rokkan Stein, Campbell Angus, Torsvik Per, Valen Henry, *Citizens, Elections, Parties*. Oslo, David McKay Company, 1970.
Safran Nadav, *From War to War*. Western Publishing, 1969.
Shimshoni Daniel, *Israeli Democracy*. New York, Free Press, 1982.
Yanai Nathan, *Party Leadership in Israel*. Ramat Gan, Turtledove Publishing, 1981.

Hebrew

Avneri Arieh L., *Hahityashvut Hayehudit Vetaanat Hanishul 1878–1948* (The Jewish Land Settlement and the Arab Claim of Dispossession 1878–1948). Tel-Aviv, Hakibbutz Hameuchad, 1980.
Arian Asher (ed.), *Yisrael, Dor Hahithavut* (Israel – A Developing Society). Tel-Aviv, Zmora, Bitan, Modan, 1979.
Bachrach Zvi, *Ideologiot Bamea Haesrim* (Ideologies in the Twentieth Century). Tel-Aviv, The Defence Ministry Publishing House, 1980.
Bar-Zohar Michael, *Ben-Gurion*. Tel-Aviv, Am Oved, 1977.
Eilon Amos, *Hayisraelim* (The Israelis). Jerusalem, Schocken, 1972.
Eisenstadt S.N., *Shinui Vehemshechiut Bachevra Hayisraelit* (Change and Continuity in Israeli Society). Jerusalem, Magnes, 1974.
Eisenstadt S.N., *Hachevra Hayisraelite* (The Israeli Society). Jerusalem, Magnes, 1967.
Friedman Menahem, *Hevra Vadat* (Society and Religion). Jerusalem, Yad Ben Zvi, 1978.
Gilboa Eytan and Naor Mordechai (eds.), *Hasichsuch Haaravi-Yisraeli* (The Arab-Israeli Conflict). Tel-Aviv, Defence Ministry Publishing House, 1981.

Gorny Yosef, *Hasheela Haaravit Vehabeaia Hayehudit* (The Arab Question and the Jewish Problem). Tel-Aviv, Am Oved, 1985.

Gutman Yechiel, *Hayoetz Hamishpati Neged Hamemshala* (The Attorney General Versus the Government). Jerusalem, Edanim Publishers, 1981.

Horovitz Moshe, *Harav Schach* (Rabbi Schach). Jerusalem, Keter, 1989.

Landau Jacob, *Haaravim Beyisrael* (The Arabs in Israel). Tel-Aviv, Ministry of Defence Publishing House, 1971.

Levi Amnon, *Hacharedim* (The Ultra Orthodox). Jerusalem, Keter, 1989.

Lissak Moshe, *Haelitot shel Hayeshuv Hayehudi Beertz Yisrael Bitkufat Hamandat* (The Elites of the Jewish Community in Palestine). Tel-Aviv, Am Oved, 1981.

Lissak Moshe and Gutman Emanuel, *Hamaarchet Hapolitit Hayisraelit* (The Israeli Political System). Tel-Aviv, Am Oved, 1977.

Padan Yechiam (ed.), *Hechalom Vehagshamato* (Dream and Realization). Tel-Aviv, Ministry of Defence Publishing House, 1979.

Peres Yochanan, *Yachasey Edot Beyisrael* (Ethnic Relations in Israel). Tel-Aviv, Sifriat Poalim, 1976.

Porath Yehoshua, *Tzmichat Hatnua Haleumit Hapalestinait 1918–1929* (The Emergence of the Palestinian-Arab National Movement 1918–1929). Tel-Aviv, Am Oved, 1976.

Rubinstein, Amnon, *Hamishpat Haconstitutzioni Shel Medinat Yisrael* (The Constitutional Law of the State of Israel). Tel-Aviv, Schocken, 1969.

Salpeter Eliahu and Elitzur Yuval, *Hamimsad* (Who Runs Israel). Tel-Aviv, Levine Epstine, 1973.

Segal Zeev, *Democratia Yisraelit* (Israeli Democracy). Tel-Aviv, Ministry of Defence Publishing House, 1988.

Shapira Anita, *Hahalicha Al Kav Haofek* (Visions in Conflict). Tel-Aviv, Am Oved, 1989.

Shapiro Yonathan, *Hademocratia Beyisrael* (Democracy in Israel). Ramat Gan, Massada, 1977.

Shapiro Yonathan, *Ilit Lelo Mamshichim* (An Elite Without Successors). Tel-Aviv, Sifriat Poalim, 1984.

Tzachor Zeev, *Baderech Lehanhagat Hayeshuv* (On the Way to the Pre-State Leadership). Jerusalem, Yad Ben Zvi, 1982.

Yaacobi Gad, *Hamemshala* (The Government). Tel-Aviv, Am Oved and Zmora, Bitan, Modan, 1980.

Index